PART OF A JOURNEY

PART OF
A JOURNEY

An Autobiographical Journal
1977–1979

PHILIP TOYNBEE

COLLINS
St James's Place, London
1981

William Collins Sons & Co Ltd
London · Glasgow · Sydney · Auckland
Toronto · Johannesburg

The author and publisher would like to thank
Oxford University Press for permission to quote from
First and Last Notebooks by Simone Weil,
translated by Sir Richard Rees;
also *The Observer* for permission to quote from
the author's reviews.

First published 1981
© Philip Toynbee 1981

ISBN 0 00 211696 0
Made and printed in Great Britain by
William Collins Sons & Co Ltd, Glasgow

For Connie Hellias
1897–1980

PREFACE

The origin of this journal was a desultory plan for writing quite a different book; but it soon turned itself into a daily account of ideas which came to me in the course of a renewed search for meaning in my life. Since I started those notes without any thought that they themselves would ever be published I wrote more frankly and intimately than I would have done if I had had future readers in mind. And by the time that I had begun to think in terms of making a real book out of those private notes the tone had already been set. What is presented here remains a frank and intimate record of my daily life over a period of just over two years; but this does not mean that it is wholly spontaneous; still less that I have 'told all'. I have been a professional writer for forty years, and as soon as I began to think of possible publication it was inevitable that I would immediately use all my acquired skills to make it as good a book as I could.

This meant not only touching up and revising the first spontaneous but very clumsy version; it also meant taking small liberties with the chronological order of events. As soon as this journal became a possible book I had to think at once of readers who knew nothing about me, and how to give them the necessary information as painlessly and unobtrusively as possible. This meant introducing the larger facts of my past into the flow of the journal's narrative whether or not these particular memories had really returned to me on that particular date.

I also learned that in a journal, as in every other kind of writing I had ever done, much of the art lay in careful juxtaposition: the order in which ideas came to me as I was living my daily life was not necessarily the *best* order when the

[7]

life was being transmuted into a literary work.

Finally, of course, I have made certain changes and omissions out of a necessary consideration for other people who appear in these pages. And I have made still larger omissions, even from the second draft of the journal, out of consideration for my readers: many passages were simply too boring, repetitious, flat and generally unprofitable.

But in spite of these various adjustments and omissions I believe that this is not only as honest a book as I could make it, but also a truthful journal. It does record, and without many of the usual reticences, the important events in my outer, still more in my inner, life during the twenty-six months between August 1977 and October 1979. By good luck rather than foresight this turned out to be a period when a great deal happened both to me and around me. I can't claim that I have been radically changed by these inner and outer events, but I am sure that I have strengthened my *will* to be changed. Although my 64th birthday is just behind me as I write this preface I usually look forward to whatever is left of my life with high hopes that I shall at least become increasingly aware of the presence of those holy mysteries which surround us all. Someone has said that mysteries are not problems to be solved but realities to be contemplated. I believe that this contemplation is the most important element in prayer; and prayer will – I hope and I pray – become a larger and larger element in my life as the years pass.

I have said that the bare outward circumstances of my present life – that I am a book reviewer leading a rather secluded existence with his wife in a country cottage – will emerge in greater detail during the early pages of the journal itself. But something should be said here about my religious background, such as it is, and the erratic, religious meanderings which brought me to the point of belief at which the journal opens.

Though both my parents were agnostics during my childhood my many schools provided me with a conventional upper-middle-class C of E background. This included confirmation during my first year at Rugby, and its effect on me was negative

[8]

in the extreme: I was strongly repelled by the institutional Christianity of half a century ago.

But when I was eleven I came to realize for the first time not only that I belonged to an intellectual family but also that this entailed certain intellectual obligations. I made it known that I was deeply interested in Comparative Religion and I began to buy very old, very cheap second-hand books with titles like *Faiths of the World* and *Thoughts and Aspirations of the Ages*. I was often to be seen apparently reading these books, but the truth was, of course, that I usually found them desperately boring. Yet this pretence, with its grain of truth within it, was kept in view for the next three years, before I rapidly dropped it under violent pressure from my public school contemporaries.

As for my own religious beliefs I accepted the thoughtful scepticism which my parents had shared until my mother, after moving rapidly through the higher reaches of Anglicanism, was received into the Roman Catholic Church soon after my seventeenth birthday. That conversion must, I think, have offended and hurt me even more deeply than I knew at the time. In any case the general effect was not to dampen my interest in religion, which had revived as soon as my prowess on the rugby field had made it permissible to exhibit it again, but to make me passionately and derisively hostile to Christianity, with a particularly sharp resentment against the Roman Church.

From that time until I was fifty-one, and fully equipped with the usual daunting experiences of adult life, I remained in a fluctuating attitude of hostile fascination towards all forms of religious belief. I read widely, if shallowly, in mythology, anthropology and religious origins; and the question of God's existence was seldom off my mind for long. There were occasional quite undramatic and unfruitful moments when it seemed to me to make slightly more sense to say that God existed than to say that he did not. I remember once putting it in these terms to my friend, Professor A. J. Ayer, and greatly enjoying his shocked face and scandalized protestations. It gradually became known to all my friends – unbelievers almost to a man and woman – that I was soft on religion and in real danger of falling into the disgraceful pit of Christian faith.

But in the year 1967 I received a shock of the same kind, though much milder in degree, as the one I had received when my mother became a Catholic. My wife, who had been going through a period of considerable stress and strain, suddenly decided that she wished to receive instruction from a friend and neighbour who was a retired priest of the Church of England. Sally had been brought up in the American Middle West, and in virtually total ignorance of the Bible and Christian doctrine; nor, until this point in her life – and after seventeen years of marriage – had she shown the faintest interest in any form of religion.

My reactions to this disturbing *volter face* were extremely mixed: I was delighted that Sally seemed to be finding the support she needed, but I was exasperated by the form which her new belief had taken. I attended her baptism and confirmation with the wryest possible emotions. To me, who had been to church only for funerals and weddings since leaving Oxford, the words of the prayers had a ghastly and poignant significance. I remembered with strong distaste, but also with that strange excitement which such distant memories often evoke, the hours of boredom and near-disgust which I had been forced to spend in my school chapel. I detected no change whatever in the Anglican Church: it seemed as dusty and unimaginative as it had showed itself at school. I probably also felt that my wife had stolen a march on me, and left me at an unexpected disadvantage.

But I concealed these reactions from Sally as best I could – not always very well – without concealing that I was following her strange progress with fascination and some sympathy, as well as with many misgivings. I now began to attend Matins with her on Sundays, first in a local Anglican church above the valley of the Severn, and then, with much more satisfaction, in a Moravian chapel on the banks of the Wye.

One day, for no special reason that I was able to detect, I made what seemed like a final decision that I too believed in

God, and was therefore ready to start examining all the religious knowledge I had acquired over the years, not just as an intellectual curiosity but as the possible approach to a livable reality. The point that needs to be made is that this 'conversion' was so unsensational, so undramatic that I doubt whether I really have the right to use the word at all. Yet by telling Sally about it I formally registered myself as a believer of sorts; and whenever arguments cropped up among our friends I now acted as a vigorous *advocatus dei*.

Nor did our two conversions seem to have had any conspicuous effect on our somewhat hectic relationship. Our churchgoing gradually faded away, until it was reduced to a formal obeisance to our formal beliefs at Christmas and Easter.

Yet during the next six years I was engaged in what now seems to have been a desperate attempt to move forward; to penetrate some sort of dark block in the processes of my mind and heart. I designed and constructed an elaborate water-garden: I devoted myself to a tropical aquarium, and to the collection of gramophone records: I took up sailing, bought a dinghy and joined a club on the Severn estuary: I became a keen photographer, even to the extent of buying a great deal of expensive equipment and printing my own pictures: I took to bicycling about our steep countryside, looking at churches and taking photographs: I became a conservationist ... And it was my conservationist passion which led me to the drastic conviction that Sally and I ought to start an organic farming community in our own house. I urged on her that since our two older children had left us this was the best possible use we could make of our partly-emptied family home.

Sally was very dubious about the capacity of either of us to endure a communal life. She knew that although I had ostensibly lived a life of almost frenzied social activity I had become no less frenziedly dependent on longer and longer intervals of total privacy.

But at this point nothing and nobody could have stopped me, and I joyfully took part in making the drastic structural changes to Barn House which would enable ten people to be accommodated instead of the original five.

I survived some nine months of increasingly communal life before gladly giving way to Sally's final insistence that we *must* get out and find a small house in the area for ourselves and our youngest daughter. It was understood that we would remain 'associate members' of the now flourishing Barn House community; and I fully intended to work in the fields which I had worked so hard at clearing of their trees and shrubs only a year before.

But by the time we moved into Woodroyd Cottage, only a mile by foot along the valley from Barn House, I had come to recognize that something else had also happened to me. I now fell into an increasingly dark and impenetrable state of depression. This was quite different from the many glooms and miseries of the past, if only because it seemed to be without any specific and obvious cause. True, our daughter Laura was now suffering from a disturbing case of anorexia nervosa: true, my inability to tolerate community life had seemed like one of my life's major failures: true, I was approaching the end of that gigantic 'tragi-comic epic' called *Pantaloon* on which I had been working for nearly a quarter of a century, and I must have felt some nervousness about how I would spend my time when that enormous labour was at last accomplished. In fact, like most other people, I could think of any number of reasons for being anxious, unhappy and dissatisfied with myself. And, of course, I still had a full array of childhood mistreatments for the benefit of any psychiatrist who might lay his hands on me.

But I could not find that any of this was enough to explain the real horror and anguish which I was experiencing in the summer of 1975. Even my vague and undulating spiritual beliefs were being crushed and ground, so it seemed, in that terrible mill of pain. Certainly they seemed utterly useless to me so long as my sole object was to escape from that condition and try to operate again as I'd been operating before the depression crept up on me and overwhelmed me. On the other hand, I was never for a moment tempted to reject my growing belief in a God of love – as a witness to this I had published a small book in 1973 called *Towards the Holy Spirit*. It would have seemed insufferably feeble to alter my beliefs simply because I myself was having a bad time. I had always known, after all, that many millions of my contemporaries are condemned to having a bad time for the whole of their lives.

But partly through my reading, and partly through some independent but slow and heavy process within my mind and heart, I gradually began to think of this depression in a quite new set of terms. Instead of looking for its causes and thinking about how to get rid of them, I began to look for its purposes and to wonder how I could fulfil them. I couldn't and still can't, tell whether God sends us such acute afflictions to bring us to some new understanding through our pain. But I am now as sure as I can be that depression is often a sign, whether human or divine, that the life of the victim needs to be drastically changed; that acts of genuine contrition are called for; that the dark block within can be dissolved only by recognizing that something like an inner death and resurrection is demanded of the sufferer.

In fact the measures that I took in the end were entirely practical. By the spring of 1977 I had begun to falter even in the writing of my book reviews for *The Observer*: this weekly task now filled me with the almost continual dread that I might be in no state to get it done. After many different pills had failed I finally persuaded my doctor to recommend me for a course of ECT (Electric Convulsion Treatment), and this was administered to me over a period of three weeks in May of that year. By the beginning of July I knew that the darkness was really lifting at last – not completely, but rather as a uniformly dark sky begins to break up into shreds and patches of cloud. A month later I began to toy with the idea of writing another book.

August 1980

PART OF
A JOURNEY

1 August 1977

More than two months have passed since I finished a course of ECT at Bristol, and for the past six weeks I have been almost entirely free of depression. No exorbitant elation, thank God, but the dazed incredulity of a prisoner suddenly let out into ordinary daylight after three years in a dungeon.

But I must beware of such extravagant images as this; for whatever purpose this diary is meant to serve it certainly won't serve any at all unless I keep it as simple and as truthful as I can. The depression, which began in a desultory way about seven years ago, was acute from 1974 to June of this year. (But the word 'acute' is also a dubious one, for although I was sometimes incapacitated for days on end I was often in reasonable working order for a week or more.)

Yes; but even on the best days there was that perpetual fear of a form of possession which sometimes came as suddenly as a blow.

3 August

How absurd it seems to me now, all that 'humane' outcry against ECT: as if a few electric shocks administered to an anaesthetized patient were more of an 'outrage against the person' than cutting open his stomach and removing his appendix. If the treatment works, as indeed it does in many cases, no experienced depressive is going to worry about the reason why.

[15]

It must be a sign of great improvement that I've begun to make serious plans for writing a new book. The title – *A Marriage of Heaven and Earth* – came to me some time last year, when I was incapable of getting much further than a title. But I do find a few notes scribbled diagonally across the great drawing book which Stephen Spender gave me for my sixtieth birthday. Inside the cover of the book Stephen had written 'Philip, it's never too late to write' – a friendly reminder, though I couldn't make much use of it at the time.

The fact that I've added the surname of my old friend in that passage shows that I must already be thinking in terms of some future reader of these pages. Reader or readers? When I started writing in this notebook on Monday I meant to clarify my own mind about my present condition before beginning to make detailed plans for *A Marriage of Heaven and Earth*. But now it seems that a second line of defence is being prepared in case that far more ambitious book should fail. So this will have to be an explanatory and public journal, not the cryptic and abbreviated kind which is written only for one's own private use or pleasure.

As for the much more grandiose work, failure seems all too likely. The idea – perhaps a sort of inflated gas balloon intended to carry me up and out of that desolation – was to express a whole theology by means which would strictly avoid the expository; the prosaic; the argumentative. I know that I wanted at all costs to suppress any note of didacticism or of personal authority.

Here are some of the notes which I wrote in a moment of hope last autumn:

A Marriage of Heaven and Earth

'Thy will be done on earth as it is in heaven.' i.e. his will is *not* now done on earth: full implications of this.

Blake inevitably in mind, but a much longer work than

Heaven and Hell. Inevitably longer, because so much more tentative; exploratory; earthbound.

Prose and poetry. Aphorisms. Pensées. Annotated quotations. The occasional 'I', but the I of an unholy fool. Mock prophetic. Enigmatic, but the enigmas not a stupid tease or a pretension to inexpressible depths. The enigmas of real doubt and searching.

Prayers. Exclamations. Runes.

9 August

It seems as if I'd set myself a task when dreaming or half-asleep; for the woken self finds these notes almost intimidating. I must have written them while still under the influence of *Pantaloon*, that huge 'tragi-comic epic', of which more than half is still unpublished. I was planning and writing that book from 1953 to 1975; and even making alterations to the last section but one (*Malcontenta*) as late as last summer. (I am very surprised now to realize how much work I *did* manage to do during the three worst years of my depression. I hardly ever failed to produce my weekly review for *The Observer*; and I even edited a book on the Spanish Civil War. Another sign that things can't have been quite so bad as they look from this side of them.)

Anyway *Pantaloon* has yet to find a publisher who will produce the whole work in a single volume; and this means that it still hangs rather uneasily round my shoulders, like unfinished business. But I feel sure that I shall never again want to write anything so monumental; or anything so consciously a 'work of art'. Whatever other lessons my confused and mutable faith may be teaching me I know that one of them is a lesson in simplicity. Simplicity of heart and mind. And enigmas, however innocently meant, may be very pleasant things for a writer to play about with, but are hardly the best means for writing a *useful* book.

Yet for me simplicity is far more daunting than contrivance and elaboration. I doubt if any field of human thought
has produced so much turgid and obscure writing as religion.
So many anguished attempts to express the inexpressible; to
make earthly sense of heavenly experience. And as for the great
simple masterpieces – St Mark's Gospel; *Everyman*; *The Pilgrim's
Progress* – all these were written at times when certain plain
religious beliefs could at least be kept clear of the perennial
babel.

But ours is an age in which a famous and formidable theologian has written an enormous commentary on the thirty pages
of St Paul's Epistle to the Romans. It is also an age when minor
theologians, driven to desperation by the general confusion,
have proposed that curious solecism, a theology without a god.
An age, too, when the whole exotic and mystifying vocabulary
of Eastern religions has clouded poor Christian heads with
strange negations and abstractions; old mysteries made even
more mysterious by the weirdness of new sounds. (Just as I was
beginning to write this entry I heard one of our community
milkers chanting '*Om Mani Padme Hum*' in time to the squeezing
of udders and the whining of milk in the pail. What would
Hardy's milkmaids have said to this!)

So the last thing I want to do in *M of H & E* is throw another
bulging packet of enigmas into the cauldron of modern religious
disputation. God forbid! And if I know anything at all about
my own religious temperament it isn't one which rejoices in
abstraction or mystification. I feel a strong urge to say simple
things and to pray simple prayers. I certainly feel something
like a moral obligation to avoid all those literary flourishes and
devices which I used, so appropriately and with so much gusto,
in *Pantaloon*.

But nothing is more repulsive than a false simplicity; which
means, in my case, any simplicity which hasn't been arduously
and painfully worked for. I know a few country people from

our own neighbourhood whose Christian faith is still untouched by Darwin; whose biblical trust has been inherited from generations of unquestioning believers. But this, for most of us, is a state of lost innocence which we may genuinely envy and admire; which we may even believe to have been the very best of earlier routes from earth to heaven; but which we can imitate ourselves only by a kind of mental bluster which cows the active mind and heart.

17 August

So I think it will be a long time before I start trying to write this ambitious book; and that my plans for it are likely to go through many changes before I feel able to begin sketching even a rudimentary text.

And in the meantime this journal will consist mainly of notes, as explicit as I can make them, of ideas which come to me either from other people's books or out of my own head. If events in my own life intrude here they will all, I hope, be relevant to this particular enterprise. It's clear that religious faith differs sharply from most other fields of speculation, and every scholarly 'discipline', in that it must be a directly personal thing. Unless I try to live what I believe, changing my life as my faith changes, then the final fabrication will be no use to me or to anyone else.

———— * ————

It seems that enquiry and commitment must go forward together hand in hand; continuously, and side by side. It is a very difficult task to keep them more or less level, but I can't see any other way to make honest progress. 'I believe in order that I may understand' (St Anselm). And now that I understand more clearly I believe more confidently. And now that I believe more confidently . . .

———— * ————

'Naked ape!' A jeering shout of contempt. Anyone who rejects

[19]

it out of hand, and with total conviction, must surely have caught at least some glimpse of man's true depth and dignity. That is, of his heavenly dimension.

———— * ————

Yang (Heaven) and Yin (Earth) meet in Man.

———— * ————

'Repentance'; 'Penitence'; 'Contrition'; – these are all good words, but haven't they come to imply a rather grandiose obsession with our own sinful selves? One Christian notion is that the past must be continuously scoured by confession, penance, and resolution to amendment. The opposite idea, with just as good Christian credentials, is of a sudden 'salvation' which obliterates past sins at a single swoop of heavenly mercy.

I like the sacrament of confession for its workaday good sense; the demand it makes for constant recollection – in the religious sense of a gathering-oneself-together; a taking-stock. I like the revivalist *coup de foudre* for its recognition that true revelation can instantly change a man, so that his sins simply fall away from him, to be replaced by present joy and future hope.

The two conceptions shouldn't exclude each other, though they are emotionally so far apart. The danger of regular confession is habituation and boredom; a dulling of the heart to any possibility of a more drastic change than mere absolution is ever likely to produce. The danger of 'seeing the light', 'being saved' etc. is that this tremendous experience may deceive the newly converted into believing that his spiritual journey is now over; that he has no more to learn: even that he's been changed 'in the twinkling of an eye' from a learner into a teacher.

The ideal, I suppose, would be a man who practises regular confession receives a sudden light; continues his confession as before. As before but with deeper insight; new joy; fuller love.

———— * ————

To replace 'Repentance' with 'Reorientation'? This is too clumsy, but I like the implication of turning towards the rising sun.

[20]

'Rebirth' should be kept for very special occasions (none of which has ever come my way, or is ever likely to).

'Salvation' has that horrid ring of spiritual arrogance: also the inevitable alternative of 'Damnation'.

I've always liked 'Amendment' for its modesty and dryness, and I used this word a lot in the later volumes of *Pantaloon*. But the word I'm looking for needs to be a little bolder.

But not so bold as 'Enlightenment'.

Perhaps 'Renewal' is the best, suggesting both a process and the possibility of sudden change. (In my case the process has been very slow, partial and recidivist; the moments of change so imperceptible that I have always doubted whether they really qualified.)

———— * ————

'Theology should be derived from a reflective interpretation of human experience' (Schleiermacher). This ought to be a truism, for where else do any valid ideas come from? But much theology is like a cube balanced on one of its corners; that corner being the original experience and all the rest a precarious intellectual superstructure.

18 August

One very simple and sad fact about Jesus is that he died 2000 years ago. And even belief in the Resurrection doesn't necessarily mean that we can believe his promise to be with us always, 'even unto the end of the world'.

I've never felt it possible to pray to Jesus; never felt the faintest flicker of his presence.

———— * ————

Whitehead's God of persuasive love rather than coercive power, who influences and is influenced by the world, and allows 'freedom in man and spontaneity in nature'.

But not even this gets away from the problem of omnipotence; therefore the problem of evil. For if God 'allows' spontaneity

[21]

in nature, but could control it if he wished, then he is just as much responsible for earthquakes as if he had planned each one of them.

I'd prefer to speak of a God who enables man to be partially free within his natural environment of iron Necessity. And I see God confronting the natural world, not as his creation but as the given material with which he has to work on Earth. Or the given domain *within which* he has to work. God/Heaven forever striving to penetrate Man/Earth. (But Man and Earth are appallingly resistant to the offered light and freedom.)

——— * ———

This leads to a strange thought. According to orthodox theology God's iron law (his 'providence') rules everywhere on Earth except in that area of freedom which he has granted to man: permission to be damned or saved. According to my tentative bundle of beliefs Necessity (Scientific Law) rules everywhere on Earth except in that area of man's heart and mind which God has been able to penetrate.

Yet although these ... visions? wild cosmic guesses? mental contraptions? differ so widely, they are agreed in their belief that man can have true freedom only by opening his heart and mind to God. Sister Paula (e.g.) would see this freedom as something *granted* by God to man; by Heaven to Earth. I see it as something *won* by God, with the help of man: and won *for* God as well as for man. A thinly scattered colonizing of Earth by Heaven; every holy man a light twinkling in the dark.

——— * ———

And any 'soul' would at least be a lesser light, for I shall use this very ambiguous word to mean a human heart and mind which have been opened to God, however narrowly.

However unconsciously?

I remember that staunch old unbeliever Barbara Wooton, getting so irritated in a television debate when some parson called her a better Christian than she knew. I shared her exasperation at what I took to be a blandly patronizing remark.

[22]

After all, Christians would not enjoy being called better unbelievers than they know.

But there is a real problem here, for wouldn't it be even worse
to say that an honest and loving atheist is rejected by God,
deprived of all heavenly light, simply because he can't believe
in God or Heaven? If we say this we take a dangerous step
towards the position of those sectarians who believe that they
alone are saved; the rest of us condemned to eternal hellfire.
Who are *we* to say through whom God is able to work on
Earth?

And yet we must think that to believe in him is at least a
little help to him; that our efforts to open our hearts to him
make it easier for him to enter us and dwell in us.

----- * -----

St Seraphim of Sarov (d. 1833). A very great saint, and recent
enough for us to know a lot about him. The evidence both for
his levitations and for his transfigurations is incontrovertible.
I haven't the least difficulty in accepting both.

But then what happens to my notion that God can work,
on Earth, only through the hearts and minds of men? Can he
also use our *bodies* in ways which contradict the laws of nature?

The lesson is that no man can prescribe the limitations of
God's power on Earth. I only know – i.e. believe with all my
heart, with all my strength, and with all my mind – that there
are such limitations. (For too many years I was prevented from
even attempting to make this journey by my revulsion against
the Omnipotent God of Christian orthodoxy.)

----- * -----

'All must know first the voice crying in the wilderness of their
hearts' (George Fox). I heard that voice again last night, though
as if from quite a long way off. I prayed that it won't come
any nearer.

[23]

A Marriage of Heaven and Earth

Perhaps the image of a pilgrim should be present somewhere; but should he be the central figure, or an intermittent device; an occasional narrator?

For many years he had pursued fame and all the pleasures of the senses.

When deeper questions confronted him, because of a death or a loss in love, he glanced at them, furrowed his brow and turned away again.

But each time that a great question was evaded in this way it entered him in the form of a pit or vacancy; a hollow pain.

So the day was bound to come when these dark pits had honeycombed his mind.

Thus I break an excellent resolution, and try out a few lines of possible text. Or rather, impossible text. Much too portentous. And if there is to be a pilgrim figure the irony of the word must be plain from the very start.

———— * ————

'By love he can be caught and held, but by thinking never' (*Cloud of Unknowing*). Yes, but though I can just believe that God loves me – since I am, after all, a tangible person – I find it very hard even to understand the words 'I love God'. The nearest I ever get is the notion of some Great Mother, incomprehensibly everywhere-at-once, who loves me and all mankind much as earthly mothers love their children.

Naively anthropomorphic? But my only experience of loving is of loving *people*. Certainly I shan't even attempt to love 'Not that, not that, not that, not that ...' the God of the so-called apophactic mystics. Nor do I feel any very strong affection for the Ground of Our Being; the Eternal I AM; the Absolute ...

And whatever God may be, he/she/it must include a person whom *we can love with simple hearts*.

[24]

Light has to be treated sometimes as particles; sometimes as waves. God, perhaps, sometimes as Pure Being; sometimes as a Loving Mother. Different approaches for different people and different occasions.

———— * ————

Resignation to inevitable ignorance must be an important element in wisdom. And probably the whole question of survival; the afterlife and so on comes into this category. 'Be Here Now!'

Yet how eagerly I still devour True Ghost Stories; almost anything at all on spirit-communication, psychical research, ESP. A rather shamefaced passion.

I have never once had any feeling that a person I have known and loved in life has been present to me after death. But then I am the least psychic of men: just as I often think, though there is no necessary connection, that I am one of the worst qualified of anyone I know to make a successful spiritual journey. Earthly. Earthy. Earthbound.

———— * ————

We played Haydn's *Nelson Mass* yesterday evening, and this was one of those rare occasions of great exaltation. But even then I felt that almost painful yearning; the sense of a vast promise not quite fulfilled. As if the rising line of the graph always reaches the end of the paper some distance from the top. And so I extrapolate from that high point of Earthly beauty, and imagine a continuation of the line in Heaven.

But I suppose the supreme secular experience is falling in love. The Beloved is praised by the Lover in terms which seem wildly extravagant, even deluded, to a friend. But perhaps this is because the Lover has seen God in the loved face: *has drawn God down* into the loved face, body, temperament, mind: soul.

———— * ————

'Religion is an attempt to live life according to the true facts of man's nature and of his place in the world.' Where did I

[25]

find this? Beautifully dry, simple and precise. Exhaustive, even.

———— * ————

And where did I find prayer described as 'the purification and making sense of our desires'?

23 *August*

Moral problems of a book reviewer. I have been brooding a little about my harsh, even snooty review of Bamber Gascoigne's *The Christians** which appeared on Sunday. In fact it was made all the snootier by the title – *Quizmaster's Christendom* – which was not my choice.

The general problem is simply that my near-Christian beliefs don't accord very well with my profession. If all my reviews were written in a spirit of sweet charity and judge-not-that-ye-be-not-judged they would soon nauseate my readers. (They'd nauseate my editor even sooner.) But shouldn't it be possible to condemn a book without jeering at the author?

Yet weighty, Olympian disapproval, without a touch of humour, falls into a moral pomposity which is even more insufferable than bitchiness.

In this case the problem was sharpened by the fact that Gascoigne wrote a very contemptuous and (of course!) shallow review of the first volume of *Pantaloon* when it appeared in 1961. I vowed, in my very early days as a reviewer, that I would never write a hostile review of a book written either by a friend or by someone whom I might be thought to regard as an enemy. To do the first is surely an unnecessary laceration. To do the second offends against the principle that justice must not only be done but also be seen to be done. (On the other hand I have taken great pleasure in heaping coals of fire on certain heads – e.g. that of Hugh Trevor Roper, the scourge of my father.)

But unfortunately this principle sometimes comes up against

* *The Christians* by Bamber Gascoigne (Jonathan Cape, London).

[26]

professional obligations; even professional competence. I was the obvious person to review Gascoigne's book; and as the only salaried reviewer on *The Observer* staff I haven't the freelance's right to refuse what my editor wants me to do.

Should I, then, have 'declared an interest' at the beginning of my review? Should I have warned readers of possible prejudice? But this seems absurdly self-important.

In this case, as in all the (few) others of the same kind, I was on the look-out for personal spite from the very beginning, when I first started reading the book. I am as sure as I can be that my judgement of the book was right, and that I was right to say so.

But a certain uneasiness remains. I wish I could review only books which I admire.

24 August

A strange digression. But I already suspect that this journal is going to become more and more personal as I become more engrossed in it. A book, perhaps, about the attempt to write another book; though in fact I feel more optimistic now about *M of H & E* than I did last week.

The great problem still is how to be simple without being silly.

———— * ————

Intercessionary prayer. Not a message sent up to Heaven for acknowledgement and action, but an attempt to transmit whatever love we have to the person in need. For all we know our loving prayer may be a means of *enabling* God to help the other.

———— * ————

God and man straining to reach each other. Michelangelo's *Creation of Adam*, fingers at full stretch towards each other. How hard for man! How hard for God!

———— * ————

'And the Lord formed man of the dust of the ground, and breathed into his nostrils the breath of life; and man became a living soul' (Genesis 2:7). It's only the first declaration which *M of H & E* is bound to reject, and surely the least important. The second declaration is a powerful metaphor for our need of the infused Spirit to make us fully human. And it's this alone which enables us to transcend apehood and become the 'living souls' of the third part.

25 August

Today Kerry, of the Barn House community, brought back the printed copies of our 'prospectus' from Monmouth, and we all feel reasonably pleased with it. No. Better say that those of us who composed the document – with what a long-bargaining over words and phrases! – are the ones who accept it. Martin and Rose tend to be ribald; and Dave is airily noncommittal.

[Decorated letter head]

BARN HOUSE COMMUNITY

'Our community was established some three years ago with the purpose of exploring a way of life which would be ecologically sound and which would lead to self-development through shared experience. Thus the people who came together during our first year were united by their wish to experience community living and by their common interest in organic gardening and farming.

'But over the years there has been a gradual, and quite unplanned, shift of emphasis in the attitudes of most members towards the deeper purposes of our living here together. Roughly, the element of shared life has become more prominent than the attempt to achieve self-sufficiency. And this has been accompanied by a growing awareness that what we are seeking is a love capable of crossing all boundaries and achieving a level of consciousness on which we can enter into true oneness with each other.

'It is not that the move towards self-sufficiency and the concern for natural rhythms and balances has become unimportant to us, but rather that we now see these things as only one part of our larger aim. We believe this "Way" is possible by opening ourselves to a higher power of love – called by whatever name best suits the individual – working both within us, between us and from outside us. This means learning to love and to give oneself to others in order to get beyond the ego-self and discover the true Self within.

'The ordering of our lives here is flexible; but at the very heart of them we put the Sunday evening "communion" at which we all meet to remind ourselves of our main purpose through readings, meditation and other methods. On the practical side it is, of course, necessary for members to earn money for the community by going out to work (e.g. part-time teaching and gardening). But we believe that a very important part of our aim is served by keeping two days a week when, after breakfasting at the same time, we all work together on our own land or inside the buildings. In addition to these common activities we also pursue our individual paths, which currently include pottery, puppetry, music, drama, herbal medicine, yoga, tai-chi and private meditation.

'It is from all this that we hope to strengthen our love, our joy and our spiritual understanding. This applies just as much to our parties, celebrations, games and expeditions.

'We feel it important to emphasize that our fellowship is not just turned inward on itself; we regard ourselves as an integral part of that wider community which consists of our neighbours, our previous members and the many good friends who have passed through Barn House during the last three years.

'It only remains to say that the community has a good-sized house and neighbouring barn; about six acres of land (two under vegetables); two cows, chickens and a beehive. At the time of writing there are five full members, and about five transients: we feel that the optimum number would be ten, both as regards living space and also in order to form a viable and closely-knit family for future growth together in love and consciousness.'

BARN HOUSE COMMUNITY
Brackweir
Nr Chepstow
Gwent
Tel. Tintern 365

A bit sloppy in parts. 'Spiritual' itself is such a vague and awkward term; even unctuous. But there seems to be no other; and the main thing is that those of us who want to go forward in this direction (Kerry, Simon and Clare within the community; Sally and I as 'associate members') should know what we mean among ourselves and what we are offering to possible future members.

As for the sturdy farming-and-no-nonsense communards, of whom young Martin has become the derisive spokesman, they are all making plans to leave in any case. No use denying that there's now a sharp and painful rift; particularly evident at our Sunday evening 'communions' when all the Martin-inclined stay rather noisily away. *Amicable* derision? Ostensibly amicable.

But we – though Sally less than I – are determined to do all we can to help the Holy Remnant through this crisis: in fact to be part of it as never before; members one of another. We've put some more cash into the very depleted funds, but for us the most important thing is our will to be *with* BH as we have never been since we moved out to Woodroyd two and a half years ago.

I shall always regret that the best years, 1975 and 1976, when the community was really humming with energy, affection, even joy, coincided with the very worst years of my depression. S believes that the depression was hastened and sharpened by my instigation of a community in our old house to which I myself was quite incapable of belonging. She may be right. This was probably the most drastic of the many occasions in my life when will and capacity have been absurdly divided. Trying, so often, to live beyond my moral means, and all the grotesque calamities of failure.

But my failure to be anything more than a weak and limping member during the good years is all the more reason why I should now throw my revived energies into the work of resurrection. A rather portentous word, but nothing less than some form of rebirth can save BH from the awful fate anticipated for it by (Australian) Mary: that of becoming what they call a 'crash pad'.

I am often aware of how much we shall miss Bim, gone off to be a street clown in London: he was one of the very first, and like all the 1975–7 'old-timers', a person of great character and strong personality. Shy but stubborn; a true artist; a charming, kind, vigorous but melancholy young man. This is another real loss to us, after Robin, Steve and Adima, Dave and Fiona. Already we begin to look back on a golden age; a classical period of the community.

Yes; but we must look forward too; and who knows what bright phoenix of the spirit may not rise from our old family house along the valley. I pray for this every night.

1 September

We load on to God compensations for all the lacks which we bemoan in ourselves. Being finite we call him infinite; a word which nobody understands. Perhaps he is only a thousand times less constricted than we are, which would *seem like* infinity to us.

———— * ————

Jesus half-perceived the God of Pure Love, but was still half held in the grip of Jehovah. Perhaps St Francis was an even more complete representative of the new God than Jesus had been. But Jesus alone was credited with the potent myth of death and rebirth for the redemption of man.

[31]

3 September

God as one: God as many. Perhaps there is no contradiction here in the arithmetic of Heaven. (How much I like the phrase 'all the company of Heaven'.)

———— * ————

It's said that man is the only self-conscious animal. He not only thinks, feels and wishes, but knows himself to be thinking, feeling and wishing. This is what Whitman hated in man, preferring the other animals because:

They do not sweat and whine about their condition;
They do not lie awake in the dark and weep for their sins;
They do not make me sick discussing their duty to God ...

He preferred those other animals for being 'so placid and self-contained'; yet it is all this whining, weeping and discussing which makes us yearn for the light of Heaven. This is the soul at work – which is often an ugly sight compared with the graces of the swan and the puma. But that ugly self-disgust is just what saves us from the frozen self-containment of those lovely creatures.

4 September

Disbelievers claim that all religious faith is subjective. Heavenly (otherworldly) reality is proved to be no better than a wishful fantasy by the contradictory accounts of it given at different times and in different places. These accounts, they say, may differ in power of expression, or moral effectiveness, or richness of imagination: they cannot differ in correspondence to objective truth.

Always remember that the realistic alternative to this sceptic is not a man who claims to know the truth about Heaven, but a man who believes that there *is* such a truth, however little of it he knows. Or is ever likely to know.

——— * ———

Laura* is in trouble with her new, and first, boyfriend. Partly because of her childhood illnesses we have always been particularly protective towards her; and she, as a result, particularly dependent on us. In fact only a few months ago it would have seemed inconceivable to any of us that she would by now be able to spend nights away at the house of Richard's parents.

Of course we know that this sort of trouble is inevitable; that she will get over it; that she must go through this necessary hardening process if she's ever to face life without our immediate and constant support. But what *aching* pain her pain gives us; worse, I think, than all the other miseries of her last two difficult years.

It is not that we love her more than the other two children (in my case, than my other four), but her vulnerability is so great that all the normal pains seem to threaten her with some crushing and irremediable disablement.

Love of children: certainly the purest and simplest kind I've ever felt. No doubt this, too, has its element of egomania, but the principal feeling is a passionate hope that they shall be happy; and with no apparent demand for anything in return. Of course I would grieve if they turned, or grew against me. But I know that this would make no difference at all to my love for them. (Love for a loved and loving wife is even stronger; but how many complexities of giving and taking enter into *that* astonishing entanglement!)

10 September

I was 'Lamplighter' at BH on Sunday and knew all the time that I was doing it wrong. Because our communions have tended to hesitancy, even confusion, I was determined to lead

* Youngest child, aged 17; the only one still living with her parents.

[33]

this one with a fine aplomb, one eye, perhaps, on the strict liturgical order of Sunday morning mass at the convent.

So it went: I lit the lamp; we passed it round the circle as usual; then a full five minutes of holding hands in silence; then the Gregorian chants on our cassette player (recorded from the stereo at Woodroyd that afternoon). Ten minutes of this before I switched off and read a passage from Merton for ten minutes more. Then a noble OM, rising, falling, dying away – say another five minutes. Prayer from the Upanishads ('From the Unreal lead me to the Real, From Darkness lead me to Light ...'), followed by Kerry and Dave striking up on their guitars for 'May the long-time sun'. I conducted this to a close: short silence again before I stood up; we all stood up to give each other our hug of peace, clockwise, with 'Peace be with you, Simon' – 'Peace be with you, Clare' ... around the circle. Circle completed – communion completed. Forty-five minutes.

Each item was good in itself; but I soon realized that the disciplined structure was all wrong; quite contrary to the natural mode of BH. When (e.g.) Bec is Lamplighter things are uncertain, unpredicted, a bit scrappy: but the rest of us share the work with her; feel our way forward together.

———— * ————

A long discussion afterwards about tensions and strains. I said that this may be a painful travail from which, God willing, something new and better will be born. But as soon as I'd said this I realized that it's easy enough for me to take this lofty view, since S and I are safely outside the immediate circle of pain.

But I also realized that none of the others had reacted to my comment in this way. How free they are from the malice, and even malignancy, of my own circle when I was in my twenties and thirties.

12 September

I bought a pair of formidable brown boots in Monmouth,

and recognized afterwards that this was the latest – and far the most modest – gesture of release. First the caravan, that most forthright symbol of freedom regained after the near-confinement of depression. This needed a new car to tow it; a new radio cassette player for music on our escapades. Which suggested a completely new hi-fi equipment for Woodroyd: what better means of taking wing than music! So a little orgy of record and cassette buying ...

Putting all this in the same category as the regeneration of BH makes it seem respectable: signs of renewal at least. Rebirth? And how should I not rejoice at this revived appetite for life? But plainly, too, my old acquisitiveness, long hunched up in the dark with every other enthusiasm, has also come prancing out again.

But not much guilt, just yet. After all I do *enjoy* these new possessions, and true enjoyment is a great solvent of guilt.

Guilt, of course, will follow: always follows. How many lives that money might have saved! Well, more of that when it comes: there's always more of *that* to come.

———— * ————

'Who are you, O Lord, and what am I?' Even St Francis had to ask himself these questions. But most of us reverse the order; we must question ourselves before we can start to question God: anthropology before theology; Earth before Heaven. (How that book of mine now plods: or wavers!)

———— * ————

Theology = Stories told on Earth about Heaven. But if none of these stories is 'true' – in the Freddie* sense – how can we decide which ones are better than others? Survival is one criterion; and the stories that survive do two things at least: they raise the hearts of many people, and they make them aware of strange inner responses. Surely I heard this story somewhere else? In a dream? Before I was born? On a different star? So surely there must be another place; another time; to which I

* A. J. Ayer; old friend and sceptical philosopher.

[35]

once belonged, half-belong to now; yearn to belong to again.

And all great art carries this same echo of another place. The tragic self-portraits of Rembrandt are lit, in spite of their sadness, by a light from Heaven.

13 September

The Sacramental (Christian) against Maya (Buddhist and Hindu). The natural world is not an illusion but the only means we have of making symbols which give us a glimpse of Heaven. God does not estrange us from Earth when he shines his light into our souls. He shows us that we can be at home here, *provided we never forget his abiding presence.* 'The gain of the Earth must be Heaven's gain too' (Browning). I am, by the grace of God, a man of the world.

———— * ————

This old monster Rajneesh; so arrogant and egotistical; lives luxuriously in Poonah, it seems, with a swarm of rich Western disciples. Yet some of his writing is very good. How can this be? It deeply offends my longing for simple and coherent truth – e.g. Good Gurus eat Gruel.

Wisdom from gruel-despising Bhagwan Shree Rajneesh: 'A teacher, as opposed to a master, can teach you everything about God. You can become a Doctor of Divinity: DD. It is simply unbelievable that things like this exist on earth – people who carry a doctorate about divinity!'

Or this:

A disciple is concerned with knowing: a student is only concerned with knowledge.'

14 September

'Beloved God; Heaven, Enlightener of earthly darkness; I pray for your help in making yet another earthly attempt to reach you. May this work also serve you in your endless attempt to enter our hearts and minds; for unless it helps you to reach us it cannot help us to reach you. I know that those on Earth who come closest to you do so without the use of earthly words. But most of us are unable to achieve the wordless communication of mystical union and visionary grace. The best we can do is to look for new words to express what can never be expressed; contrive new forms through which our love may pass more easily to you, and yours to us ...'

In fact, devise some single prayer – far tidier than this one with which to infuse the whole book. A devotional work rather than an explanatory or descriptive one. (For who am I to explain or to describe?)

On the other hand who am I to pray, either: there's *nothing* so hard as prayer.

'Whatever appears in this text as a bold statement of fact is a cry for heavenly enlightenment out of the depths of earthly darkness. I write about something of which I know nothing. I am like an illiterate pushing wooden letters about in the hope that they will happen to make an intelligible word.'

And the fault of *that* is obsequiousness and melodramatic excess. If the metaphor were apt I'd simply resign myself to automatic writing: never make a single correction. (And of course there are those who believe that automatic writing does give the best chance of communicating with another world. But which other world? There may be millions of them.)

After all, if God is *infinitely* beyond our highest conceptions nothing we say about him would be truer than anything else. To say that he's a green clockwork mouse with red claws would be just as good as all the high stutterings of St John of the Cross.

Best, perhaps, to do what all popular religion has always done; create a bold mythology which has real sacramental value, real holiness. But we must always call it sharply to heel whenever it starts behaving as if it were literal truth.

The trouble with all creeds is that they try to deny the rich story-telling of legitimate myth-theology by dessicating the story into a set of factual propositions.

15 September

A good afternoon at BH transplanting spring cabbages with Rose, Martin and Kerry. Through the tension, and beyond it, there's much affection still. What's more I respond easily to Martin's sardonic attitude to meditation, zikr, yoga, etc., although I also try to practice them. I even respond to his derisive irreligion. It's generally recognized nowadays that every good Christian must bear his quota of doubt. Perhaps periodical outbursts of downright blasphemous mockery might also help to freshen us up a bit.

Donne on Doubt

To adore, or scorn an image, or protest,
May all be bad. Doubt wisely; in strange way
To stand inquiring right is not to stray;
To sleep or run wrong is. On a huge hill
Cragged and steep, Truth stands, and he that will
Reach her, about must and about must go,
And what the hill's suddenness resists, win so.

———— * ————

M of H & E

To start with a string of defining propositions. A *dry* beginning. Blake does much better:

RINTRAH roars and shakes his fires in the burden'd air;
Hungry clouds swag on the deep.

But I doubt if I could ever rise to that; or whether I want to. Nothing could be more ludicrous than the prophetic stance adopted by someone with no prophetic insight.

In any case quite a lot of Blake's grandiloquence was a take-off of Swedenborg. Probably best to think about Blake as little as possible. Though I do rather like the recurring side-heads.

What about IMPERMISSIBLE SPECULATIONS and VISIONS OF A BLIND MAN?

No getting away from it: this must be a highly patterned work of literary craft. Inner shapes to be very carefully devised.

IRATUS (or FURIOSO) – the man forever in a rage; and others of this order.

'By God,' said Iratus, between his black teeth,
'There is no kindness nor honesty left in Babylon.'

A journey being made behind it all? Dimly seen, but providing a narrative backbone. (But *not* allegorical. Why is allegory so impossible for us now?)

Section of pure homage; paid to all my particular heroes and heroines.

Not to be shy of contradiction. A work of cheerful and fruitful contradiction.

One eye on *Faust. Dynasts?* Working towards oldest literary form of all – Sacred Drama. An angel as chorus, unseen/unheard by Hero, but heard by us. His guardian angel, with him everywhere.

16 September

Some fears lately that Laura's anorexia might be getting a grip on her again. Oh, this mixture of loving tenderness and irritation! How hard it is to suffer the obsessions of others, however keenly we may be aware of our own. S is very good with L, though always afraid of being an over-fussy parent. (But S is wonderfully good with anyone in trouble. Except herself, of course!)

17 September

'Phenomena of psychological transference and combinations. If people were told: What makes carnal desire imperious in you is not its carnal element. It is the fact that

[39]

you put into it the essential part of yourselves – the need for unity, the need for God – they wouldn't believe it ... To make the Christian faith palpable, it must be shown to be implicitly present, in a degraded form, even in the basest passions. What we are talking to you about is the very thing you are longing for with your whole soul, at this moment, in your present state. But you give it a false name. Don't give it the name we suggest. Simply stop giving it any name at all. Persevere in this interior silence. And one day you will hear a voice that will tell you the true name' (Simone Weil).

There is a crude answer to all this; and crude answers aren't always the worst ones – 'You can't fob off a randy man with Holy Communion'. Nor, perhaps, ought you to try.

For Simone W this passage is fairly tolerant about lust; but she still calls such desires 'base' and 'degraded'. So I'd say that she's writing about the sexual urge in its purest and least discriminating form. And though I use 'pure' here in the sense of 'unmixed'; 'undiluted', I mean to give it a positive moral sense as well. Two strangers meet; please each other both as persons and as bodies; sleep together with friendly joy; part forever in the morning. To me this is a genuinely pure and delightful encounter; a marvellous reciprocity of giving and receiving. Therefore *holy*, to those of pure heart and mind unpolluted by prurient guilt.

This view of what is disparagingly called 'casual sex' makes it easier for me than for SW to think that such an act will be blessed by God. Any intense and guiltless *sharing* must be at least a minor experience of the Kingdom. But SW is saying both more and less than this: that carnal desire is base in itself, but is *really* a longing not for another body but for God. One of those theories which tempts me to apply Freddie's Verification Principle. And under that severe instrument – 'putting to the question' as the Inquisition described torture – SW's proposition fails as surely as any other psychological theory. (Try verifying the Oedipus Complex!)

Agreed that every earthly desire may be an *incipient* desire

[40]

for Heaven: but not a *mistaken* desire for Heaven. I really do want that woman: I am mistaken only if I treat this desire as base and degraded. Seen as a step towards God – not as a substitute for taking such a step – shared sexual joy may be a genuine act of worship.

19 September

Last week I reviewed John Heilpern's extraordinary book on Peter Brook's theatrical expedition through darkest Africa. (*Conference of the Birds: The Story of Peter Brook in Africa* (Faber & Faber, London).) Never having been a theatre-goer it had never occurred to me that modern theatre could, as it were, rediscover its sacred origins. As I wrote in my review I had always regarded Brook as a monster of trendy self-advertisement: which shows again how wrong it is to form judgements without adequate evidence. I now see that 'audience participation' has a real and important meaning; the kind of theatre, I suppose, which is furthest removed from Racine. Furthest removed, also, from Brecht's Alienation Principle, which insists that the play is never anything other than a play.

The best moments of Brook's strange international troupe in Africa suggest a joyful, as well as a sacred, communication across deep barriers of language and culture.

———— * ————

The form of 'belief' which makes God 'the depth of our being', etc., is simply old Atheism writ large. Religious trappings, the mutilation of religious language, make it all the worse. If they are anything at all these people are florid psychologists; anthropocentrics who fill out that empty centre with the language of profundity.

And all this talk of God 'including within himself' both good and evil; darkness and light. This sounds dramatic, sophisticated, even impressive so long as you stick to the grand abstractions. Let them come down to earth; tell us that God worked through Himmler just as surely as through St Francis. And what

[41]

about the sheer squalor, meanness, *meagreness* of everyday vanity, greed, jealousy, malice. Are these as godlike as the life and death of Dietrich Bonhoeffer?

The dreadful dread of 'above' and 'beyond'. *Of course* Heaven is above Earth, and God is beyond man. That is the primary fact: penetration of Earth by Heaven, Man by God is the (blessed) secondary fact.

———— * ————

New Testament scholarship. An essential task performed. But what remains when every doubt has been thrown on the person and words of Jesus is that *certain people* wrote all the words of the New Testament in the course of about seventy years. And the greater the number of human minds which contributed to the telling of those stories, the writing of those letters, the more amazing the revelation. Perhaps, as my friend Gerry Richards has suggested, the greatest event of the New Testament was not the Crucifixion or the Resurrection, but Pentecost.

21 September

Nor is God 'in' that much-loved, ever-changing view of the Wye at Bigsweir – far below me, over falling woods and fields. But he is in my loving it and praising it: in everything which makes me treat this valley as something more than an environment.

Bewitched by beautiful and gentle valleys, pantheists and nature mystics forget the arctic waste; and sweet valleys such as this one ravaged by an earthquake, such as I saw in Ithaca twenty years ago.

———— * ————

Evensong at Tymawr. Holy and loving sisters singing the psalms. Because St Benedict started the practice 1400 years ago. And this antiquity of the tradition is impressive. But what contortions of mind and heart must be needed to convert so much brazen self-righteousness, so much whining self-pity, so much bloodthirsty vindictiveness into a 'type' of Christ's passion – or whatever meaning they give it.

———— * ————

M of H & E

Jerusalem still a permissible symbol of the Good City; *Babylon* of Bad City.

But how do I feel about Babylon now, where I spent so many years of my young life? Its stews and gutters, The Gargoyle Club and all my bad companions – Brian, Dylan, Guy, David ... *their boyfriends and their molls. The friends of my dereliction: permanent tenants of my mind.

We were 'sinners', of course; drunken, gluttonous and lustful creatures who gave not a thought to our souls. And most of them dead in their desolation; not a relish of salvation in them. But how dare we say that even those lives were wasted? And as for my own apprenticeship in Babylon? Perhaps there is a Time for Excess and a Time for Moderation: a Time for Earthly Pleasure (and all its pains) and a Time for Heavenly Striving (and all its pains).

(Not sure how much I really believe all this. Certainly there was no need to spend *so long* in Babylon; ten years in the stews, at least, and many later returns.)

———— * ————

A blasphemous joke. In Times Square a vast crucifixion in garish lights: the Roman soldier is reaching up the sponge to Jesus, but from the mouth of the Crucified emerge the words, 'Not unless it's Sarson's'.

I find this very funny; and feel no shame in doing so. This is partly because the joke is not against Jesus but against the ruthless vulgarity of the advertising world. But wildly inappropriate associations are surely the root of all humour. The Crucifixion evokes deep reverence; perhaps anguish; perhaps holy joy: an ad for Sarson's vinegar is like a bottle-nosed clown in

* Brian Howard, Dylan Thomas, Guy Burgess, David Tennant.

[43]

baggy trousers suddenly appearing at the foot of the cross.

—— * ——

'Man is like a castaway, clinging to a spar and tossed by the waves. He has no control over the movement imposed on him by the water. From the highest heaven God throws a rope. The man either grasps it or not. If he does, he is still subject to pressures imposed by the sea, but these pressures are combined with the new mechanical factor of the rope, so that the mechanical relations between the man and the sea have changed. His hands bleed from the pressure of the rope, and he is sometimes so buffeted by the sea that he lets go and then catches it again.

But if he voluntarily pushes it away, God withdraws it.'

Simone Weil at her very best and very worst. The whole first paragraph is a magnificent image; but what perversity, what melodramatic love of 'hard sayings', makes her turn God into a monster? (Jesus said we are to forgive not seven times but seventy times seven; i.e. forever. Will God do less?)

24 September

Time to take stock. I've been making serious efforts to pray and meditate for about eighteen months. With what results, if any?

Loved ones – S and the children – all agree I'm less impatient than I used to be. And that was no minor failing. An intolerant, and intolerable, demand that things happen, people act, just when I wanted them to happen and act. I never really thought that the whole line of traffic in the jam ahead should immediately get on to the verge and let us pass; but I spoke and behaved as if I did think this. Possessed by a noxious demon of furious impatience. The rampant, tumescent self.

Not that I'm now a model of saintly patience; far from that. I doubt if I've even reached the average level. But now, when held up on the road, I get out my rosary and repeat my mantra – 'The Peace of God' – and nearly always manage at least to keep my mouth shut – instead of taking it out on poor S. (Though at bad times the beads get rough treatment and the unspoken mantra sounds more like a curse than a blessing.)

Ah, but should I take any pleasure from this improvement? Well, the self-congratulation is wry enough, surely, and scarcely involves me in the sin of pride. Relief at not behaving like an insufferable lunatic is hardly the fault by which the angels fell.

And what other benefits from so much arduous concentration, sitting cross-legged with my back against the bed? Certainly not a speck of enlightenment; but at least I had the sense from the start to have no such high expectations. It is something – perhaps quite a lot – that without any conscious act of the will I find that I've stopped biting my nails.

25 September

Present regime: Twenty minutes yoga exercises in the morning, followed by five minutes prone and silent on the floor. In the evening the imitation lotus, concentrating on a few (personally sacred) objects set out on the little shrine I made last summer. Half an hour.

26 September

M of H & E

Theology is the strangest and hardest to place of all the subjects which have exercised the curiosity and passions of mankind. (As Gibbon might almost have written.) Can't be called a 'discipline' in the academic sense, as History, Physics and English Literature are all legitimate disciplines. Nature of scholarly discipline is necessary agreement among practitioners; agreed method by which its assertions can be verified. Historians of opposite sympathies describe the English Civil War in very different terms; but all agree that the battle of Naseby was fought in 1645. And if challenged they can produce contemporary documents to prove it. In the strict sciences disagreement is virtually limited to the fringes of new discovery and speculation.

But on a major theological issue – e.g. relationship of Holy Spirit to Father and Son – there has been violent and enduring disagreement; and neither party can devise a means of confuting the other.

The very reason, perhaps, why theological disputes have been so bitter and bloody, whereas rival historians have never done worse than be rude to each other in learned journals. Since neither theological opponent can prove the other wrong the only way of settling the dispute seemed to be by sword or stake.

This resistance of theological statements to any form of verification has led to the current dismissal of the whole subject as literally nonsensical. When Christians declare that Jesus was 'begotten, not made, one in essence with the Father' they may seem to be making a factual statement; in reality, say Freddie et al., they are talking gibberish. And many modern theologians would now agree.

> 'One route away from this impasse is to decide that God-language is not to be measured against God, but against the human attitudes which reach out to God. We can say, that is, that it does not at all refer to God and, indeed, that reference is not its business. The grammar of "God" is a non-referential grammar. Its absolute intentionality arises, not from an absolute object that it is meant to describe, but from the quality of the adoration, faith, patience and self-giving that it is meant to express.' (?)

In Cyril's* memorable words – 'He's groggy; he can't last'.

It's wise to recognize that theology is not about God but about Man seeking for God; Heaven guessed at from Earth. But whoever wrote that typical piece of modern Christian argument is trying to wrench a statement out of one language and into another. To express adoration of Heaven I can think of

* Cyril Connolly: from *The Rock Pool*.

[46]

better ways than to quote a piece of subtle Greek theologizing of the fourth century.

27 September

So a crude man of the world, when told that Jesus was born of the Holy Ghost and the Virgin Mary, might ask, 'Do you mean that this ghost of yours copulated with a Galilean peasant girl two thousand years ago? If so, what did he do it with?'

'Obscene blasphemy!' answers the ordinary Christian. 'Not only grossly offensive but also stupidly misunderstanding. That is not what I meant at all. That is not it at all.' If he is a simple Christian he might get no further than this echo of poor bewildered Prufrock. If more sophisticated he'd start talking about myth and symbol.

And it's true, of course, that many orders of language elude those hatchet men of modern philosophy. Poetry conveys vivid meaning, but is under no obligation whatever to submit it to verification/falsification. 'April is the cruellest month ...'

Would it be better then, if theologians finally withdrew their subject from the sciences ('Queen of the Sciences') and placed it among the arts? Is theology more like a dance than a proof; more like a poem than a logical proposition?

More like, perhaps; but few theologians would be satisfied with what they'd consider a form of demotion. A demotion from the literal to the metaphorical. Few would accept the suggestion that 'Jesus is the Son of God' is a statement of the same order as 'April is the cruellest month'. All except the most radical theologians would feel that the statement about Jesus is 'true' as Eliot's statement about April can't be regarded as true. So the creeds, they say, are more than 'poetically' or 'metaphorically' true.

It seems, then, that theology may be something quite on its own; *sui generis*; unfittable into any category of human discourse. For it is trying, as most of us would admit, to say the unsayable; to find words for an experience which is beyond all words.

[47]

(April, on the other hand, is easily describable in literal and prosaic terms; it is the fourth month of our year; weather of a certain type; vegetation at a certain stage ...)

So we fall back on 'Faith'. The uniqueness of a religious doctrine is that it depends on an act of belief which is itself a moral quality.

But how grotesque, they say, to claim that it's morally praiseworthy to believe something simply because there are no grounds for believing it! So we answer, nowadays, by saying that 'trust' is a better word than 'faith': and indeed the faith to be expressed in *M of H & E* will be based almost entirely on my own trust in the witness of others.

How to explain the New Testament; the great saints; the enduring assurance of Another Order of Reality in all parts of the world, etc.

Most of the Christian saints were not only very good men but also very intelligent ones. But what is most striking about them is not their intelligence; not even their goodness; but, precisely, their *sanctity*. A ridiculously circular argument? Not if you understand the word. Their *holiness*. Their *blessedness*. Their *otherworldliness*.

So there *are* words, after all, which we can use and with which we can communicate among ourselves. Myself unsanctified, unholy, unblest and this-worldly I know perfectly well what the opposite words mean. I can recognize those qualities in men and women I meet, or read about. And if the opponent still says that the words are meaningless he is behaving like a tone-deaf man who insists that the words 'harmony' and 'melody' have no meaning.

29 September

I must have got carried away on Tuesday, and in quite the wrong direction. I fell into the pit of apologetics, though that is the last place I want to be when writing *M of H & E*. No didactic arguments, please. I don't even want a rational

[48]

sequence of thought; but pungent juxtapositions; crafty echoes and repetitions; the gnomically shrewd.

———— * ————

A very good communion at BH on Wednesday – called by Michele in special need – helped me to see how far I'd been going astray. A little chanting, but a lot of silence. And my agitation of that afternoon was marvellously calmed. An apt and loving reminder that what we do matters much more than what we say. For how crassly that last entry would have fallen into our silence, sitting hand-in-hand, all eyes on the still flame of the lamp.

30 September

M of H & E

Yet what have I got but words?

Theology is a false science but a true experience.

All theology, all the dogmas and doctrines of religion, are stories told on Earth about Heaven.

In this story Heaven and Earth are distinct but related domains (continuums; spheres; realms; fields; planes; levels).

The word 'Heaven' includes the words 'God' and 'Spirit': the Holy and the Sacred.

But Hell is one extremity of man's condition on Earth.

Hell is a dramatic term for a man in a state of extreme affliction.

Hell is not the opposite of Heaven but of Holy Bliss and Heavenly Light on Earth.

(Scarcely gnomic!)

Three parts: The Quest
The Drama
The Teaching

The modern Tempters. Job. The Apocalypse. From the NT Apocalypse 'we get the assurance that human history must flow into the glory of eternity'.

[49]

Render unto Science; and *with real generosity.* For all truth is truth under God.

M *of* H *&* E

Heaven is the light of earthly man's enlightenment.

Heaven is the source of all that's described on Earth as Holiness.

But in particular Heaven is the God of Love and the City of God; the Kingdom and the Holy Spirit; the Risen and Ascended Christ.

Earth is the order of space and time.

Earth is the continuum of Space-Time.

Earth is the whole material universe.

But in particular Earth is this planet, inhabited by Man.

A bit more like it, perhaps. But how hard to go on from there without falling back into either argument or waffle!

In any case too overtly Christian. Surely my heart and mind are at least as much engaged by our eclectic communions at BH as by mass at Tymawr. The incompetent stutter is no less valid than the calm, antique assurance?

Watching that Buddhist monk on TV, walking along the path from his monastery *I couldn't doubt* his holiness; his vision; his knowledge; his blessed state. It was clever of the director to keep the camera fixed on those holy feet for fully five minutes, and to end the programme there. How to convey what it was that made those feet so deeply impressive; more eloquent than any words?

8 October

And then the banana skin! Always well-placed: never foreseen.

I got roaringly-boringly drunk on an evening out; felt, next

[50]

morning, that I'd been set back months and months. And this was followed by several days of pain and fear.

But today I begin to wonder whether that cropper – or any other – need be a setback. Not that such mishaps teach lessons of future abstinence, or I'd have learned *this* lesson forty years ago. But that break-out, that foolery, and all the fearful days that followed – surely they should somehow be *incorporated*. Perhaps it's part of *my* dance to fall flat on my face from time to time.

A rare event now, in any case. This hermit-life provides so few occasions for relapses into Babylonian habits.

(Or is that the wrong way round? Wasn't I driven into seclusion by the constant pains of social drinking; wildly exhibited humiliations; such troughs, in both senses, of self-disgust and remorse?)

———— * ————

Days of doubt too, of course. Always lurking in the mind the mocking suspicion that this whole religious to-do is simply an old man's hobby. Something to fill the empty space. A warding-off of senile apathy.

10 October

Rereading yesterday's review has been a rather ludicrous experience. The book was a life of Elizabeth Bowen, and the reviewer's tone of quiet authority and dignified self-confidence suggests a very different provenance from the bedroom of a man sick with a hangover and groaning with remorse. The comic discordance between appearance and reality.

The book also reminded me of the several different worlds I used to half-belong-to in my earlier years; in this case the proud, respectable upper-class intelligentsia. And now it really seems that S and I belong to no 'world' at all – except perhaps the heterogeneous world of Monmouth and District. Peripheral even to that.

'God is everywhere, but not everywhere to us. There is but one point in the Universe where God communicates with us, and that is the centre of our own soul' (St Augustine).

From this, perhaps, a whole new Christian mythology could be created. (No adequate new Christian myth since fifth century?)

Evolution as the Descent of God. Fall of Man = increasing ability of God to enter man's evolving soul. For (mythical) convenience imagine a single mutated man (Adam) who first distinguished himself from clan, tribe, totem ... whole environment, and said, 'I am I'. So God entered Adam at the very moment of a terrifying loss – the loss of his close solidarity with Earth. And God then set him the alarming but exhilarating task of regaining what he had lost – his true sense of belonging here – but of knowing from now on that he also belongs to the Kingdom. Transfiguring love of God and his neighbour was now man's proper goal; his only adequate ambition ...

———— * ————

M of H & E

Shortest possible units. Single lines; or very short paras. No continuous narrative. 'The Lost Traveller's dream under the hill.'

At last I decided to remove a single snow-brick from the roof of my igloo.

I saw nothing but darkness.

Perhaps this was because my igloo was enclosed in another one which was only a little larger than mine.

Perhaps there is an infinite series of igloos around me and above me: endless, inescapable constriction, cold and dark.

But it is also possible that the darkness which fills that

little brick-shaped opening is the dark of infinite space and freedom.

And it is possible that if I continue to stare at the opening which I have made a single star may appear there to confirm the freedom of those skies.

Or perhaps a sequence of *very few* descriptive statements: cross-heads. To be followed in each case by any amount of filling out in form of comment; parallels; exclamations; denials; quotations; justifications; mockery; dreams; fantasies ...

Hero born of the Devil and the BVM. The result, a prophetic impostor; but one who plays himself into a *perfect* imitation of real thing.

Long confession of sins, but not the expected ones: or expected ones in very peculiar form.

'At this stage of my journey it seems that I am to be severely belaboured by self-contempt.'

Must avoid a dreary procession through Ideas and Ideologies of the Age.

———— * ————

'In scientific research you make progress, because the end, however distant, is a complete and finite model of the universe. In spiritual exercises you may cover a certain amount of ground, but you can make no *progress* since the object of your understanding is infinite, and therefore you never come closer to its centre.'

Hmmmmmmmmmm! But what if the physical world *extends into* the spiritual, with no hard line between them. Having constructed a telescope fifty times bigger than the last one, an astronomer puts his eye to it and sees a bright angel flitting by. Or within the smallest particle of all LOVE is discovered to be vibrating.

[53]

M of H & E

Narrative *form*, at least.
'Father! Father! I saw a drunk lady in the park today!'
He turned to me from the rainy window-pane,
Showing the lean clown's face of immutable grief.
'Your intonation of wonder and expectancy
'Is disproportionate to the facts as you present them.'
There was no mockery in this use of language,
Only a refusal, or incapacity,
To diminish even a child by condescension.

Clear in my mind, the sadly disbelieving Jewish father. Whole work could be interrogation by son.

28 October

On the contrary, WHOLE SCHEME ABANDONED! And with what relief; joyful release! Just as I often felt after struggling for months with some intractable section of *Pantaloon*, and suddenly recognizing that it was a misbegotten mess.

Atrocious, those lame or strutting attempts at a beginning. Like feeble echoes of *Pantaloon*. In other words, attempts at another *literary creation*. But perhaps I'm done with literary creation.

7 November

Back to Tymawr for mass yesterday, after the sisters' annual October holiday from all intruders. Calmed and strengthened. To write or not to write no longer seemed an issue of great importance.

It's not, I confess, the sacred moment itself which greatly affects me, but the whole process. Alarm at 6.45; morning dusk; quick shave and coffee. The swoop into the valley from St

Briavels, on to the empty valley road and over Bigsweir bridge (sun just rising yesterday as I crossed the river). Up the misty Whitebrook valley; stopping to open the white convent gate; up the drive between cows and the little unmarked cemetery under the chestnut tree.

Coming into the chapel, and taking the place where 'Brother Philip' has been written on a slip by Sister Mary Jean. Grave faces, but not solemn, all in their expected places. My growing familiarity with the strict order of the mass. 'We are all partakers of the one bread.' *That* being the heart of it for me.

Down the chapel steps and into the hall, to be greeted by the happily smiling faces of Sister Paula and the Reverend Mother. My little chat with them both, before the delicious – silent – breakfast with ladies on retreat. Those home-made rolls, home-made butter, home-made marmalade more sacramental to me than any wine or wafer.

Then the library, and a quick devouring of the shelves before Sister Paula comes in from Terce. We settle down for forty minutes' talk; sometimes deep theological matters, but always interspersed with pleasant chitchat on convent, or Toynbee family, affairs. Never a disputation, though so many important disagreements. Exploration, explanation ...

Being an associate of this holy place gives me immense satisfaction; the sisterhood of the nuns I know; even a growing sense that the Reverend Mother is indeed a true mother to me – though she must be ten years younger.

They have their problems, of course, but how strong the sense of stability I get there! It seems inconceivable that the convent should ever collapse and disintegrate.

Strange to think that we lived so close to this heavenly place for fifteen years without even knowing of its existence. It took Kerry and Michele to find it for Barn House; and so for me. Another roundabout blessing of recent years.

My only regret is that S is still unwilling to come. Not that I ever press her: I'm often tempted, but common sense – or holy guidance – just prevents me. She won't come until she needs to.

8 November

When I was made an associate of the convent, last September, I spent the whole day there, and attended all the offices. I was still so ignorant about religious orders – in spite of those weird, semi-immured months at Ampleforth in 1934 – that I was startled to discover how much time is devoted to reciting the psalms. Startled and alarmed; particularly as we'd had one of the more horrific ones that morning.

So I paced about those beautiful grounds for at least two hours, wondering whether I could honestly go through with the ceremony that evening. I prayed frantically for the word to be given; but received nothing that I was aware of, and was impelled to submit to my initiation more for fear of causing pain and embarrassment than by any wisely-holy calculation.

But this may be one of God's mysterious ways. I've never for a moment regretted my close association with Tymawr.

12 November

Pouring with rain yesterday made gardening impossible; so I put on my ferocious boots and set out for a serious walk. The first for months. The boots splendidly increased my sense of purpose; not of destination, but of walking for walking's sake. And the walking stick in my hand again, pushing me firmly forward along the roads. A free and purposeful man!

And a changed world!

For years all visual beauty has been tangled up with nostalgia. 'Tears at the heart of things': poignancy: carried back by a tree to some half-memory of a childhood tree, so *freshly* seen so long ago! A florid and deeply satisfying melancholy. Or the tree was a *memento mori*; my melancholy softly expanding into a future of no trees at all.

But now, on this walk, I stopped several times and looked at a single tree as I haven't done for years. No; as I've never done in my life before. The tree was there and now, in its own immediate and peculiar right: *that* tree and no other. And I was acutely here-and-now as I stared at it, unhampered by past or future: freed from the corruption of the ever-intrusive ME. Intense happiness.

13 November

A much wilder walk today; white flecks on the turbulent brown river when I paused, as always, in front of Birchfield House.

I can now repeat the tree experience almost at will. It is in no way pantheistic; or even 'spiritual'. No feeling whatever that the tree and I are One, and parts of a Great Whole which is the Unity of All Things. Quite the contrary: a sharp awareness of the tree's individual identity.

Perhaps the mystical emotions are yet to come; more likely not. But if they do I hope never to lose that vision of the tree's 'inscape': its very potent self and presence. If anything the tree might become so intensely, blazingly real that it would have acquired a heavenly status. Or rather my God-given vision would have seen heaven in the tree. And the tree would be more a tree than ever: through the transfiguring eye.

It's surely a false mysticism, the kind which turns against the physical world instead of transfiguring it. The heresy known as 'angelism'; an excellent word with its implication of kindly ridicule.

14 November

And in Monmouth shops, houses and people were clarified and dignified in the same way. My shopping itself is now very deliberate and considered; trying to acquire grace through strict attention. (And how I used to hate shopping before I took it up when S started working at the Citizens' Advice Bureau.)

[57]

The CAB. She is discreet, of course, about the individual cases but from the general account she gives me of her work I know better than ever that she is a good counsellor. Patience, sympathy, shrewdness.

15 November

Perhaps this new attention is a movement towards Zen. Yet I find the paradoxes and denials of Zen very tiresome; no use to me at all. Besides, my metaphysics of transfiguration would be rewarded with a beating if I tried it in a Zen monastery. And old Rajneesh has harsh words for me too: 'You can exist either as a head-orientated person, or you can exist as a heart-orientated person. When your energy, your life-energy, falls from the head towards the heart, you become a Sufi ... A Sufi means a man of the heart, a man of love; a man who doesn't bother from where this universe comes, who doesn't bother who created it, who doesn't bother where it is leading: in fact who doesn't ask any questions – rather, on the contrary, he starts living ... You are here, throbbing, alive – dance with existence! Live it! Be it! And allow it to happen in its total mystery within you.'

Yes, but just as the dancer needs hours of practice to free her body into its natural – but lost – grace and spontaneity, so the man of the head, the man of words, may have to fumble and fight with words for years before he can be silent without a sense of unnatural constraint.

Wisdom from *The English Auden** which I reviewed on Sunday: 'Distrust the man who says, "First things first! First let us raise the material standard of living among the masses, and then we will see what we can do about spiritual problems." In accomplishing the first without considering the second he will have created an enormous industrial machine which cannot be altered without economic dislocation and ruin.'

---

* *The English Auden*, Ed. Edward Mendelson (Faber & Faber, London).

16 November

Sitting in the car outside St Briavels castle, rain deluging the valley, awaiting the prospective buyer of our Mork Hill fields. Succeeded (I *think*) in actually relishing her delay.

Sale of fields. Another move in BH's withdrawal from its farming origins. (Also a move which greatly improves our own finances!) This still leaves plenty of land for cows, fruit, vegetables; but not if the enthusiasm continues to wane. Lip service is still paid to work as prayer, the holy soil, etc., but meditation, yoga, zikr, even astrology, now take up much time and energy. A threat of angelism here?

19 November

Tree-scrutiny more an *Entfremdung* (Brecht) than audience-participation. I stand apart and look; looking I respect, almost to the point of love. But what I hope to be loving is God; not because he 'made' the tree but because he gives me the power to see it with such intensity and clarity.

Always remember *nature is neutral*. Never praise the 'natural' for that alone. (Though it's certainly true that we've moved too far from what is appropriate to our minds and bodies simply by the fact of our long earthly inheritance.)

'Nature gets credit which in truth should be reserved for ourselves; the rose for its scent, the nightingale for his song, and the sun for its radiance. The poets are entirely mistaken. They should address their lyrics to themselves and should turn them into odes of self-congratulation on the excellence of the human mind. Nature is a dull affair, soundless, scentless, colourless, merely the hurrying of material endlessly, meaninglessly' (Whitehead).

But Whitehead knows that those self-praising poets would be grotesque; and in other passages he seems to know why: that even the world perceived by the senses would still be a

[59]

dull affair unless we *give value* to what we receive from rose, nightingale and sun. For what's the conceivable use – evolutionary/utilitarian – of standing entranced by the rose and the nightingale as the sun sets?

The *only* use of this state is that it can turn us into conscious receivers of heavenly light; and then transmitters of the light received.

20 November

T. H. Huxley admitted that human ethics are directly opposed to the jungle laws of evolution. He might have gone further and seen that true, exorbitant *goodness* is equally opposed to the urbane laws of enlightened self-interest.

21 November

Sudden, lacerating row with S; of a kind we'd hoped and believed we were done with. Horrible, the dread familiarity: same old skeletons dragged from each other's cupboards and the bones thrown in each other's faces. How can our love and respect for each other be true if we still behave towards each other like angry children?

S claims that her long-accumulated resentments at last burst out of her. This may be so: perhaps she has more cause for stored-up resentment than I have. Certainly she is the more self-repressive; and if little of this anger builds up in me it's probably because I nearly always release it as soon as I feel it. (Or at least I used to do so.)

But it seems simpler to remind ourselves of how hard a task co-habitation must always be: the sheer intensity of the other's presence. And this is all the more so in our case, the husband forever at home; the husband and wife doing scarcely anything apart.

But resignation to these wretched quarrels would be abominable. Radical change is not only possible; it is *demanded*. And if I didn't believe that we can and shall change – by humbly opening ourselves to God – I would find life meaningless: perhaps unlivable.

Resolution to love better – that is, more thoughtfully.

———— * ————

We've been left in a raw, rueful state, licking each other's wounds. And that's a great improvement, anyway, for in the worst of the old times the horror would sometimes linger on for days.

But even now we still can't pray together.

———— * ————

Such different temperaments, in so many ways: but *complementary* we tell ourselves. Almost the mythical male and female: her natural good sense and unforced 'givingness'; a born counsellor with a sharp, practical, unintellectual mind. My rash, energetic zigzags through life. Her greater ease in casual company; outward calmness, tending to a melancholy resignation which is sometimes relieved by bouts of self-defensive fury. My selfishness; intemperance, in the widest as well as the narrow sense; near-pathological need of privacy, relieved by outbursts of boon companionship ...

A strange couple, I suppose. But no stranger than many we know. And surely we're closer now than ever before.

Do I imprison her, I asked, by my close and constant presence; by the extreme unsociability of our present life? She said that the way we live is as much her creation as mine: and certainly she seems just as averse to social life as I am. She is just as likely to be disturbed by the racketing around as I am; though in a different way.

But it is not only our weaknesses which keep us close together – and alone together – for so much of our time.

Two full mornings writing letters to depressed ladies in Sussex and Hampshire; part of my DA (Depressive Anonymous) stint. I quite enjoy this, and know that I do it well. But if I had to invite these correspondents into the house, with no means of getting them out by a given time, I'd be frantic with misery and anger.

(But S, who hates writing letters, would gladly welcome them in and try to talk to them as long as they chose to stay.

Jack Spratt and his wife.)

———— * ————

On Saturday over to Ledbury again for one of our regular meetings with Keith and Sheila.* Ploughman's lunch in the hotel, talking of DA. Just now this organization is going through many teething troubles, and much goodwill is needed between the organizers; as well as time and energy. But what closer bond than shared experience of the Blue Devil? What greater need than to expand our groups as widely as we can?

For me – for both of us – this work not only provides a social purpose, but also drives us out of the house to Working Parties all over the country.

———— * ————

Yesterday afternoon, sawing logs at BH with Kerry, Clare and Richard, I felt that dreadful surging up of the dark spirit, almost like a physical tide in the head. For half an hour I gritted my teeth; kept up the chatter and the work. Then, with some embarrassment, I told them my condition and asked for their help. On my suggestion we went down to the barn, sat in a ring, silent and holding hands, as on our Sunday evenings. It seemed to work – which means that it did work – their affection and goodwill so strongly felt.

It's surprising, perhaps, that they don't practise such therapy

———

*Keith Middleton, co-founder of DA, and his wife.

themselves, for it fits well with their mode of life and thinking. But they retain a strange reserve among themselves; communicate best by writing passages to each other in the community diary. (The splendid parties – pot, guitars, *a little* booze – are something else: openness, spontaneity; even a sort of love.)

How much I owe them! How much I respect their tolerance for us and for each other – a tolerance which is certainly no sign of indifference. When I note, with indignation, that X is causing trouble and avoiding work the rest of them see him simply as 'doing his thing'; as supplying something-or-other which nobody else can offer. (Such as bloodymindedness, I think but don't say.)

Another curious difference between S and me. I remember our meeting with a rancid old friend of mine in Ankara when we were travelling about the Middle East together in 1950; just before we got married. Arrogant and dogmatic with drink J accused S of being typically American in her plump, blue-eyed innocence; her crude imperviousness to tragedy. And though I defended her against this charge I think at the time I half-agreed with J; for I was still feeling world-weary with grief for Anne* and saw myself as a sad old monster dragging this callow maid from Cleveland, Ohio, around the Ancient World.

But now the shoe's on the other foot; with a vengeance; perhaps a literal vengeance. I'm again the unsinkable enthusiast; seeker; self-amender – at least by constantly-renewed resolve. But for many years – due to the lowering experience of her married life? – S has sometimes alarmed me by her stoical resignation to the facts of life and death. She even used to insist that no adult is ever capable of change. And when she had *her* short bout of depression, eight or nine years ago, it took the form of extreme listlessness; the sense of being insulated from everything and everyone; almost anaesthetized. Whereas although I was equally immobilized I suffered acute and violent pain as well.

* PT's first wife to whom he was married from 1939 to 1949.

[63]

25 November

Just back from our first caravan trip, camping in the Shropshire hills above Church Stretton. Over the Long Mynd in a blizzard; home-brewed beer in Bishop's Castle (a little magic town); Worcester Cathedral on the way home (looking; really *looking* now; 'a keen ecclesiologist'; even prayers in the noisy nave).

And what good companions we are on journeys. How charming those two evenings in the caravan; Beethoven on the cassette player; scrambled eggs and a bottle of wine; love, with great love, on a narrow bunk and the wild, snowy wind thudding and squealing against the windows.

My best and boldest adventure for years.

29 November

But days of dryness now; moving back into the rusty old prison of my own skull. Love not strong or true enough. But how to love better? Certainly not by trying; straining, like a constipated man; tensing the muscles: 'I will! I will! I *will!*'

By submission, then. Not submission to the way things are. The very opposite of that; submitting to God's will, and to being changed according to his will. Pray for the fructifying peace of God, which the world cannot give.

Yet all this is so contrary to my nervy and hectic temperament. (I see very well how easy it was to blame outer devils, demons, Satan, etc., for the devils we nurture inside us.)

—— * ——

But still a sense of relief, surely, at having no plans for another book to distract my attention from this one true task of opening my heart and mind to God. (Or do I discern a new idea already, no bigger than a man's hand: a purple smudge at the very edge of my attention?)

In spite of this dryness, and the physical depletion that comes with it, I must continue to go through the proper motions of daily life. *As if* there were faith and energy behind them. I must try to avoid putting this heavy burden of my gloom on S's willing shoulders.

30 November

So much Eastern wisdom harps on the absurdity of striving; all effort worse than useless; nowhere to go since we're already there ... Yet how they belie this by all that savage Zen discipline; trying so hard not to try; being punished if they show the least sign of effort!

I love Gurdjieff's notion of 'the work'; all metaphors of labours to be done, journeys to be made. And the goal – if there is one; if I ever reach it – will certainly be seen, *then*, as something marvellously simple. Not a child's simplicity, but the simplicity of childhood regained. So many accretions to be cut out or planed away.

'Those who seek God have already found him.' Sometimes it's a great comfort to read this: sometimes an irritation. 'What do you *mean*, I've already found him? *Where*? *I* can't see him. Or do you mean that I haven't really started to seek yet? Well, in that case, *hell*! what I must be seeking for is *how to seek*. The same, impossible task, with a different name; and a much more discouraging one.'

———— * ————

But it is important to get rid of the disastrous Christian notion of 'merits' to be acquired; like so many good conduct marks collected through a term at school. If there are stages on this journey, and if I have reached even the first of them, then I know that whatever is new seems much more like a gift than an achievement.

The working is in the waiting; but the waiting is far from passive.

Back, with renewed irritation, to the Zen insistence that

[65]

enlightenment has nothing to do with good and evil. Or this, from rotten old Rajneesh: 'If you are a real man by all means drive off the farmer's ox or grab the food from a starving man.'

But if I've learned anything it's that true love is a recognition of reality: that wicked actions and self-centred thinking deny and conceal the truth. 'Love rejoiceth in the truth.' 'The truth shall make you free.' 'God is spirit, and those that would come to him must come in spirit and in truth.'

First, humility; which is a clearing the way for love: a scraping out of the encrusted heart. And humility is not a demand that we should esteem ourselves at less than we are. (All those early Christian saints – moaning that they were the worst sinners in the world? Surely they'd simply fallen over backwards into another kind of self-conceit.) Humility must mean trying to see ourselves as we really are. And pride is always a denial of the (painful yet exhilarating) truth about ourselves.

How can I love S properly until I know her?

———— * ————

Faced with the Inexpressible the West has tried to describe it in absurdly concrete terms: the whole traditional theology is a case of the misplaced concrete. Faced with the Inexpressible the fault of the East has been to play about with paradox and negation.

1 December

Good, Evil and God. All that is good is intimately, in-extricably tied together. To walk well is an aid to loving well: better perception makes it easier to avoid wrong or foolish action; courtesy may need courage to support it. (I stayed downstairs for two hours with our unexpected visitor, *excruciated* by that mixture of claustrophobia and embarrassment which is so much worse than any 'boredom'. Pined for the stronghold of my room.) Beauty, when fully received, is always a revelation of truth. (But concentration camp guards went home at night and listened to Bach. No doubt with rapture. Yet surely every

[66]

note of Bach is a rejection of wickedness and stupidity. To think that I used to find such contradictions richly intriguing!)

2 December

Reading *The Imitation of Christ* again, and finding it just as barren as I did before. So narrowly hortatory and moralizing; a sterile strategy. Thus we might become better behaved, but only at the cost of hopeless inner turmoil.

This goes with à Kempis's hatred of the world; his simple dualism. We must indeed be reborn, as they all say, but in *this* world first: *into* this world first. Right action only from right thinking and right feeling. Undeviating right action only from right being. Which demands a discriminating love of earthly people: even earthly things. (No! Never use 'love' for *things*. The aesthetic fallacy.)

———— * ————

Yet preoccupation with the physical person of Christ is a most repulsive Catholic obsession. To dwell in his holy wounds . . . The Sacred Heart. Corpus Christi. Drinking the blood. So flesh obstructs the spirit. (What name for this heresy; the opposite of Angelism? Corporalism? Carnalism?)

Zen and Yoga are better here, seeing the body as ally and counterpart of the soul: both to be kept in their right proportion and relationship.

———— * ————

I'm trying now to hear even the most familiar music as if for the first time. Karajan's new recording of Beethoven symphonies – his third! But in fact I haven't the ear to distinguish one performance from another, and I find that I'm in danger of actually *hating* the all-too-familiar thumping and booming away.

Better luck with this book of Sisley reproductions. *The Flood at Port Marley*, stared and stared at every evening in bed. Chosen for its very 'straightness'; ordinariness; unselfconsciousness. (I

[67]

know very well that Sisley was one of a band of highly conscious revolutionaries, but *now* this picture looks back at me with perfect calmness, moderation and assurance.)

When I bought this series (*The Masters*), week by week, about ten years ago, the idea was to mitigate my shameful ignorance of the visual arts. (What a great self-educator I have been, at least in constantly renewed intention!) – But now all I want is to look harder and see better and I've no wish to be even the most amateur of art historians. For me – how Ben* would hate this! – every good picture is a medium for the grace of God.

Last week my delightful correspondent, Ann Horne, sent me Sullivan's little book on Beethoven; the only critical work I've ever read which studies works of art wholly in terms of the artist's spiritual development. And how well this is done; with what vigour, perception and total lack of sentimentality, or even special pleading. (In much of the book Beethoven is speaking for himself.)

———— * ————

Driving back from Gloucester yesterday the sun had begun to go down, and the trees, which I'd stared at so hard and respectfully on the way over, were now silhouetted against a radiant sunset. How much they had lost by this gaudy treatment! As if Beauty had blundered crudely on to the scene, like a bad painter who must touch up whatever he sees. 'Isn't this simply *lovely*!' instead of 'See what is there!'

But as for the Spirit, the Transcendent, I sometimes suspect that I must be almost tone-deaf in such high matters.

3 December

Bad dreams again. The appalling lifelessness: worse – a positive draining away of all meaning, hope or motive. These are not conventional nightmares, but the horror of subtraction; reduction: and myself always in a state of shame and odium.

*Benedict Nicolson, Editor of *The Burlington Magazine*; PT's oldest friend.

Yet I have written on the edge of the shelf by my bed a stirring vesperal couplet by Sir Thomas Browne:

> 'When I do rest my soul advance:
> Make my sleep an holy trance.'

I try to repeat this at the last possible moment before my (always broken and disordered) sleep begins. But the trance remains stubbornly unholy. Unless, of course, the horror-dream is another of God's mysterious ways.

———— * ————

The absurd but painful struggle against smoking. I first 'gave up' about twenty years ago, and once achieved an unbroken abstinence of nearly six months. Usually, now, the cycle is five or six weeks off; a week or two on. And usually too, the relapse is excused by some family mishap; or simply by too many people being around.

What is so strange is that I deeply hate the wretched little poisonous tubes, and positively look forward, on smoking days, to the day I've set myself for renouncing them again.

———— * ————

Sometimes it seems that the only thing I must do now is to slow myself down. I keep finding that I've speeded up again; almost regressed to those totally unregenerate days of obsessive, and ultimately prostrating, activity. That blind and desperate busyness which so many of our prophets have diagnosed as the principal addiction of Western Man. How to kick it without falling into our self-created inner void?

But at least when prostration came this time, and I was in bed for two days, I rejoiced in the enforced calm and used it for a sort of meandering meditation.

———— * ————

New mantra:

> 'Peace.
> Heavenly Grace.
> God lives in me.
> God is my life.'

[69]

This ought to be not only a programme but a description of what is always there. My tendency is to use it as a cry for help.

———— * ————

That outside world of business and politics, wars and city streets, which I both hate and fear. But I never forget that I am in no position to despise it. This is partly because our seclusion here is an extraordinary privilege; but even more because I know very well that I am exempt from none of the wicked world's vices. I thought of adding 'except lust for power', but the truth is that anyone who writes for a public is trying to impose his will on his readers. (My ancient joke with Terry* – that he is always trying to keep me out of the pulpit.)

———— * ————

Once or twice lately there has been that sudden discolouring of the senses; the threat of vacancy. I felt a sharp fear of the real depression which used to follow. So I concentrate on whatever I happen to be doing, to ward off the danger by hard attention. Even shaving: 'The Peace of God. The Peace of God. *The Peace of God* ...' A very meticulous scraping of chin and cheeks.

———— * ————

Walking today, and tree gazing, I thought with real horror of trying to *write* about one of those well-studied trees. A sense both of disgust and of utter incapacity. Why? Because any attempt to describe it would at once prejudice, betray, the tree's superb and individual reality. Words would generalize the tree; decorate it yet blur it. A good photograph would be best; or rather least offensive.

Even in this notebook I find words a burden, and hate the business of searching for an apt one. In fact the only writing which gives me real satisfaction now is my weekly review – whether in or out of the pulpit. At least this is a professional

*Terence Kilmartin; old friend and Literary Editor of *The Observer*.

[70]

activity; demanded of me; ungratuitous; best thought of, perhaps, as filling a space on the page of a newspaper.

4 December

Piero della Francesca's *Resurrection*. The only representation of Jesus I know which seems to do him justice. Staring at that amazing face and trying to discover its particular quality I came at last on the word 'knowledge'. It is significant that this is the *risen* Christ because the face reveals a knowledge of something beyond our world. It is also a sad face but a very strong one. Almost tough in its strength and courage, but full of pity.

Even if Jesus never existed Piero's vision is an astonishing revelation of God working through man. *There* is an incarnation, Piero in the act of painting; we in the act of looking.

——— * ———

For some time I have been planning a long letter to my brother in which, with infinite tact and all the wisdom I can command, I would show him how necessary it is that he, too, should set out on the Way. Yet when he came here to stay the night I found the utmost difficulty even in sitting up and talking to him about such things. In fact it was at his invitation that I began, but I soon felt disgusted by the stumbling inadequacy of everything I said: a sense of constantly missing the real point and saying something weak and false instead. Yet in the morning Lawrence thanked me for having spoken 'so well'; and said he'd resolved to think it all over again.

So pride – in the planned letter – was followed by a fall on that painful evening. But the humility which resulted from the fall was rewarded by a pat on the back! (And what, I wonder, will be the punishment for *that* complacency?)

6 December

I was trying to persuade Lawrence that true religion never

starts with moral exhortation or resolutions; it always starts from the felt need for renewal; the hope of seeing a known face in a new light; the hope that a familiar sound will suddenly recede or advance into a new space, producing echoes never heard before. And sin is an obstruction to this new awareness. Sin is resignation to a stale and opaque world without depth or meaning.

And I suspect that each of us suffers from some *besetting* sin, which we must diagnose with great care and much hard thought. Often that dominant sin is not what seems the most obvious one; or rather it lies half-concealed behind some of its more ostentatious forms. In my own case it might seem that lust (in the years of lust in action!) and gluttony (drunkenness) have been my major sins; but now I believe that what lies behind these, and most of my other faults, is a sort of wilful metabolic frenzy; the constant urge to hurry as quickly as possible out of the present moment and into the next one. Get this woman *now*; *at once*! Drink these drinks *immediately* in order to take instant possession of the whole evening ahead.

7 December

Jason and Lucy* came yesterday, and amiably (but seriously) criticized S, Laura and me for living in a hothouse of torrid and cultivated emotion. Well, I've put it more strongly than they did, but I think this is what they might have said, but for their filial love and piety.

I see the truth of this: what with my depression, L's anorexia and S's anxiety for us and for herself there has been a feeling of emotional claustrophobia in this cottage: emphasized, perhaps, by the woods which so nearly enclose us. How the three of us have *thrashed out* our troubles; flayed them until the poor dead horses must look very ragged and gory to outside eyes!

But I think our older children are a little out of date. We're

* Son, aged 24 and daughter, aged 22.

not quite so self-enclosed as we used to be, and Laura has flown at least half-way out of the nest. The time might even come when visitors to this house will get some strength and hope from being here.

If I can't believe in that possibility I'd surely be failing in the great Christian virtue of Hope.

(Yes; but if I do believe in it am I failing in the great Christian virtues of Truth and Humility?)

9 December

Now this is like a surrender; a resolution broken; the habit of a lifetime forcing its way back after a very short and uneasy period of expulsion. For the plan to write another book has now reached a stage where I can't any longer avoid describing it here.

What I hope to do, then, is to write a journal and an autobiography simultaneously, devoting to each day a section of journal and sharply dividing this from a following section of autobiography. I plan to relate the two in many ingenious ways; but my chief delight is in the notion of *convergence*. For the autobiography will be gradually catching up on the journal until at last it brings the reader to the very day when the journal started – and the writing of the autobiography also started.

The journal, in which hardly any background information will be given, is bound to be eliptical; enigmatic; question-raising. But as the autobiography develops the enigmas will be clarified and all the questions will at last be answered.

So many enticing possibilities.

And the search for God will be the covert theme of the whole work; eventually the main and obvious theme.

(Yes, but I must keep it implicit for as long as possible, knowing only too well from my failure with that wretched *Marriage of Heaven and Earth* how little equipped I am to write directly about heavenly aspirations.)

——— * ———

As if to atone for the breaking of one resolution I have now made another – to give up booze entirely. Not that there have been any dramas lately; but it still remains a source of constant, nagging anxiety. Shall we go out to the pub this evening, or ought I to stay at home with my ginger beer? Will there be enough at X's house when we go there? Will there be too much at Y's? Is one Guinness before lunch too much? What about two, then? If I stay at the convent for Compline how much time will that leave me for The Crown on the way home?

A heavy burden for even the most sluggish pilgrim to bear. *Entbehren sollst man: sollst entbehren.* For true freedom, they say, comes only from ridding ourselves of physical indulgences. No; of *dependences.*

Yet this is perhaps the hardest task I've ever set myself, and I can't pretend that I look forward to it with excited relish: a new experience, hurrah! It seems more like parting from an old, well-tried companion who, for all the injuries he's done me (and others), has also given me much comfort in need and many, many moments of unspoiled happiness.

10 December

An exception will be made, of course, on Christmas Day. *At Christmas time.*

Well, this first Monmouth Thursday, dreaded so much, passed off a little more smoothly than I'd feared. Much amazement all round at my Cokes and bitter lemons. And I certainly found it desperately hard *to talk*; diving at one fell swoop from one extreme to another, as is my habit; swooping from garrulity to near-taciturnity. Was I a spectre at their feast of pints? Not quite that, perhaps, but when we left them, half an hour earlier than usual, I felt an immense release of tension at being alone in the car with S. (And how good she was to me! How understanding!)

[74]

Several curious results of all these attempts at change and growth. For example I can no longer enjoy the musical form of theme and variations, because it seems to make the composer's ingenuity so boastfully conspicuous. What I want from art now is a tremendous and lucid simplicity (which probably means, in the case of music, an ingenuity so great that I can't detect or understand it).

————— * —————

We went to Tymawr for the life vows of our friend Sister Susan Benedicta. Afterwards a stand-up lunch with several strangers; then extended coffee with nuns and others. Just the sort of occasion for which I would have stoked up thoroughly beforehand: I might even have taken the precaution of a small bottle in my pocket. In fact there was champagne on offer, but this was no great temptation.

The happy truth is that I glided through the whole affair with scarcely a tremor of nervous impatience or parched anxiety. 'Be here now.' 'The Peace of God.' Also the constant reminder that when it was over I'd be safe at home in no time, digging the garden, enjoyably reimmersed in the ordered routine which I have always loved so much.

Loved *too* much.

————— * —————

How can one react to (e.g.) the beautiful final duet of Nero and Poppeia? Or to *La ci darem la mano*? Or to the *Dies Irae* in Verdi's *Requiem*? Sublime beauty to clothe (a) unrepentant satisfaction with the outcome of wicked and murderous actions: (b) the lovemaking of a brutal womanizer and a silly little flirt: (c) threats of loathsome punishment by a God of Vengeance. This is an old problem; and an unsolved one so far as I'm concerned. For I'm sure that Tolstoy's solution is no good at all – which is to condemn all the famously great works in favour of an inferior, but moralistic art.

[75]

O for a tankard full of the true, the swarthy Guinness!

———— * ————

Most of my conscious attempts to change have no necessary connection whatever with religious faith. Most of them could be made by a non-believer with equal benefit. Deceleration; attention; meditation ... all these are steps towards 'integration', or whatever the current psychological term may be. And therefore to greater calm and authority in factory, office or boardroom.

Yet I could never have tried to make these changes except as a means of searching for God; and to do his will.

O Guardian Angel, comfort me with ginger beer!

———— * ————

We like to make models for the mysteries which bewilder us so much. After reading many books about the unreality of time, and how we should try to inhabit the eternal depth of the present moment, I imagined a great wooden ring slowly revolving, illuminated by a still lantern high up above its centre. We are all walking on the ring, as the ring itself is moving through time, our heads usually bent down to watch the changing patterns of the grain. But sometimes we are able to catch a glimpse of the great central light, out of the corner of an eye.

Like all models this one breaks down as soon as I try to elaborate it. But it helps a little in the preposterous task of conceiving the inconceivable.

15 December

A Pilgrim of Our Time

I imagine the journal will be a bit more formal than this one; but I rather dread that extra formality. As for the autobiography the great task will be one of ruthless omission: I want to put down only what's relevant to this present journey, which means an absolute ban on decoration. But to distinguish the relevant from the ornamental will be the daunting problem.

And how much fudging shall I allow myself – e.g. transferring material already used in these pages to the months when the book is being written? Fudge to your heart's content, say all my instincts as a writer. To reach the Truth, or even to approach it, you must go by the way of many little lies.

———— * ————

Stace's *Mysticism and Philosophy*. A good book; severe yet generously open-minded. He accepts the absolute reality of mystical experience, but refuses to label it either objective or subjective. 'Trans-subjective' is his rather awkward neologism; but Heaven knows the linguistic problem is real enough.

One thing which he strangely omits is the *joy* which all the great mystics talk about.

———— * ————

I can get no help at all from the occult. Perhaps there do exist intermediate orders of reality between Earth and Heaven. Yet when I try to read Steiner or Gurdjieff I am immediately irritated by their purple gateways, green-clad guides and magic runes. Such super-confidence in the way they map out these areas for us! What's more, the different shamans differ so widely in their reports. Surely this is the same fault which leads to the strict elaboration of creeds and dogmas. Such dusty answers the soul gets when hot for certainties in matters of the spirit.

———— * ————

I used to get a peculiar satisfaction when dressing from pushing my feet into my shoes while pulling up my trousers or pulling my shirt on. *To be doing two things at once*, and thus increasing the speed of the whole tiresome process made me feel that I was saving time with admirable dexterity. Now I try to dress almost in slow motion.

Last night I went down to the kitchen to make myself a

sandwich, and back in bed I began to gobble it as I always do, never finishing one mouthful before taking another; and reading, of course, at the same time. *With real difficulty* I put down the book and began to munch with the greatest possible awareness, scrupulously emptying my mouth before taking another bite.

A multitude of such trivial restraints make up a large part of the work. Boys who gulp their food will *never* get to Heaven.

16 December

Now I remember something else about the moving and impressive ceremony of Sister Benedicta's vows. After it was over – she lying flat on the chapel floor and all the rest of it – she came over to kiss her parents who were sitting in the front row of the guest pews. Her father is a wry, clownish little disbeliever, who made several caustic remarks during the reception. But by far the best was reported by Sister Benedicta afterwards. As she stooped to kiss her father in chapel – a moment for not-a-dry-eye if ever there was one – all he whispered to her was, 'What a caper!'

Laughter in heaven, I hope.

17 December

Bad dreams continue. Perhaps they act as a sort of drainage system for waking life, saving our fully-conscious minds from at least some part of their desolations and self-disgust.

——— * ———

A Pilgrim of Our Time

But would the echo of Lermontov's irony be recognized?

Anyway, plans for the book continue, with the usual ups and downs of confidence. Many difficulties loom. If only the heavy old load of *Pantaloon*, still languishing at the Oxford University

[78]

Press, were off my shoulders one way or the other. (A third refusal and I might simply shut it away in a drawer and leave it for the delighted discovery of a more appreciative generation. The Happy Few!)

18 December

What are we to make of the vision of Bernadette, and all other stories of the same kind? She reported that the lady in the grotto spoke the words 'I am the Immaculate Conception'. Yet though she was a devout daughter of the Church she was a peasant girl who had never consciously heard of this recent and very recherché doctrine. Yet her later life shows that she was a true saint, and it is hard to doubt the truth of what she reported.

Pious Roman Catholics take this as a heavenly confirmation of the doctrine; a supreme confirmation of the virgin birth and the present status of Mary in Heaven.

Dyed-in-the-wool non-believers speak of hysteria, or even pious fraud.

The problem for a non-Catholic who nevertheless believes that Bernadette saw and heard just what she said she saw and heard is that (e.g.) Ramakrishna's visions of Mother Kali are every bit as well authenticated as this vision at Lourdes in 1858. Is there room in Heaven for both Mother Kali and Mary the Queen?

Can it be that Heaven is protean in all its aspects; and that the forms which it produces for earthly visionaries are drawn from the formless substance of that other world to accord with our inadequate earthly approximations? 'If this is the best they can see then let them see it.'

In other words the simple vision of Bernadette could be conjured out of Heaven by the simple but beautiful mind of the saint. Because the belief in a Virgin unspotted by any taint of sin is *consonant* with the glories of Heaven it was possible for Heaven and Bernadette to create this vision between them.

[79]

But what are we to make of diabolical manifestations, which are every bit as well attested as visions of Heaven? I can make no sense of them at all, for the notion of an evil spirit is surely a contradiction in terms. A spirit, by definition, is wiser, knows more, than any man; and evil is so closely bound up with stupidity and ignorance. (Lucifer would have perfectly foreseen his own defeat, so his rebellion would have been an absurdity.)

The true cosmic struggle is not between good and evil spirits but the struggle of good spirits (Heaven) to infuse their loving light into earthly minds and hearts. This struggle is against the blind forces of Necessity which control not only all the matter of the universe but also most of the minds in it most of the time.

For all we know there may be planets in the universe where this battle has already been won: earths to which the Kingdom has come; where God's will is already being done. In which case the material universe may contain areas which are true colonies of Heaven because the fleshly creatures on those planets have evolved into pure spirits. Our own great mystics have indeed retained their fleshly bodies; but there were times when these seemed no more than abandoned husks. A saint in ecstasy is far more spirit than mind or body.

The highest purpose of human life is to co-operate with Heaven by the force of our own loving faith. Every prayer is an attempt to admit a little more of Heaven to Earth. This is also true of every loving action.

Although this conception of Heaven and Earth differs in many important ways from orthodox Christianity there is a great deal of Christian writing which conforms to it. There is a great deal more which can be made to conform to it by a change which scarcely disturbs the force of the original.

'Those who are so advanced as to go to God direct and without the images of the imagination should follow this method; others, in turn, are helped by a different one; for we cannot all be eyes in the Lord's body. Each one for himself must thus pray just as God ordains, and in deep love and quiet peace. Whoever serves God as He wills, to him shall God respond according to that man's own will ... Outwardly practised and inwardly cherished virtue produces peace of soul; though it is to be said that the peace that arises from the more interior exercises of religion is a treasure of which no man can rob you. Men wise in their own conceit will bid you do this and do that to become perfect – and it is all a set of observances of their own contrivance.'

This was written by Blessed John Tauler, the fourteenth-century German mystic. He knew from his own experiences that although certain images may be used in earthly communications with Heaven, the supreme mystical vision is direct and imageless. He also knew that particular images and observances can be positively harmful if they are imposed on others as the only truth and the only way.

19 December

Simone Weil's careful distinction between Temperance and Privation. The first is much to be preferred, but if we can't manage it privation is far better than intemperance.

I suppose I ought to applaud this with happy enthusiasm; after all, it seems to conform to my present practice. But how alien it is to Blake's splendid recommendations to excess, and persistence in folly.

——— * ———

Meditation. One hour a day now, usually between five and six. It still seems more like an endurance test than a journey towards Light and Peace. But I won't think the worse of it on that account. If it's only a means of enforcing patience that should be good enough for me.

28 December

It was a very good Christmas, with all the immediate family

here; Josephine and Pip* as well. A pleasantly patriarchal sense, greatly aided by the temporary abandonment of my self-imposed prohibition. No trouble *there*, of course, as there hardly ever is on such occasions. Other people's houses have been the scenes of my worst performances.

But I can't say that the effect of these dry days has been particularly good. My normal unsociability has become a mania for solitude, and although I've proved that I can meet people, and even talk to them, without the help of booze, I certainly haven't proved that I can do so with pleasure.

Having Paddy and Joan† for the weekend was an insanely heroic enterprise; and all the time I was painfully acting the part of the boon companion I used to be in their infinitely exhilarating company. (Paddy and I – perfect foils for each other's clownish extravagances.) The strain was almost un-remitting; and I saw these dear old friends drive away at last with a sense of melting relief: retreated instantly to bed and a day's collapse.

So I must choose, it begins to seem, between abstention from both drink and company, or keeping my friends and risking the desperate old perils of folly, illness and remorse.

But I can't abandon the new regime on such facile grounds as these. Time may solve the horrid dilemma. (In fact I've even added a total Friday fast to the greater privation. Excess is all!)

A PILGRIM OF OUR TIME

7 January 1978

Thomas Merton writes of 'the soul wounded by inordinate self-expression'. Alerted by that splendid phrase I resolved about six weeks ago to renounce writing books, at least for several months: perhaps for ever. Too much of my writing over the

* PT's eldest daughter and 3-year-old grandson.
† Patrick and Joan Leigh-Fermor; old friends.

last forty years has been tainted with pride; or has demanded that support and reassurance which only the respect of readers, known and unknown, seemed able to give me. So I thought that the time had come to quieten down and try to dissolve the inordinate self instead of exhibiting and inflating it.

Yet Merton wrote and published about forty books during his cut-short life. I know this caused him much heart-searching when he first entered the monastery; but he had the rare advantage of being under obedience and all his early books were written on the direct orders of his superior.

But not, I suspect, his later books. Towards the end of his life he was exhibiting a freedom of speculation, and a breadth of concern, which cannot have been altogether congenial even to the most liberal of Cistercian abbots. Merton would never have disobeyed a direct order to stop writing, so such an order can never have been given. But the tone of those magnificent late works is of a truly free man, freely communicating his thoughts to people far outside his earliest readership of faithful Roman Catholics or potential converts. I doubt if he was much bothered, at the time, by the perils of self-expression. His heart and mind overflowed with new things seen and understood; and he was impelled by a generous longing to share them with 'Those gathering multitudes outside/Whose glances hunger worsens'.

Heaven knows I am no Merton, and can never expect to reach his final state of loving self-assurance (which is the result and not the denial of true humility, the self being now humbly assured of its God-given task). But so much has happened to me, and within me, during the last four years that I feel a strong urge to transmit whatever I can to others. And if, being human and no saint, my motives for trying to write another book are far from pure, the refusal to do so on that account would itself be a kind of self-righteousness. Yes, an example of those *scruples* which are so rightly deplored in the Catholic Church; a mean-minded claim to unearned merit and a spurious virtue.

In any case St Augustine put the opposite case very

persuasively in the *Confessions*: 'What have I now said, my God, my life, my holy joy? Or what says any man when he speaks of Thee? Yet woe to him that speaketh not, since even the most eloquent are mute.'

So this book will be an attempt to tell anyone willing to listen all that I've learned about Earth and guessed about Heaven. No less.

*   *   *

The bare plot is biblical in the extreme: or so it seems at this moment, as I start to tell it. A long period of Captivity: a painful Exodus through the Wilderness: arrival at last in the Promised Land. But – as for the Israelites so for me – the Promised Land is not Eden, Paradise or Heaven, but simply the *right place* for a true work to be begun.

There is even the vague, half-mythical memory of a time before the Captivity; in biblical terms the patriarchal age of Abraham, Isaac and Jacob, not wholly innocent but fresh and primordial: *in memory* happy and free. During the first six years of my life I was fully aware of only two people; my mother and my two-years-older brother. I was nicknamed 'Fatmouse', and photographs reveal a face and body chubby with benign contentment. It's true that there was the normal tension between my brother and me, but this, in all my later memories, is dwarfed into triviality by the great figure of our own Good Judge, my wise and loving mother.

Hindsight, and long, resentful brooding, suggest that this period was abruptly brought to an end by the birth of my brother Lawrence. But although this seems to be one true reason for the change, I've also learned, by looking carefully backwards, that I was never aware of any sudden cataclysm in the life of our family. In my memory I can detect bad things beginning to happen, but while they were happening I never even thought of looking for a cause. I doubt if many children do: what happens is seldom questioned, however deeply it may implant certain dumb and unrecognized emotions. A family

[84]

friend saw very clearly that my mother transferred much of her overt love from Tony and me to the third-born son. The same friend also saw that while Tony seemed almost unaffected by this – perhaps he had already worked off his quota of jealousy on me – I was soon disturbed by obvious though confused resentments.

And so, the much-told story continues, I was made captive to these emotions, and remained their captive for forty years. Forty years of *Basic Insecurity*, according to the language of our time, in which I was propelled from childhood into late middle age unremittingly bedevilled by that more and more distant withdrawal of my mother's love.

Surely the case is too classical to be quite convincing.

But, keeping for the moment to the traditional account, it would seem that a deep impulse to escape from my desert confinement must have been growing in my unconscious mind, perhaps at a fairly steady rate but more likely in a succession of subterranean quakes and tremors. Certainly the surface of those forty years is marked by several periods of more-than-usual upheaval and disorder. Until, at the age of fifty-eight, a period began of what seemed at the time to be some sort of terminal collapse; an ultimate tremor which shook me so savagely that I felt threatened with irreparable disintegration.

The possibility that this extreme distress might be both a sign and a means of liberation stumbled into my shaken and clouded mind only after about two years of that condition. But by the summer of 1977, when the darkness had begun to clear, I was not surprised to find myself in a different place from before, looking in a new direction, equipped with fresh purposes and happier beliefs.

During the six months which have passed since then my new hope and changed understanding have become clearer to me almost week by week. But so too, as a result of that partial clarification, has become an uneasy vision of the endless journey which lies ahead of me.

[85]

That was the first account. In the rest of this book I shall try to fill out what has been misleadingly over-simplified here; perhaps giving different as well as fuller interpretations; hoping to draw from this material of my life a faith, a hope and a love which have played very little obvious part in my life until now.

So the book which I foresee will not be a decorated or discursive autobiography, telling of comic uncles and sighing over long-ago picnics set in charmingly repainted landscapes. What I hope to put down here is not what happened to happen to me, but my present search for a meaning in all that long bewilderment.

Perhaps too much has been made of myths in our time, but the myth of Exodus came very smoothly into my mind when I sat down at my desk yesterday morning. A remote Canaan before the Captivity: many years in Egypt, and many of those in a bondage which was quite cheerfully accepted: the miseries of an *enforced* escape: Canaan again, but now with at least a groping awareness of what I am supposed to do here. (If certain elements of early childhood seem to be given back in later life we should never forget how much they have been changed. To try to make simple returns is bound to corrupt and falsify the present as well as the past.)

———— * ————

I had been digging hard in the garden on this rainy afternoon, and believed, until my evening recollection, that the time had been well spent. It was only when I looked back on it that I realized how much I had been thinking about my *Observer* review which had appeared that morning; how warmly I'd been congratulating myself on its wit and well-turned phrases, even to the extent of imagining certain friends reading and admiring it.

I've often caught myself at such childish vanities before, and blushed to think of them. Not that it's the sort of thing to be heavily dwelled upon and penitentially regretted. But it is a useful reminder of how much old Adam-the-Ego is still in charge. *That* self, the one the world sees, is still my chief concern: the concern last week, for example, that my friends at Barn House should see me as a wise and kindly older man, who can act quite naturally in their 'space', but who also has certain graces of age which are still beyond them.

*   *   *

All that period of my youngest childhood is filled and suffused with love of my mother. She seemed a wise, strong and tender giantess, holding my hand on a walk or swinging me high above her head; a tall figure in doorways or towering beside my bed. During those years, and probably for many years afterwards, the thought that she might be wrong in anything she did or said was as far outside the reach of my mind as the idea that she was capable of dying. (It wasn't until I saw her dead body, nearly fifty years later, that I realized what a small woman she had been.)

So my mother was also a storybook queen, except that she was so palpably present to Tony and me, warm-fleshed, always sweet-scented and often singing. Although she reproached us when we behaved badly, and sometimes punished us, *that* mother was never angry. To have lost her temper would have been a breach of the impeccable serenity which belonged to her as closely as her beautiful hair and face.

Tony's two-year seniority was not quite enough to make him my indisputable superior. But he claimed that it was, and my frequent rejections of this claim were the principal cause of our rows. Yet I must have recognized that he was my better in certain ways, and at certain times, for I remember a sporadic respect for his larger size and greater knowledge.

But Tony was much more shy and withdrawn than I was. He was terrified of being made to look foolish in public, while I was a natural clown, and always happy to attract attention. I was also the more quick-tempered of the two, and my mother

[87]

used the same device to tease Tony out of his sullen self-consciousness and me from my noisy tantrums. She would raise her first fingers to her temples, point them down at us like horns, purse up her mouth as if in awe of us and waggle her fingers at our angry faces. We understood that this forbade us to sulk or rage any longer: her gesture was almost an order to us to laugh at ourselves.

Although Tony and I often quarrelled I know now, as I have always known, that we were closely bound to each other under all the apparent ferocity of our rows and arguments. In fact the very idea that these rows might be a reason for loving my brother less was as far outside my way of thinking and feeling as the idea that my mother might be wrong; or mortal.

Yet our quarrelling was the usual cause of my mother's displeasure, and in most cases she was shrewd in deciding who was the more to be blamed. So we were usually in disgrace separately, and in a disgrace which divided us even further. This may be why I remember so clearly an afternoon when we had been equal accomplices in some nursery crime. My mother had spoken to us with that air of amazed disgust which was the worst punishment we ever received; and even my father had been called to our bedroom to add his uneasy quota of disapproval. After they had left us alone to our shame, with the curtain drawn to emphasize the darkness of our condition, Tony came across and sat on my bed beside me. He said, 'Now we're together against them *all*,' and he seemed to get some fierce satisfaction from this state of hopeless embattlement. I felt that he was not only the brother I loved so much but also my great superior in courage and pugnacity.

10 January

I heard yesterday that my cousin Edward, a turbulent Border Baron, has died in an illicit bed. My first memory of Edward and his sisters was when they, Tony and I, and another group of cousins used to play together on the lawns of Castle Howard. Our notorious great-grandmother, Rosalind Carlisle, sat in a tall window of the South Front and threw down chocolates among us for the pleasure of seeing us fight for them.

But we knew Edward much better when we were all in our late teens, and he shocked and enthralled us by being the first of us to go to bed with women. At this time the women were German tarts, but he continued, and greatly widened, the practice until his death at the age of sixty-three. So there was something both suitable and macabre about Edward's end. 'A good way to go' is the robust and perfectly appropriate comment. Yet the event also has its Grand Guignol aspect, and might even, I suppose, be the text for a hellfire sermon. There is also a tragic side, for Edward, in spite of his bluster, was a lonely man who had been twice divorced and lived rather gloomily in his Bluebeard's Castle.

Is it the habit of writing fiction which makes it so natural for me to see an event like this in so many different lights? And should I, if I make some progress on this journey, be able to see it at last with a single eye? To have seen Edward, in this case, with the eye of love alone?

*   *   *

I spent part of each summer at Castle Howard from a very early age. My mother's mother was a member of that great landed family which owned so many square miles of Cumberland and the North Riding. My father, on the other hand, came from the professional middle class on the Toynbee side, and his mother was the daughter of a Birmingham manufacturer. It seems odd to me now that I grew up with so many Howard cousins but never met a single Birmingham Marshall except my paternal grandmother herself. The social distinction between my parents was something of which both were keenly, though seldom openly, aware.

But we spent those summer holidays not in the great palace

itself but in a separate flat above the estate office; and I never for a moment felt that I belonged with all that grandeur. Tony and I went barefoot in those summers, and our Aunt Kitty, who had followed our great-grandmother as the incumbent châtelaine of Castle Howard, treated us with angry disgust whenever she found us padding across those splendid floors.

But for most of the year during my early childhood we lived close to the Thames and the Chelsea Embankment. The great, grey tidal river, with its mudbanks and swirling current, was a constant source of terror from which only my mother could protect me. Once I had seen two policemen dragging a bundle of dripping wet sackcloth up a flight of the river steps; and Miss Otway, nanny and governess, a richly morbid woman, told me that this was the dead body of a man who had jumped off Westminster Bridge. The scene, and the little crowd that had gathered round it, stayed in my mind and my dreams for many years.

But the dream which recurred most often was of a high wind blowing down the river as we crossed the Albert Bridge for our afternoon walk in Battersea Park. I was clawing at the smooth surface of the bridge as the wind blew me back and back towards an edge which no longer had any protective paling. But my mother always saved me before I fell down into the wrinkled water.

Miss Otway's face seemed to have been worn and roughened by years of care. She had pink eyes which were often flooded with tears, and great earphones of plaited grey hair at each side of her head. She involved Tony and me very closely in her own strong emotions; and particularly in her loving and pitiful concern for her sister Norah. We never saw Norah, but we understood that she was a beautiful but impossible charmer, always in trouble and always a dreadful worry to Miss Otway's mother. Once there was even talk of Norah being sent to prison; and once she ran away for a week with a greengrocer. Tony and I shared the distress of Norah's sister, and listened with suspense to each new instalment of these troubles.

Miss Otway was a vivid storyteller, and most of her stories

were either about her family in Leatherhead or else about an endless and legendary struggle between the Good Poor and the Wicked Rich. This conflict was not in the least political, or even social: it was more like the conflict in fairy stories between the honest young woodcutter and the wicked king. It had no application at all to anything we saw around us.

———— * ————

My father was a much more shadowy figure to us than Miss Otway. He must have been at his college most of the day, and his vague benevolence when we saw him was too unchanging to be memorable. I think his rimless spectacles made us think him weak, and unheroic. But sometimes he played little jokes on us which we enjoyed.

Sometimes, too, we were allowed to come into our parents' bedroom in the morning; and when I saw them sitting side by side in that great bed I was deeply assured of their strong and unbreakable union. Or rather I was never aware of my need for such assurance. We used to climb into the foot of the bed, pulling the eiderdown over our legs; and when the whole family of four were together there I imagined the bed to be a boat which would sail down the river and over the sea.

Certainly this concept of the close family was deeply planted in my mind, and my father was just as necessary a part of it as either my mother or my brother. I never admitted to myself that I loved him less than the other two, for I knew from as early as I can remember that such inequality in love is a terrible and dangerous thing.

———— * ————

This may have originated in the prayers which my mother had taught us to say every evening. I remember a time when she sat on my bed, or Tony's according to turn, and we knelt beside her leaning our heads against her bosom. 'God bless Mummy, Daddy and Tony; Grandmother, Grandfather and Granny; Uncle Denis, Aunt Aggie ...' The proper order of love was laid down in this prayer, and although I certainly loved

Tony more than I loved my father the first three on the list were joined together in a unique priority.

———— * ————

At this period my father and mother were conventionally liberal-minded agnostics, but I think my mother must have already regretted the severe and dogmatic rationalism of her own upbringing. The prayers which she taught us were a sign of her divided mind, for apart from them we heard very little about God or Jesus. Certainly those vague beings meant much less to us than the heroes and heroines of Miss Otway's dramas.

But our few religious fantasies were never discouraged. The bedroom which Tony and I shared looked out on the embankment and the dark river beyond it. Our curtains were always drawn together in such a way that two bars of light from the streetlamp outside fell across the ceiling and down the opposite wall. These long, bright rectangles, sharply bent towards the ends, were known as our angels; the larger one Tony's and the smaller one mine. They were our protectors during the night, and once, when the streetlamp failed, we were seriously upset by their absence. My mother lit a night-light for us and put it on a table between our beds.

12 January

We tend to think that it must be harder for older people to change and grow than it is for those who are still young and, presumably, more flexible and uncommitted. So I sometimes pride myself on at least the *efforts* I make to change my life in accordance with certain radical changes of belief.

Yet in India it's often assumed that when a man has reached retiring age, when a woman has done with her children, they will move together into an ashram and spend their remaining years under the direction of a guru.

At least I now have a better idea of what a well-ordered

life would be like. In the past I've been fanatically attached to an unchanging daily routine; but I always knew that this was largely to protect myself from a congenital disorder within; partly a wholly practical device for getting my work done without any office hours to keep. Now I would like always to walk with the magical care and attention, yet utter naturalness, of that Buddhist monk we saw on TV not long ago. To do everything as if it were a ritual; to do nothing without attention and respect.

At first, of course, such behaviour is bound to seem grotesquely *un*natural; self-conscious in the worst sense. But I must put up with this until my attention becomes as natural to me as my constant and busy distraction has seemed to be until now.

Attendant Dieu, as best I can.

———— * ————

Last night S and I watched a TV programme on anorexia, Laura coming in half-way through and staring at those emaciated figures with an alarming intensity. With envy? Two out of the three psychiatrists who were interviewed believed that the dread disease is *always* caused by some tension or disturbance within the family. Certainly poor L has had plenty of that.

But how hard it is at this particular time to know how much responsibility parents must bear for the misfortunes of their children! We mustn't be afraid to accept it, but nor must we grab too much blame for ourselves, thus depriving our children of all credit for their own faults.

In the fashion of the age I used to blame my mother for most of my troubles. Now that I'm beginning to reject that facile convention it would be absurd if I started to load myself with guilt for the troubles of my own children.

*   *   *

At some very early point in our shared nights I had begun to tell stories to Tony before we went to sleep. Soon I had created a small but complete mythology based on a country called Ponham which was ruled over by a lady of the same name. There was a shark pond and a single-line railway which crossed it by a precarious bridge. There was a good man called Barley, and a swarm of bad, loutish boys called the Disobedients ... Probably there were not more than six stories altogether, and no variations were attempted, or even allowed, in any of them.

—— * ——

But the most powerful mythology of all had grown up around the Germans – the 'GERM-MANS'. Tony had been born at the beginning of the First War and I in 1916, a few days before the opening of the Battle of the Somme. I have often claimed that my earliest memory is of the Armistice in November 1918, when I was taken across the Albert Bridge on our usual walk and saw white millers dancing in a ring outside the Battersea flour mills. But this is more likely to be a memory of that scene as it was often described to me by my mother in later years.

Yet the war and its aftermath provided Miss Otway with some of her best material; and there were also maids in the Chelsea flat – still only one at a time – who contributed their own vivid accounts of the Kaiser and his frightful soldiers. One of these young girls had a sweetheart called Earny who had lost an arm in battle, and I still believe that I can remember his single arm, in hospital blue, supporting me against the embankment wall.

The Germans were grey ogres, capable of every wickedness, and the Kaiser was Satan himself. A year or two after the war a German professor came to stay with my parents, and when he told me what he was I shrank away from him and said, 'But Germans eat us!'

—— * ——

As for the conventional terror-figures of our childhood I was far more frightened of witches than of ogres, trolls or dragons. Another dream which recurred was of witches in the basement of a Chelsea house, gloating over haunches of bright crimson meat. I knew that these were the haunches of boys.

A true midwinter, worst-of-winter afternoon, digging the garden. A dead day when it was hard to believe that life would ever return to the woods and garden. In tune with this I felt a faint shiver of depression; but this immediately set me digging with great deliberation; not faster but much more slowly than before. 'Digging!' I said, 'Digging – Dig-ging – Dig-ging ...' As I shall hope to murmur 'Dy-ing Dy-ing Dy-ing' when that time comes.

(And was it one motive for trying to change my life – that I wanted to prepare myself for death? Or has it been a result of my attempted change that I no longer seem to fear death quite so much as I did?)

——— * ———

At least it seems clear to me now that this turning towards God – this turning towards where I hope God is, or might be – couldn't have happened at any earlier period of my life. We are only conscious of any freedom of choice in the present moment; and when we look back on our past it seems to make little sense to say, I might have done this or that instead of what I did do.

So although those long years of energetic sinning were often so painful to myself and others I can't honestly say that I'm 'ashamed' of them. The person I see back there seems, from here, to have been acting as he had to act, and seems to have been bringing me, however clumsily and blindly, to my present state of at least lesser blindness and partially-changed desires.

But it is also true, of course, that the route which brought me here was not simply traversed and left behind: that confused and roundabout journey has cluttered me up with wrong ways of thinking and feeling: stupidities have grown all over me like horny skins: I am beset by wrong habits and foolish expectations.

Today, for example, I worried away at our finances like a dog worrying a dirty old bone. Not that there's any cause to

[95]

worry; but even if we were threatened with imminent destitution how gratifying it would be if I could face that prospect with perfect equanimity. Better still, with joy and exultation in the knowledge that dispossession is a famous old way of arriving at true possession. (My emendation of the famous *East Coker* lines has been:

> 'In order to dispossess yourself of what you possess
> You must go by the way of a surfeit of possessions.')

* * *

In the spring of 1921 my mother and father went out to Turkey, where he was to cover the Graeco-Turkish war for the *Manchester Guardian*. They were away for six months, and we spent the whole of that time at our grandparents' house on Boar's Hill. My grandfather, Gilbert Murray, was Regius Professor of Greek at Oxford, and although this meant nothing at all to Tony and me we knew that he was in some way more splendid than other people. My grandmother was a small, eternally bustling woman, in principle a total egalitarian but an unashamed aristocrat in her dictatorial treatment of everyone except her husband.

Tony and I were fond of them both, but fonder of our grandfather, who interfered with us so much less. He used to come back from Oxford, or descend from his study, like a gentle and pacifying god. He was a charming and amusing man; and he kept up a running story for us about the activities of the Boar which had given its name to that academic hillside.

Certainly we had no sense at all of being abandoned by our parents, who wrote to us often and sent funny drawings of their adventures in Turkey. Yatscombe was a very hospitable house, and I shall always remember it for the almost continuous talk; for its large bright windows and the smell of lavender and roses.

But a strange and alarming episode still stands out blackly from that pleasant blur of summer lawns, hazel woods, bamboos and delicious vegetarian meals. All that I can now *see* is my grandfather bursting through my bedroom door, pulling me out of bed and across his lap and slapping my bottom hard and often with his open hand. I must have known very well at the time that this wasn't the arbitary and inexplicable event which it still seems while it stays on the edge of my memory. The truth is that for a long time I had been bellowing interminably after being put to bed, and at last even my grandfather's patience had been tried too hard.

I don't for a moment suppose that this punishment left a scar on my mind; but the shock of witnessing that transformation from gentle storyteller into ferocious chastiser was unforgettable. Perhaps it was the best possible treatment, for it seems that there was no bellowing after it, and I certainly bóre no grudge against my grandfather.

I still believe that the background of these sometimes abrasive memories was one of love and good order; for me, if not for Tony. Many years later my mother told me that she had found me the more endearing of the two, but she gave no sign of this at the time and, in my passion for equality of love, I would have been shocked and alarmed if she had shown her preference in any way. But perhaps Tony did see signs of it; though if he did he never said so, either then or later.

17 January

As I make a little progress in meditation, control, attention, so my interest in speculative theology (what other legitimate kind is there?) seems to be dying away. Mercifully so, for I often had a sense of futility when I tried to think in those terms. 'The transfer of faith from the dimension of a personal encounter into the dimension of factual instruction is the great tragedy of Christianity.' (Bultmann – who devoted his life to instruction!)

——— * ———

'Neo-Scholasticism.' A frightful word, in sound, meaning and associations. It sounds pompous, arrogant and esoterically intellectual. It instantly brings back to my mind the black Christianity of forty years ago – to which my mother, also, so

[97]

intimately belonged. It involved a contorted, almost analytical approach to religious experience which now seems desperately arid and unattractive.

Recollections of Christmas, 1977

The presence of Jason with Chrissie, Lucy with Bernard, Josephine with Pip gave us again that warming sense of the enlarged family reassembled in unbroken closeness and affection. But perhaps the most memorable event was the carol singing at Tymawr. The Reverend Mother had invited the whole Barn House community, and every one of them went. We settled down in the big sitting room at Michaelgarth, most of the guests being elderly lady-associates of the convent. Kerry and Novice Sister Karen sat on the floor together with their guitars; and among many familiar carols Barn House sang two of their own, to a very different rhythm and accompanied by both guitarists.

At first, as on earlier occasions, the mingling of black habits and hoods with frayed jeans and bright jerseys seemed almost comical. But these two very different communities have much more in common than anyone outside them would expect. When they meet like this they love to compare notes, and each seems almost ready to learn lessons from the other. My position as an associate of both communities makes these meetings very delightful and inspiriting. Freaks and enclosed Anglican nuns!

——— * ———

I have been trying to persuade some of my Depressive Anonymous correspondents to get together and form groups. But this has never worked; and I see quite clearly now that it never will work. What we need is a paid organizer, of great charismatic power, who can race about the country, not only forming groups, but sustaining them whenever they begin to flag. Keith is the obvious person.

——— * ———

I've now done three Friday fasts – in fact from Thursday supper to Saturday lunch – without any great difficulty, but also without any notable benefit, either physical or spiritual. In fact the main effect of these privations has been to present me with a new temptation to complacency. Perhaps I needed that, since I don't have a great many of *them*. But what curious and convoluted forms this journey sometimes takes!

The real object of all my new activities is to keep 'the fool of the house' under better control – St Teresa's term for the topmost level of our busy, discursive, aimless consciousness.

* * *

I have a very clear memory of my grandmother skipping across the hall at Yatscombe, holding a piece of paper above her head and singing, 'A new-born baby! A new-born baby brother for Tony and Philip!' I suppose we must have been warned of this, but all I remember was a feeling of mildly uncomprehending surprise. There was certainly no conscious shock of jealousy, and not the least apprehension of what this birth would mean to us.

When we came back to London we came not only to a new baby but also to a new house. Presumably my father was earning more by now – he had held a professorship at London University, but had recently begun his career at the Royal Institute of International Affairs – for this St John's Wood house was much larger than the Chelsea flat. There was even a patchy lawn, some blackened lime trees and a castor-oil bush.

What I remember best is coming into a bedroom and seeing the new baby at my mother's breast; but even at this moment of confrontation I can remember no very strong emotion. I said that the baby looked weak, and asked my mother whether it was going to die. Today the 'true' meaning of my question seems too obvious to mention; yet I know that I felt a quite genuine concern for the wrinkled fragility of that tiny, spluttering creature. And I would guess that this concern was at least as real as any fratricidal impulse in my unconscious mind.

But how did it come about that within a year of that birth I was boarding at a private school only half a mile from our St John's Wood house? I wasn't even a weekly boarder, although my mother must have paid occasional visits to the school in term-time.

Children usually accept whatever happens to them without question, and I doubt if it even seemed odd to me that I was boarding at a school where Tony was a dayboy, and where the parents of all the other boarders seemed to be living in Africa or India.

Many years afterwards, when this state of affairs, and many others that followed it, *had* begun to seem strange to me, my mother explained that I had become so intolerable soon after the birth of my brother Lawrence that it was impossible to keep me at home. Indeed she had always dreaded the holidays, when the exiled monster would again start to raise hell in a house which had been a bower of peace in his absence.

What I do remember is that I was often in trouble now, and that the notion of my exceptional naughtiness was one which I learned to accept as a fact of life. I told the dirtiest stories in the dormitory. I was often beaten by the tough but charming Mr Campbell, whom all of us wished to please. I got myself lost whenever we went on school outings to Hampstead Heath.

Most home memories of those years have been obliterated; but I remember that my mother, who had never seemed capable of ill-temper in Chelsea, was often fiercely angry with me in St John's Wood. And still it never crossed my mind that she might be wrong, or even mistaken, in anything she said or did. (How curious it seems to me now that we were brought up to believe that all the adults we knew were good, and that both our parents were impeccable.)

Yet my memories of that school are not particularly harrowing. In fact the clearest of them all is a very happy one. On one of the school expeditions to Hampstead Heath a larger boy had steered me away from the others into an arena concealed by surrounding bushes. There he was just about to inflict some form of schoolboy torture on me when Tony suddenly jumped through the gorse and attacked my tormentor with flailing arms. The bigger boy ran away at once.

Some time in my ninth year, and second year at Arnold House, the headmistress was taking a group of parents round the garden when they came upon Toynbee Minor peeing into a flowerpot. This had been, of course, the culmination of many offences, the last straw on that broad back which made her decide that her school could tolerate me no better than my mother could.

This first expulsion from school must have greatly strengthened my conviction of sin, for my mother's accusations had now been endorsed by a quite separate authority.

After this, with a minimum delay, I was sent off to board at the Dragon School in Oxford, an institution which prided itself on being able to lick even the most misshapen boys into shape.

*   *   *

20 January

And there, for the second time in a few months, I abandon a book with a sense of almost unqualified relief. The prospect of starting to describe the second of my five interminable schools had begun to loom over me like a menacing cloud of boredom and meaningless effort. But the conviction must have been growing in me for several days that I would never be able to finish the autobiography which I had begun with such a deceptive flourish of self-confidence.

Perhaps it was that little description of the dirty lime trees and the castor-oil bush which did the trick. That little decorative, utterly irrelevant, utterly pointless touch of local colour. Who cares what that garden looked like? Who cares what that small boy did, or who his parents were, or where he went to school?

I know there are certain magicians who can make the most trivial scenes and episodes of their own past seem of vital concern to the rest of us. But I see very clearly now that I don't belong to that tribe.

What's more the journal, too, seems to have suffered from trying to keep company with that consequential narrator. I should have remembered how much I've hated, and eschewed, all forms of narrative ever since I finished the last of the three conventional novels which I wrote in my twenties. 'And then ... and then ... and then ...' Worse still – 'then I ... then I ... then I ...'

Ever since I began to plan *Tea with Mrs Goodman* – which appeared in 1947 – I've seen that for me the only way of writing is to string together a necklace of sharp occasions and to conceal as best I can any narrative or explanatory thread.

So if ever I turn back to my own past again for something to write about I shall treat it not as a story to tell but as a mine to be quarried.

21 January

The only justification I shall ever find for exploring my past life is to find moments, episodes, annunciations which can be made to blaze with the light of some universal truth and meaning. *Annunciations!* A possible title, perhaps, for that dimly-conceived future book. And in many cases the title would have a perfectly literal meaning: My mother coming into my bedroom in the early morning to tell me that Tony had shot himself. The casual announcement by a friend at a party that my parents had separated. Anne's unwilling admission that she wanted to leave me for Richard. S accepting my love in Tel Aviv. Mary at the encounter group. The letter from Connie Hellins after fifty years ...

Such moments of joy and horror are not just episodes in *my* life but openings into the light and darkness which everyone else has seen.

No; not *Annunciations*, which is much too grand and biblical. Perhaps *Reconstructions*, since I certainly mean to take liberties with those moments of truth.

But this is incorrigible! My wretched soul still craving for the wounds of self-expression. Better stick to this diary, after all, in the hope that it may one day be fit for others to see. Honest enough and interesting enough. A humble job, by my present good intentions, in which the flamboyant self will be shot down at once as soon as he starts to fly too high. Clarity before elegance. Truth before both. I hope so.

26 January

I do keep in mind my extraordinary privileges. Money, to start with, which has not only bought us this pleasant cottage to live in but also allowed us to lend our larger house for a useful, though some would say a dottily idiosyncratic purpose. (Be frank! Be frank! S would say it herself, and often does, and often angrily. How much did I impose the community on her by my own overweening enthusiasm? Certain it was ruthlessly imposed on poor Laura, who was never consulted at all. No wonder she resents the loss of her old home.)

Anyway, I am, in the most obvious ways, an unusually lucky man. Not just money for my pet high-minded scheme, but a happy family life (by and large); an enjoyable job; a satisfying talent; many good friends – though I see them so seldom; no urban obligations; *plenty of time*. I can now add good health to the list, after nearly seven months without deep depression. And most important of all, I hope and believe, is this new freedom of the spirit: a real liberation of the heart and mind. However little it shows.

Yes, but how harshly uncompromising they've all been about this, the great saints and gurus. We must give *all* to the poor: if we remain *the least bit* attached to physical possessions we shall

[103]

never come to the Kingdom; to Enlightenment; Samadhi ...

Yet I also know only too well that neither S nor I is fit to make this sacrifice. As for me, a self-inflicted poverty would impoverish not only my body but also my heart and mind. I wouldn't be a holy beggar but a whining, angry and resentful one.

So perhaps there is a certain humility in recognizing that we are like the rich young man in the gospel, incapable of the heroism which is needed for true discipleship.

But was Jesus right in that case? He also said, after all, that in his father's house are many mansions; and surely there was a humble mansion even for that young man. Perhaps he was destroyed by having too great a demand made on him: driven to despair, and in the end to total moral collapse. Whereas a less stringent demand might have led him at least *towards* the light of the Kingdom.

25 January

After sawing wood at BH and sitting down for our tea an unusual discussion began between Phil and me. It was unusual in being a debate about religious first principles, and such debates are very rare. This is partly because all the communards (except Kerry) have a deep suspicion of words, and partly because they want to believe that to be 'spiritually minded' is a state which necessarily unites us all in love and (undefined; unformulated) faith. But I believe as much as I ever did that some of these differences are important and that to pretend they don't exist is dangerously soft-headed.

Phil, though he read PPE at Oxford (he and Kerry are the only communards ever to have completed a university course) announced that he took no interest whatever in history. He used our (overused?) *Be Here Now* as an excuse for this indifference. But history, I said, is simply the study of what human beings have done and thought and felt and said before our own time; and isn't it a strange form of arrogance to treat these people as unworthy of our attention; undeserving of our respect; even of our love?

Then there was talk of that ridiculous so-called 'Essene' gospel which has been handed round at BH for the last few weeks. This document transforms Jesus into a militant vegetarian, and tells us that before his ministry in Palestine he had travelled widely in the Far East and sat at the feet of many Buddhist and Hindu sages. I told them that there isn't a scrap of evidence for this, and what's more that the whole ridiculous effusion bears all the marks of having been written between 1880 and 1920 (it reeks of Blavatsky and Annie Besant and the Brahmo-Somaj). But it was clear that they weren't much interested in evidence; or even in provenance. Their 'truth' doesn't depend on such mundane matters as these.

One of their worst tendencies is to believe something simply because they want to believe it. Just as one of their best tendencies is the corollary to this – open-mindedness to any living truth, coming from any source. I wish they could manage the second without the first.

A little later Phil and I were travelling the old Buddhist versus Judaeo-Christian road – he being a relapsed Jew and now an approximate Buddhist. In fact this road has almost disappeared from view under the rich growth of ecumenical goodwill, and I think we all felt a certain discomfort as I began to uncover it again. It was the *blandness* of Buddhism that I attacked, the serene indifference, for example, to the hungry and destitute of their own countries. To which Phil answered that the body, starving or replete, is only a phantasm of the unenlightened mind: the spirit is all that matters. To which I answered ... No, I can't bear to trundle through it all again.

But I'm glad that Christians go to the starving with *bread*, as well as with love and the Holy Spirit. Presumably Phil's Buddhist would have passed by on the other side with the priest and the Levite. Worse still, he might have stopped beside the poor beaten-up traveller and gently instructed him to endure his bad karma with a good grace, since he was only paying for the sins and follies of his earlier lives.

[105]

The argument was always friendly and good-humoured, but it leaves me dissatisfied with myself as well as with BH. By inheritance, upbringing and strong natural inclination I've acquired a respect for words and the mind which none of them shares. But I often feel that they're nearer the truth than I am, however inarticulate their truth may be. They seem to know that the best truth is silent.

God, how I wish – at times – that I could keep my mind still; put all the nagging questions aside and wait until they're silently answered. Or silently dissolved.

26 January

On the telly Russian soldiers doing the goose step. It's hardly credible that *anyone* would have wanted to imitate this monstrosity of the German army: such a blasphemous misuse of the human body, turning it into a vile machine for kicking and stamping at the same time. The very opposite of a holy dance like the tai-chi.

——— * ———

'Every real creation of art is independent, more powerful than the artist himself, and returns to the divine through its own manifestation. It is one with man only in this, that it bears testimony to the mediation of the divine within him' (Beethoven).

——— * ———

I have now become a perfectionist about gramophone records, discarding all the old ones which have the slightest flaw in them. Yet before we got our new speakers I used to collect records quite indiscriminately, and in huge quantities.

The point, I'm afraid, is that the records interest me more than the music does. How different from S: but then her ear is twice as good as mine, and her pleasure in listening is certainly twice as great. (When I *do* listen I listen as if with knitted brow.)

From *Observer* review of *Natural and Supernatural: A History of the Paranormal*, by Brian Inglis (Hodder & Stoughton, London).

The word 'paranormal' suggests that the whole area must be subject to the basic postulates of science about the essential orderliness of nature; its susceptibility *in every field* to the application of laws and to the method of repeatable experiment. What is deeply disturbing to the scientific mind, even in a period where deep disturbances have to be constantly lived with, is that during more than a century of increasingly careful investigation no more is understood about telepathy, clairvoyance, poltergeist, communication with the dead, etc., than was understood when the investigations began. *Evidence* has mounted so high that there seems little point in continually adding to the disorderly heap. *Explanations* remain jejune, laboured, often tautological.

But if scientists are disturbed, so also should be all those who believe in a spiritual reality above, as well as within the reality perceived by the senses. I have no doubt at all that several saints have levitated themselves: but so have several most earthly ladies and gentlemen who were not above attempted fraud when their genuine powers deserted them. If spirits exist as well as, or as part of, *the* Spirit, and if they are responsible for some, at least, of these goings-on, then why do they bother to do it? If, on the other hand, these miracles – for that is what they should still be called – are performed by purely human means why is it that the miracle-making capacity remains as mysterious and inexplicable as ever?

A letter from Connie reminds me, as always, of *the* letter from Connie, and persuades me that I ought to write that strange story here.

After my expulsion from the Dragon School when I was ten, and the subsequent ravaging from a child psychologist, my mother decided to send me away to a semi-reformatory farm in Kent. In fact all the other delinquents were public schoolboys, and the youngest was 17. I was put in the particular charge of a Miss Hellins, who was the under-manager of the farm; an agriculturalist and no sort of authority on reformation. I lived with her for six months in the farmhouse and grew to love her not only as a mother but as a small boy's dream-wife.

All of this ended in muddle and misfortune, but ever since I saw Miss Hellins ('Slellins' was my endearment) for the last time, in August 1926, I had been trying to find her again – however spasmodically; vaguely; even unconsciously. Quite often I thought I'd seen her on a station platform or a London street; but the face had never been quite the right one. At two of the saddest moments of my grown-up life I made the journey back to Seal Chart Farm, although I knew very well that Miss Hellins had left there long ago. And what seems strangest to me now is that I had no idea why I was going back there; what it was that I was trying to find there.

But in the late summer of 1976 I found her again, at the very time, perhaps, when I needed her most since our separation almost exactly fifty years before. Dorothy Hobhouse, the sister of an old friend, came to Tymawr for a weekend retreat, and then to visit us here at Woodroyd. Over tea she said, 'Does the name Constance Hellins mean anything to you?' and if metaphors could come to life I would have fallen off my chair. When I said that the name meant more to me than any other she could have mentioned Dorothy told me that 'Connie' was not only alive and well but a friend and neighbour of hers in Somerset.

We wrote to each other, and arranged that S, Laura and I would drive down to Bridgewater, half-way between her house and ours, and meet her for lunch in a hotel. On that journey I was in a state of extreme nervous excitement; expectation: almost fear. But as soon as I saw that good, round face and the grey bobbed hair I knew that everything would be all right. And indeed I've found in Connie – as I now, almost naturally, call her – all the charms and virtues which I remember in Slellins, my six-month mother and wife. Such affectionate good sense and unpretentious dignity; respect for the dignity of others; humour and self-reliance ...

It was more difficult for her, of course, to find the ten-year-old boy in the sixty-year-old man; but sometimes when I've made some remark she's said that it brings back the child she knew.

Apart from the simple joy of finding her again; of sharing such ancient memories; of experiencing that strange and rich conjunction of two far-separated times – more than all these, my meeting with Connie has redeemed my childhood. For up to her death, ten years ago, my mother still insisted that I had been an impossible small boy; almost a perverted monster. But not only did Connie talk of our past together with obvious delight; she wrote me a letter soon after that first meeting in which she told me that I had been 'a delightful little boy, mischievous, imaginative and affectionate'. The words amazed me; but as I gradually absorbed them I felt as if my mind had been cleared of a black fog which had hung there so long that I was no longer aware of how much it was darkening the present as well as the distant past.

Not that I could dismiss the monster altogether, or even that I wanted to. But if the boy who was monstrous at home could be delightful in the delightful company of Slellins, then he was at least half-angel as well as half-beast, like everybody else.

I can't think it was an accident that I found Connie when I did. Not that my depression marvellously lifted when she brought me her news, and her own inspiring person; but at least a new light was shone in that darkness and a new chance was given me of making some progress on this mysterious journey. (Mysterious, in this context, because although we have to work against the great inner lump of the self it's no use starting with a self-disgust which has been imposed by someone else. A sane and rational self-respect is the very beginning of that wisdom which makes us fit to set out on a journey whose continuous purpose is to lose our respected selves in God.)

———— * ————

The meeting with Connie is not the only event of these last years which has given me a sharp sense that my life is being at least partially directed. As much as God *wills*? As much as God *can*? As much, perhaps, *as he wills when he can*. I've been so inordinately 'lucky' lately, in meeting the right person at the right time; finding the right book; seeing the right programme on television.

At BH there is a strong tendency towards a total fatalism – of the most cheerful kind: what will be will be, and what will be will be for the best. I can't accept this, of course; and perhaps I should urge them to read *Candide*. God helps those who help themselves seems a sounder old motto to me; but none of us can solve the mystery of God's intervention in our lives, and therefore none of us should try. Perhaps I should recite this passage from Brother Lawrence (Herman) once a day: 'We ought to make a great difference between the acts of the *understanding* and those of the *will*; the first are of comparatively little value, and the others all. Our only business is to love and delight ourselves in God.'

30 January

Was that Tale of Connie a return of the autobiographical itch? I don't think so: I think it's a story which had to be told because it belongs so much to my present condition. Once I'd decided that this work was not to be a collection of ostensibly impersonal aphorisms, pensées, etc., there was no way of keeping the person out. The problem will be to prevent him from making too many appearances: he has that tendency.

3 February

On Sunday we hauled the caravan through a blizzard to visit Barbara, a D A friend who lives near Liverpool. Misunderstandings quickly cleared up; and between S and me, there was the usual love and happiness of journeys.

But by yesterday – dreary Thursday and soft drinks with hard-drinking friends – I was in a thoroughly jangled state. And how much better I would have felt if I'd been able to down three or four pints of draught Guinness. As for the supposed satisfaction of not doing this I felt scarcely any at all: perhaps none: perhaps more than anything a sense of my perverse folly in refusing the only medicine which could have done me any good.

Now I must go back to the fruitful new regime of prayer and calm. But I must try to get back to it without that frenzied clamping down of a fixed pattern which has always followed such times of trouble in the past. Ah, to *glide* back into a blessed and unforced good order; not scuttle back like a rabbit into its hole.

Remember that nothing of this need be wasted. Remember that love prevailed over inner chaos most of the time. Remember that I endured the conversation of KG in Monmouth with self-conscious but exemplary good humour: even encouraged him with laughter, grunts, nods and so on. Even *tried* – though failed miserably in this – to love him as a brother in the fellowship of all God's sons.

5 February

Jason and Chrissie came for the night, and I was again reminded of how much better and nicer he is than I was at his age. No false modesty whatever in this. I was obsessed by fame: he is content to work as a builder in the hope of forming a building co-operative in Coventry when he's fully trained. He is devoted to Chrissie in a responsible and cheering way; whereas most of my devotion to Anne was infantile, dependent and altogether self-centred.

———— * ————

When Jason asked me why I believed, I said that what had begun as a half-frivolous hypothesis – let's see how things would look if we think of man as a spiritual being – had become the best illumination of any that I'd ever tried. In this light the whole of human life becomes – not intelligible, but alive with meaning; many-dimensional; vividly-coloured. All the old problems have been changed into a single great luminous mystery. ('A mystery is not a problem to be solved but a condition of life to be experienced.')

Or this, at least, is what I *tried* to say to Jason.

6 February

England-Wales match on the telly. The annual occasion when I used to make a more frantic fool of myself than at any other time. All that howling and stamping and shrieking abuse; savage contempt for the English team and bitter hatred against the Welsh.

The result of this match was as usual, but at least I watched it with a certain melancholy restraint. Absurdly, though, the melancholy, the sense of personal depletion, lasted the rest of the day. I am diminished by the defeat of fifteen unknown young men in white jerseys by fifteen unknown young men in red jerseys. How readily we send out our ego and attach it to someone or something in the hope that they will inflate it for us like a balloon and carry it up into the sky with them. How readily we risk the opposite – deflation and the abysmal dust.

I should like to see a great stadium filled with Buddhist monks watching a football match played by two teams of

Enlightened Ones. (Or would they, too, give way to the ludicrous passion of partisanship?)

7 February

Last night I walked through the woods to BH for Rose's *zikr*. Eight of us knelt in a circle, hands tightly clasped, and as Rose chanted Arabic words we bowed our heads deeply towards the centre; then threw them back as far as we could. The chanting and the movements got faster and faster – until my ankles were hurting so much that I had to disengage myself and sit down panting outside the circle.

But this was a good experience while it lasted, though nothing wonderful. The best was sitting silently afterwards, all our faces dancing gently in the light of Simon's stove: closely companionable, to put it no higher.

Walking back over the snow, between the black trees, under a full and bright moon ... a dog barking from across the valley; the moonlit mare and her foal munching hay in the field at Copwell ... Everything was set for high emotions: but we seldom respond to the traditional, or over-perfect, stimuli. All I achieved was a firm resolution not to be disappointed at feeling so little.

8 February

What does seem plain to me is that in our time the real challenge to a thinking Christian comes, not from his non-believing friends and associates – humanists; atheists; agnostics, whatever they call themselves – but from the more tough-minded forms of Buddhism. Forced into an argument with a raucous atheist in Monmouth I had a sense of total futility; as if we were quite literally talking different languages. For him the words 'holy' and 'sacred' are simply nonsense sounds; or, at another point in the idiot exchange of old counters, no more than inflated equivalents of the word 'good'.

[113]

Buddhists, on the other hand, use such words with every bit as much confidence as Christians do; and no open-minded Christian could possibly deny the term 'holy' to a Truly Enlightened Buddhist. Yet this experience – of joy; of peace; of deep understanding – leads the Buddhist to quite different conclusions from the Christian's. He is not aware of a loving God penetrating his soul with light: for him the light comes solely from within himself; from the depths of his own being.

The challenge is formidable. The difference between the two religions is very deep. Contrast the sublime calm of the Buddha seated in meditation with the contorted Jesus on the cross.

Prejudiced as I inevitably am I find the Christian attitude to suffering far the richer and deeper of the two. To reach a state of no-more-pain is a primary objective of the good Buddhist – even if the very best of them, having attained Nirvana, choose to come back into this suffering world in order to help their more backward brothers to escape from it as well.

But to the Christian suffering is by no means the worst thing there is. Pain and affliction are not good in themselves, but they are necessary means to the ultimate good. And the ultimate good is not some place, or condition, in which suffering is no more, but a state of holy love and devotion: of adoration. It is only the crudest (hymn book) Heaven which is defined as a place where there is no more pain but only everlasting bliss. If to be in Heaven is to love as fully as possible then it is hard to see how pain could be banished so long as any suffering creature remains in any place.

Perhaps it is possible to make an amalgam of Buddhism and Christianity – but only by fudging them both. The whole moral, intellectual and spiritual attitudes are utterly different. The deepest beliefs – in a transcendent God of love: in the enlightened self-sufficiency of man – are irreconcilable: even contradictory.

We should bow to each other, with true respect. We should recognize that each has something to offer the other, but that those offerings which can be exchanged and absorbed are only peripheral elements of both religions.

Unless and until the world receives a new Revelation/ Illumination which transcends all these apparent differences and shows us the crucified Christ and the meditating Buddha as a single sublime figure. (But I am a little mistrustful of those who claim that this unifying vision has already been granted them. Even Merton becomes strangely turgid and opaque when he writes about Zen and the Cross. Or perhaps it's just that he becomes too difficult for me; that he has moved at this point into a realm of the spirit where I can't follow him.)

10 February

On Monday evening, moved by a true, even agonizing pity I drove to Gloucester on a Samaritan type of mission. Jason came with me, and as we drove through the dark I realized that although an action of this kind is rare for me it is second nature to him, to Lucy and to their mother. And will soon be so, it's already clear, to Laura too. But now I began to commend myself for joining their company: to reproach myself for this complacency ... commend myself for this clear-sightedness ... reproach myself ... the smelly old spiral of self-consciousness (Catch 1).

I escaped from it at last by realizing that the Spirit had probably been hard at work to produce even this minimal act of good conduct. I also used mockery against that rosy tableau of virtue, and gradually shamed it away by ridicule.

Though I don't for a moment believe in exterior devils it's often convenient to treat the loveless brute within as if he had a certain autonomy. And then to speak to him, not in anger, which he enjoys and thrives on, but with derision, which he dislikes as much as we all do.

------ * ------

'Sacrifice' is another of those dead Christian terms which modern churchmen are forever trying to dress up in more respectable clothes. Its original meaning is simply 'to make holy'; but since we can never return to that without hopeless

[115]

confusion we'd surely do better to drop it altogether. To use it of the Crucifixion (Atonement) is a blasphemy against God the Father: to use it to describe some act of abstinence or renunciation on our own part is absurdly portentous. My Friday fast, for example, is intended to improve my physical condition; to strengthen my long-enfeebled will; and, only as a very uncertain bonus, to liven up the dormant spirit within. In other words I do it because I want to do it; and for nobody's sake except my own. (Unless one anticipates all those eventual beneficiaries of a transformed and highly-spiritualized PT, radiating love wherever he goes!)

The *Sacrifice* of the mass. Nothing that I've read on this has made any sense to me at all. (Unless, of course, we use the word in its primal but obsolete meaning.)

12 February

There are messy days – days of fluster and bluster; and there are grinding days – days of gritted teeth. Sometimes, but not very often now, there are days of cheerful indifference to all deep and weighty matters, when pleasure wipes the mind clean of God and all his wiles.

For the flustered state the best cure is to go to Tymawr for evensong and compline: coolness and loving calm. For the grinding days there is no alleviation except in the knowledge that they have to come: they also serve. As for the days of careless pleasure, I take them gladly, and without apology. (Perhaps I should thank God for those genial hours when he has allowed me to forget all about him.)

But the best days are the ones which are most ritually formal; most constantly aware. Inspired by these I've been toying lately with the idea of trying out a simplified version of the Japanese tea ceremony. To be held in my room – and inside a pavilion constructed of curtained screens. S snorts loudly at this, of course, and I know perfectly well that she'd never dream of attending. And indeed I recognize it as yet

[116]

another of my extravagances; perhaps one of my idiocies. (Though certainly three or four of the dear communards would join me in those elaborate and tranquillizing motions.)

The little illustrated book on the Ceremony, which I've added to my small pile of pre-meditation reading, certainly delights me by the comic formality of the language – e.g. 'Men of Tea' – and by the cool ritualization (unification) of life which it suggests. Ah, to become a Man of Tea instead of the Man of Booze that I used to be: the Man Longing for Booze that I am today! For alcohol, in spite of its jolly pretensions, is surely the most *disintegrating* force I've ever known. (Or are these the sour grapes of a still reluctant, and sometimes resentful abstainer?)

——— * ———

Stephen (he has some other, Thai name which I can never get hold of) is a Barn House visitor who spent five years as a Buddhist monk in Thailand and northern India. The sort of quietly impressive man one would expect. He talked to us over coffee this morning about the urgent need for BH to give itself a firmer structure; a disciplined work to be done: he even spoke of learning and study-groups. I was delighted to hear that this man, so much respected by the whole community, believes in the need for a deliberate, purposive endeavour. This has never been BH's way; and in the best years the place seemed almost to run itself, by a sort of collective instinct (or direction). But now, when there seems to be a real danger of disintegration, I'm sure they need to find a new structure of this kind.

——— * ———

Robert Powell (*Zen and Reality*) writes scornfully of the traditional Judaeo-Christian attitude: 'At present I recognize that I am "evil" and that I must be "good", and I think that for this transformation I need time, which means that through certain efforts I can gradually accumulate goodness and change from bad to good.' For this Powell substitutes: 'Fear can only go spontaneously, and this happens when the mind has become utterly still. The mind cannot be forced to become still, but

[117]

it is spontaneously quiet when the whole process of consciousness has been completely understood.'

He travesties the Christian position, since the wisest Christians have never recommended trying to haul oneself out of 'badness' and into 'goodness': they've always insisted on the need to be reborn; the need for a total change of vision and understanding.

Yet after rereading Ram Dass (the popular American teacher of Eastern Wisdom) I do see that there's an element in the whole process which Christians tend to leave out; or at best to minimize. This is the element of 'letting go'; of all that is represented by the phrase 'take it easy!' when that phrase is understood in its deepest sense. It is so common for the busy, ever-active Westerner simply to turn his busyness from making money to making himself into a 'good Christian'. And so he will strain away at this as if it's the same kind of task as all the others he's done before.

But as for 'the whole process of consciousness' being 'completely understood', this is the kind of Zen-talk which has no meaning for me at all.

Merton comes to the rescue again:

'The Law of Love (supernatural) tends to break into the Law of Nature, which we assume is contrary to it. With a sigh we renounce that to which we are spontaneously inclined and turn away to "duty" – the duty of love, imposed for some inscrutable reason by God in order to "save us". Well, of course, we do want to be saved, don't we?

'Because the Law of Love is presented in this grey light, fewer and fewer people are able to keep alive a genuine interest in salvation.

'Let us forget this travesty, and try to understand the Christian view of love.

'First of all, the Law of Love *is the deepest law of our nature*, not something extraneous and alien to our nature. Our nature itself inclines us to love, and to love freely.

[118]

'The deepest and most fundamental exigency of the divine law in our hearts is that we should reach our fulfilment by loving.'

———— * ————

Meditation. I suppose I've 'made progress' within my original terms of reference; but I've never for a moment escaped from those terms. 'It's all *preliminary*, damn it!' I said to myself last night: but this was quickly followed by, 'And so it always will be.'

It is wise to be humble about this; right, and even fruitful, to accept the limitations of one's spiritual poverty. But there is always the very quiet (and surely legitimate) reservation – 'Perhaps, all the same, a new light may one day shine for me too.'

———— * ————

One evening last week I settled down to listen – *very hard* – to the *Hammerklavier Sonata* – on my new-found principle that only the best is good enough. And what a sweat it was, my attention wandering – and being sharply recalled – even more wilfully than during meditation.

It so happened that in the course of testing old records for flaws I had just reached Rachmaninov's *Rhapsody on a Theme by Paganini*; and I put this on as soon as the Beethoven was finished. What joyful relief – like plunging into cool green water after drilling for hours in a hot sun.

A happy lesson in taking it easy.

13 February

A wedge of wild geese flying above us and over the Severn sands at Newnham. An ice-clear sky, of the palest violet. Such yearning in those long necks stretched towards the east; and yet such ease and grace in the movement of the wings.

But watch that symbol-hunting! Geese are best at being geese.

———— * ————

Michelangelo's *Pietà*, sculpted when he was still in his early twenties. As a work of art I find it equivocal; but as a technical feat it seems miraculous. A superhuman skill.

As for the BVM I find that I'm still a little embarrassed by the cult of her at Tymawr. I think this distaste is partly due to the historical falsity which underlies it. Nearly all NT scholars are agreed that the whole nativity story is a pious invention; and in the gospels themselves Jesus had no special relationship with his mother. Indeed he seems to have harshly rejected even that special relationship which is usual between mothers and their sons.

But I now see that this isn't the only reason for my discomfort with the cult of Mary: too often there seems to be something mawkish about it; and I think this is just *because* Mary is worshipped as a virgin-mother – i.e. as a monstrosity conjured up by the lamentable belief that ordinary sexual reproduction is impure; shameful; too disgusting to produce a Saviour. If only we could resurrect – revivify – the fruitful and fructifying Magna Mater of late antiquity. My only formal prayer of the day begins with the words 'Heavenly Mother', if only because I feel more need of a mother than of a father. And perhaps a great many people would be easier with God the Mother than they are with God the Father.

———— * ————

Discrimination! It is in this that BH fails; and has no wish to succeed. Yet my whole working life has depended on the exercise of this faculty, and it's one which I value very highly. To discriminate; to differentiate; to distinguish – what elegances, even nobilities of human thought have been produced by this subtle and crafty feat!

I must accept, though, that this isn't the highest human faculty. The mystics all speak of a unity which is above and beyond all differences. Yet just because my own mind is so remote from this great vision I find that it fills me with a sort of horror – the Void: the Formless: Nirvana ... I find it impossible to distinguish all this from simple oblivion, which isn't a concept which has any appeal for me at all. Or any great mystery for me either, since I experience it – if that's the word – every night of my life.

Such naiveté! But I fear that naiveté is the best instrument I have on this journey. I'm reminded of my friend Ralph Izzard of the *Daily Mail*, who followed the Hillary-Tensing expedition wearing gym shoes, and with Sherpas carrying crates of whisky behind him. He wrote a book about it which he called *A Fool on Everest*. And this one might be called *A Fool on the Mystic Way*. Or better still, in the footsteps of St John of the Cross, *A Fool on Carmel*.

———— * ————

In Monmouth I congratulated myself on my half-hour conversation with old Mrs K in The Angel: resolved that I must do the old woman this kindness again some time. I wasn't alerted to the patronizing complacency of these thoughts until my recollection of the day, in bed that evening. As if Mrs K, with her long, active and thoughtful religious life, doesn't have far more to offer me than I her!

No! *Get it right!* We have much to offer each other.

———— * ————

S and I were naggingly contentious over the weekend. A reminder of the terrible homogeneity of the life we used to lead. The same bad old pattern repeated again and again and again; and I doubt if we ever really considered the possibility of changing it.

But be careful there. Catch One, in a crafty form. To condemn one's past is a most enticing way of praising one's present state.

Yes, but it is true that we are no longer *resigned* to that terrible litany of 'What about *you*, then!' 'Well then, what about *you*!' 'At least I never ...' 'No, but at least *I* never ...'

———— * ————

Bitterly cold days, and minor revelations all the time: such as the snow falling very very slowly against those rough Scotch pines above the Bennett farm. A little later I passed Mr Bennett on his tractor, the snow tumbling and swirling between us, and we laughed at each other in a sort of wry delight.

———— * ————

Hacking down the old hawthorn hedge behind the space I've cleared and levelled for the new formal garden. This is the sixth garden I shall have made in the last thirty years; and I've made them all out of a wilderness. I love this activity; but once the garden's made I would like to hand it over immediately to somebody else, and make another. To maintain a garden is a duty, and often a very burdensome one. To make a garden is almost unalloyed happiness.

(I now have a plan, not yet divulged, to build a little wooden tea pavilion in the furthest south-west corner, at the end of the paving and just beyond the formal pond.)

———— * ————

A *self-respecting* humility is what I need now: clearing the way so that love and faith may – perhaps – travel along it later. Yet the true Masters know they are Masters, and must proclaim it: for them, I suppose, humility lies in the *unremitting* knowledge that God is proclaiming himself by means of their words and actions.

(Yes; but they must also be aware that he could not proclaim himself *in just that way* without them.)

I sometimes allow myself to wonder why it is that I am no sort of Master, or even teacher, to the BH community. Being twice the age of the oldest resident member I should surely have acquired more wisdom than the rest.

The answer is that I do indeed have rather more practical wisdom than any of them; the common sense use of experience to warn and guide. I certainly have more *knowledge*. But this is where Rajneesh's distinction between Knowledge and Knowing is so useful: is essential. As a Knower I am no more advanced than anyone else; very likely more backward than two or three of them.

———— * ————

The snow had prevented us from getting to Monmouth on Thursday but we just managed to skid and slither up the hill yesterday. A very cheerful meeting with Lucy and Bernard, and then we drove cheerfully home through the slush and under a clearing sky. To find awaiting me a civil little letter from the OUP regretfully turning down *Pantaloon*: this after holding on to it, and no doubt thoroughly perusing it, for more than six months.

I had been keeping this well away from my attention most of the time; and my immediate reaction was a quick, defensive resistance to pain and disappointment. Since Chatto's abandonment at the half-way stage this makes the third rejection: but I tell myself that such treatment of such a book is only to be expected. It is 'difficult'; could never sell well, unless and until it became a classic: it would be appallingly expensive to produce; and might not even win a *succès d'estime* the way things now are with books and readers ... And yet, I add, it *will* be recognized one day as the great work which I know it to be. (*Know* it to be? *Know* it to be!)

But the real pain had only been postponed, and began to attack me quite viciously in bed last night. For in spite of trying to expect the worst I'd put quite a lot of hope into this latest attempt. I repelled the attack by reminding myself that at least half my distress is due to disappointed expectations of admiration and applause. An unregenerate longing, in fact, for that 'inordinate self-expression' which Merton so rightly reproves.

It happened, also, that I was reading the life of a heroic, wise and saintly sixteenth-century Jesuit – Matthew Ricci – serving God and man in China against enormous odds and a succession of overwhelming disappointments. Yet he was never overwhelmed; preserved not only his Christian faith but also his loving respect for the alien civilization of which he had almost become a member. In this light my disappointment became laughably trivial. Better still; it became another test; a fruitful affliction; a source of active joy. It really seemed, to me, before I went to sleep, that I had been strengthened and refreshed by a Heaven-sent message of reassurance and revival.

[123]

After all, I say to myself this morning, if *Pantaloon* is indeed what I think it is then it will surely see the light some day, and do whatever it has to do. Nor should it matter in the least whether this happens after my death or before it. It may appear at a better time than this, when people are more ready to read such a book and listen to what it's saying.

Bloody hell, all the same!

———— * ————

It might seem, perhaps, that my certainty about the great qualities of *Pantaloon* is an offence against humility. I don't think it is. Should a carpenter who knows that he's made a good table pretend to himself and to God that he's made a bad one? It would be a strange God who would approve of such dishonourable servility.

Even if I'm wrong about *Pantaloon* my faith in it would not be arrogant; for it's a faith which I've reached, and kept, only after many humble recognitions of faults which had to be corrected: only after long reflection about the completed work.

———— * ————

Perspective. The amazing brilliance of this arrangement, which prevents our vision being totally blocked by the nearest object. Driving to Lydney I saw a tree rushing towards the car, swelling as fast as it approached me. How terrifying this would be to somebody just cured of lifelong blindness.

———— * ————

Yes, it is sensible to eat wholemeal bread and margarine, as I do now; sensible to eat apple and grated carrot for lunch (grating my carrot with a Gandhian grin); sensible to fast on Fridays ... But it would be very foolish to become obsessed with diet and fasting. A wretched form of narcissism, as S pointed out in the case of certain food-fads who passed through BH last month.

15 February

From *Observer* review of *King of the Castle* by Gai Eaton. (Bodley Head, London):

Sometimes Mr Eaton's God is a sublime mystery who may be approached by any number of different but valid ways. Sometimes his God is a god of anger and vengeance who will severely punish all those who don't believe in him properly. The notion that a devoted but agnostic scientist may be making his own way towards God would be utterly detestable to Mr Eaton. He wants his sheep to be sheep and his goats to be goats.

'The least deserving of mercy when the swords are unsheathed is the humanist who supposes he can cherish humanity while excluding religion ...'

'Whatever tends towards the unification of what was formerly separated and brings a glimmer of light – the light of understanding, of fellow feeling, of attention – into what was formerly a place of darkness carries with it some faint stamp of nobility ...'

The contradiction of tone, of feeling, of general attitude to God and man is surely glaring. And yet Mr Eaton is genuinely and passionately concerned for the nobility of man, and sees very clearly how it is threatened, both blatantly and insidiously, by the complacency and blindness of so many modern pundits and rulers. He defends the living truth perceived by 'primitive' man against the trivialization of life in those societies which treat primitive myths, not as visions of the holy but as puerile attempts to do what adult scientists do so much better. How close Mr Eaton is to the heart of all spiritual endeavour when he writes that 'the basic command of religion is not "Do this!" or "Do not do that!" but simply "Look!"'

Yet his splendid vision of God is terribly marred by the sheer hatred, the black malignity, which Mr Eaton evidently feels towards so many of his fellow-men.

Although he is not a Christian he would surely subscribe to the great religious command that we should love our enemies. He may claim that he hates the sin and not the sinner, but this is not the impression which this violently striated book is likely to leave on a reader.

20 February

I now suspect that the real reason why I copied out part of that review was to give myself a mild consolation for the rejection of *Pantaloon*. A little salve applied to my wounded vanity.

———— * ————

The Portinari Altarpiece

Like all great pictures of the Annunciation this one gives the luminous sense of a completely new kind of truth and hope entering the world. But the best pictures of the Crucifixion show what the world did to that hope, and emphasize that so long as the natural world remains, anguish will lie at the very heart of it. The hope was not destroyed by the killing of Jesus; but attempts to destroy it have never ceased from that time to this.

———— * ————

Once, on my walk, I looked up through the green pools in a thundery sky and called aloud to God: an acclamation, not an appeal.

> Why look up there?
> Where better?

———— * ————

Perhaps the nearest Christianity comes to Ram Dass's Take it Easy is in such phrases as Thy Will be Done and The Peace of God. But the usual form of Christian resignation is an obsequious acceptance of every horror as a portion of God's inscrutable but unquestionable providence.

[126]

'My child has meningitis. This must be good because it must be the will of God. Therefore I praise and thank him for the anguish of my dying child.'

This seems quite mad to me; as well as blasphemous.

'My child has meningitis. God suffers as I do for this cruel affliction which he could do nothing to prevent. What he *can* do, though, is to sanctify *even this*, both for my child (?) and for myself, if we do all we can to help him.'

Still too strong? Then at least there may be comfort for the mother (transferred to the child) in the knowledge that their pain is shared in Heaven. (Perhaps one message of the Crucifixion is that God suffered on the cross as well as man; not because Jesus was a special sort of Man-God but because God suffers in every suffering man.)

———— * ————

Trying hard to reduce pill-intake. I'm now down to one Ativan a day – to pacify – and one Ludomil – to ward off the blues. How splendid if I could be pill-free by midsummer – the first time for at least 30 years. (But as for those wretched cigarettes, forty days of untroubled abstention were broken yesterday with total frivolity; in the pleasure of our friend Guy Farrer's company.)

———— * ————

A tiny shift in the mind, and the Sistine ceiling ceases to be sublime and becomes ridiculous. Worse than ridiculous – gross and repulsive. Now that this has happened to me (as I was reading Hibbard's *Michelangelo*) I wonder whether I shall ever be able to get that colossal work back into its accepted place.

———— * ————

Be Here Now as one means of holding the entrance to the mind against despair. For these have been very threatening days. I've been moving about like someone who is aware that a gun is pointing at him from the bushes. He must pretend not to know that it's there and concentrate his whole attention on every step he takes across the lawn.

——— * ———

Yes, but what if the Here and the Now contains S dying in great pain before my eyes? Detachment is recommended by many religious pundits: even by some Christian ones. But to me *Be Here Now* in such a case would be a demand that I should face the full anguish of the situation, in anguished love. An anguished love which would allay her own misery by the love; not add to it by the anguish. And how could I possibly rise to that without the help of God; without somehow becoming a vehicle for God to reach both me and her.

Perhaps I've been playing with this fantasy just because the boot is really on the other foot: for S is my constant help in trouble. Fearing to impose the frightful burden of my depression on her – she bore it so bravely and lovingly during all those bad years – I usually try to conceal it from her whenever I feel it beginning again. But I seldom succeed; seldom, perhaps, really want to succeed, since her loving concern is what I need most when the darkness threatens to come down.

1 March

Last month I reviewed, on successive Sundays, a new edition of Broch's *Death of Virgil* and three republished novels of Henry Green. Green was a resolutely light novelist, though not a flippant one: worldly in the sense that no hint of any other world is ever given. Broch, on the other hand, is a monument of profundity; mystical feeling; brooding awareness of God ... I praised Green, as I'd done so many times so many years ago, but confessed, with regret, to finding Broch almost unbearably ponderous, turgid and humourless.

Easy enough to remember that deep intentions are not enough to make deep art: but there is still a mystery here. The real puzzle, I suppose, is not that great beliefs often fail to make great books, but that a casual or amused indifference to all forms of serious faith can 'inspire' so many very good books. Firbank. What is that extra something which so nearly makes him a great writer? Wit? Elegance? Verbal agility? None of these is enough: all together they are not enough. The daunting thought is that the utmost frivolity *contains a truth of its own*.

5 March

A full day yesterday. In the morning I had two Merton books to review, and I realized that this is the first time I've ever written anything about him in public. I said that he was the greatest religious writer in the English language since Von Hügel (and might have added that what Von Hügel wrote was scarcely English!). I also said that I not only admired Merton, but loved and mourned him without ever having met him.

But how inadequate they were, those twelve hundred words; how inadequate they were bound to be. These are the times when my profession seems almost farcical.

——— * ———

To BH after lunch, and as I walked through the wood I felt the spring for the first time this year. The trees looked as if they were just about to explode in the warm sun. And again I felt none of that old nostalgia for the springs of yesteryear: for a moment I nearly understood what it might mean to speak of spring as 'eternal'.

Taking long strides between the little sunlit oaks and birches; but I was glad to recognize that these strides weren't *purposeful*, in the sense of trying to hasten my arrival. They were attentive strides.

A desultory bit of work with Kerry on the still cold and sodden seedbeds, where the old terrace used to be. Not much sense of real purpose there either, though that would have been welcome. Merton quotes Vinoba Bhave on this, with strong approval: 'The action of the person who acts without desire should be much better than that of the person who acts with

[129]

desire. This is only proper, for the latter is attracted to the fruit, and part, much or little, of his time and attention will be spent on thoughts and dreams of the fruit. But all the time and all the strength of the man who has no desire for fruit is devoted to the action.' Merton comments: 'This neatly disposes of the myth that "Spirituality" is not practical!'

I would like to agree heartily with Bhave and Merton, as Kerry certainly does; but there are difficulties. The main one is that unless we are thinking of the 'fruit' – in our case the seeding vegetables – it's hard to see how the 'action' can be done as it should be done. In other words the action of trying to make a seedbed in very difficult conditions has no real sense or meaning without a constant awareness of what those seeds are going to need in order to make them germinate, sprout and grow.

Anyway things got much merrier after this. When we'd all had tea we moved a dozen prepared seedboxes into the middle of the sitting room and sat round them in meditation for half an hour. The assumption is that the seeds we were about to sow in the boxes would respond to this spiritual preparation of the sowers; and my immediate impulse, of course, was to treat the whole thing as a piece of rather wet hocus-pocus. (Martin's coarse giggles, as we stood in helpful silence round the runner bean bed last year!) But I found, to my surprise, that I was joining in this ceremony with goodwill and sympathy, if not with absolute faith. For who can tell what the meditation may have done for the sowers, and how much their loving attention may have been transmitted to the seeds through fingers made gentler by this preparation?

———— * ————

But as for the astrology, which is booming away over there as never before, I find this not only absurd but harmful. It manages to be both a false science and a false religion; a malign superstition in that it encourages foolish notions of predestined characters and lives. At the moment this takes the form of assuming that the spring work on the land will somehow get itself done; and that making plans to do it would be crude and wrong. Presumptuous, I suppose.

(This last passage is unfair; the result of suppressed exasperation at their holy optimism combined with my view, on the way home, of the bedraggled fields in all their ruin.)

———— * ————

Two fine passages from Alan Ecclestone's *A Staircase for Silence* (Darton, Longman & Todd, London): 'Prayer is concerned with making meaningful all that has passed through our experience.' 'Péguy's spirituality was not dependent upon the experience of mystical states or visions but laboriously apprehended from the field of his everyday working life.'

These are the only kinds of prayer and spirituality which I'm ever likely to experience.

———— * ————

Yes, but what dangers there are in the kind of book which Ecclestone has tried to write – a high-flown poetical meditation.

'He presented the Beauce to Our Lady of Chartres. It was hers already by age-long right but Péguy meant the acknowledgement to confirm her title as a gesture of gratitude and hope. "The earth is the Lord's" – the truth could never be named too often, but that special bit belonged to the Queen, and that too needed to be said again.'

Slush! I would like to sick Freddie or Russell on to Christian writers when they go in for this sort of thing.

6 March

Thinking sadly of Jason and Lucy the phrase 'an amputated family' came into my mind. Of course their departure was perfectly right and proper; quite in the natural way of the world. Yes; but so is the sense of loss and sadness which we feel. I sometimes find it almost unbearable to look at pictures of them – and my other three – when they were small children. It is like looking at pictures of the dead.

———— * ————

Christ in You. This mysterious, anonymous little book, first published in 1910 and reprinted thirteen times since then, up to 1975. It purports to be written from beyond the grave, which I find a rather tiresome device. But how very good it is; a marvel of simplicity without mawkishness. S and I now read it aloud to each other before going to bed. (For several weeks we've been reading Merton's *No Man is an Island* after coffee in the morning.)

Yesterday we came on the marvellous image, in *Christ in You*, of the seed responding in darkness to the unseen light of the sun. We, like the seed, have a mysterious capacity within us which enables us to respond to the unseen light of God; to grow through the dark towards it and (if we are very lucky or very holy) to flower at last in the radiance of the Kingdom.

———— * ————

Also we've just read an eloquent passage from Merton: 'The silence of the sky remains when the plane has gone. The tranquillity of the clouds will remain when the plane has fallen apart. It is the silence of the world that is real. Our noise is the illusion.'

But last night I was harrowed, as so often, by long, repeated, agonized screams from the woods: some small creature caught by an owl, and dying very slowly and very noisily. And only a few days ago there were pictures in the paper of high seas raging over pathetic little seaside houses in Devon. How easy it is to fall into a sentimentalization of nature; even, it seems, for that least sentimental of writers.

———— * ————

Clare was leading our communion at BH last night when she was suddenly overcome by an irrepressible fit of the giggles. Kerry was grumpy about this, for which he was immediately, and quite violently, assaulted by the others. They accused him of constantly putting pressure on them to move in the direction which *he* thinks best. My sympathies were divided. I suggested that we ought to be able to incorporate Clare's giggles into our ceremony: that any enforced solemnity must be wrong.

[132]

Yet in some ways I know that I am closer to Kerry than to any of the others: he is the only one I can really talk to about spiritual matters, and I sympathize with his constant efforts to get the community better organized. This insistence on 'doing one's own thing' can be simply a form of selfishness. Only a desert hermit can live according to that rule without 'his thing' ever conflicting with other people's interests.

Mary, for example, of whom S and I are both extremely fond, is going off for her third meditation course next week just at the time when intensive work on the land must be under way. The boring old facts of social life are just as unavoidable in a spiritual community as they are in a family or a workshop. Easy to say that the individual shouldn't be subordinated to the group; but very easy, also, to see that no group can survive unless the individual is sometimes willing to do what he *doesn't* want.

———— * ————

Tymawr was very good yesterday. It seems that I always get more from mass when I am least concerned with getting anything. So what about those constant resolutions to pay better attention?

Sitting in the garden with S I told her that I'm sometimes oppressed by a growing lack of spontaneity in my present life. I look back almost with longing to those pre-depression years when I was taking up one hobby after another, and revelling in the pleasure of each in turn. *Then* when I spent two years making the water garden, contrasted with *now* when I am making this little formal garden along the lower edge of our plot. I made the BH water garden with simple pleasure, as well as with great energy: now I am working because it seems a right and proper thing to do; another useful means of helping me forward on the Way. *Then* the strong pains and pleasures of writing *Pantaloon*, almost for its own sake alone: *now* I write this journal chiefly because there are things I want to tell people.

It seemed to me, as I was talking, that I've successfully anchored myself to a faith and its practice against the danger

[133]

of being swept back into those frightening seas. But the chain is constantly tautening. In so far as this carefully thoughtful and attentive way of life is only a means of defending myself against depression then it will surely fail to do even this.

S said she feared that I was once again going to extremes: but what is one to say, then, of those holy sisters at Tymawr who have gone hundreds of miles further in that direction than I could possibly go?

The old problem of how to combine self-discipline with letting go. I put the question to Sister Paula, who said that the relaxation can come only after the discipline has been so well established that one is scarcely aware of it any longer. This seems right to me; but, reading a history of China, I'm also aware of the danger of getting frozen into a formal and stiffly ritualized way of life.

Anyway by yesterday, when S and I were gardening together in the sun, I had one of those sudden reversals of mood which are still common enough. I dug away with cheerful zest and listened to a Mozart piano concerto with unfurrowed brow.

———— * ————

Sister Paula and I also talked about Cranmer and the various Anglican liturgies. I've never taken much interest in the Church to which I happen to belong. Since I was baptized and confirmed in the Church of England and since it is the most physically accessible of Churches, it seemed natural to return to it when I began to feel the need for communal worship. I know, from my own experience and from the writings of several gloomy parsons, that there is still an awful deadness in many parishes and in much of the hierarchy. And surely the very fact of establishment is bound to be a deadening thing.

When S and I first started going to Hewelsfield Church – on *her* initiative – I was carried straight back to Rugby and the truly appalling ordeal of compulsory chapel. I've never known anything so dead as those droning pantomimes.

But Tymawr has changed all that, not only because of my admiration for the sisters but also through my meetings with many interesting priests there, young and old. And subscribing to that excellent magazine, *Theology*, has shown how much new life is still sprouting from the gnarled old trunk of our Church. By now I feel a positive affection for it; and a positive conviction that it is the best Church for me.

Gerry Richards, my very intelligent and independent-minded Quaker friend, finds it hard to understand this. But I like the well-ordered ritual of mass at Tymawr; and Quaker meetings, which I have sometimes attended, are much too austere for me.

8 March

Alas, my stupidity is unabated. Coming back from Gloucester in the early afternoon I was agitated all the time by the immense problem of whether or not I should try to do an hour's digging when we got back, or add that hour to my hour of meditation. This torment of indecision led to my being mildly disagreeable to S and Laura; also to a mad scramble into my working clothes as soon as we got home, followed by an hour's ferocious digging which left me not only exhausted but also in a state of irritated self-mockery. Nor was the hasty meditation which I crammed in afterwards much help in relieving my condition.

So reminiscent of the bad old days when I always did everything too much and too fast, and wore myself out rushing dementedly to nowhere. But at least I'd slowed myself down to a heavy plod before I went to bed.

———— * ————

Astonishing autobiography of Lois Lang-Sims which I found in the library at Tymawr. Her passionate spiritual intensity makes this journal seem very thin gruel. She writes well, too, and presents her tremendous material with a skill which I can't yet begin to emulate. (Why *emulate*, anyway!) But the main thing is that she has a natural perception of the holy, and this

[135]

has sustained her triumphantly through periods of appalling misery and anger.

I read the first two volumes until three o'clock in the morning last night and the night before, agog as I haven't been for a long, long time. And as I read I felt myself drawn closer and closer to this unknown woman, who is about my own age but seems so far ahead of me on this journey. Here are two quotations: 'Sometimes I found convent life mildly absurd; but I was never even momentarily irritated by it. I perceived that even its absurdities served a single end: the restoration of the order of the world by means of the establishment of order in a single line of time flowing through a single place. The life of a religious community resembles a dance, its significance depending on the perfect timing of the various movements.'

I have never found Tymawr absurd, chiefly perhaps because the sisters themselves are perfectly aware of this element in their lives, and know how to incorporate it in their own dance.

This, too, from her book: 'I have had very little awareness of "growing up" but rather of perpetually chasing, finding and losing myself amid a crowd of ghosts. The essence of the self is immortal; the manifestations of a sick mind, like those of a sick body, will die when at last the consequences they set in motion have worked themselves out.'

And one more passage which goes straight to my heart: 'True choice is a breaking into something new, translating one permanently on to another level of existence.' Alas, for that 'permanently': I sometimes feel as if I've heaved myself out of a muddy sea, with a great deal of panting and groaning, only to find that I keep slipping back again into the thick, turbulent water. But I suppose I do feel that I'm a little more free than I used to be; a little more capable of making choices.

9 *March*

Another assault of anger and doubt in bed last night when I could no longer avoid mulling over the OUP's rejection of

Pantaloon. So I forcefully recalled Frank Kermode's great enthusiasm; and Stephen's review of *A Learned City* ('One of the most remarkable poems of the century'); and Michael Wood's admiration; and the constant, warm encouragement of Robert Nye as I sent him each of the six unpublished volumes in turn.

I also cheered myself up by recognizing how much I now enjoy keeping this journal. I implied on Monday that my only purpose in writing here is to make a report for others who might be stumbling about in the same general direction as myself. And it's true that I'm more conscious of possible readers than I've ever been when writing my earlier books; but this imposes a certain pleasant discipline, after all, and keeps my feet quite firmly on the ground. Where they belong; unlike those of lucky Miss Lang-Sims, who makes so many successful flights into higher realms.

Anyway this black morning should be seen as an opportunity for exercising unfamiliar virtues: courage and calm. I need the courage to be calm; and then the calm will remove the need for courage.

Neither, of course, is a primal virtue, for calm could be the deadly serenity of perfect arrogance or total despair; and courage is often used in the service of the worst evil. Yet without those two what hope of practising the great virtues – the faith to be reborn; hope of the Kingdom; that love of God which always includes the love of man?

———— * ————

A bare apple tree in the bright wind. How graceless, that writhing and straining; all elbows; a tree that seems to be trying to push itself up against a crushing weight of air. Yet it is as good for scrutiny as the most elegantly sweeping beech. Not beauty but *entity* is the thing.

———— * ————

The New Testament. Whoever wrote what, and however much of it is 'true', it seems to me more and more like a huge primordial explosion of dazzling light and reverberating words. The Big Bang of astronomy, which was the beginning of the universe, so they say. And in the same way the light and sound of the New Testament have shone and echoed down the centuries; never diminishing; often expanding into new constellations and stranger music.

'Behold, I make all things new,' and not just then and there, but always and everywhere. People are constantly trying to turn the new things into old things; to catch the light and the holy words and imprison them in a sacred and immutable Law. Yet it was against just this that Jesus died; and Christians of every age should be ready to die rather than submit to it happening again.

Yes, but how wretchedly this is misunderstood by all those who are so concerned with keeping Christianity 'up to date'; cutting it down to a size which will be acceptable to 'the modern mind'. If the process of constant renewal isn't also a process of constant expansion then it's simply a dimming of the light and a muffling of the holy words.

10 March

Now that I've had a little time to think about Lois Lang-Sims's autobiography I realize that I've been even more deeply moved by it than I'd thought when I was reading it. There is something almost Dostoevskian about the violence of her nature, both for good and evil. She suffers greatly, and causes others to suffer, but everything she does seems like a sacred drama: nothing is trivial.

Her knowledge of God is not just an extension or enlargement of that 'belief' in God which I, for example, would claim to share with her. Belief by itself is simply the taking up of one human position among many; something which can be argued for and against in the ordinary language of argument. Knowledge of God is beyond argument; even, in some strange way, beyond belief and unbelief.

No sooner written than I find this, as I thumb again through her first volume: 'I had failed to understand that religious faith is a state of being, a form of knowledge, not an exercise in mental acrobatics.'

When I begin to wonder, in the light of these marvellous books, what possible point there can be in continuing to write this journal I remind myself of a story which Cyril used to tell about a Sufi saint. 'There are some,' said the saint, 'who ride on white chargers and leap over the moon. There are others who plod along a muddy road on their own two feet, often slipping back in a day as far as they have advanced in the past month. But both sorts of traveller arrive at the same place in the end.' (Cyril was talking about writers, of course, and not about seekers.)

'The same place' doesn't mean that everybody reaches an equal degree of illumination. It must mean that all true travellers get as far as they can, and that this furthest possible point for each traveller is as bright for him (and perhaps for God) as the ecstatic union of St Teresa. To be fully extended according to one's own unique nature and capacities – that's the only thing that matters. And the beauty of it is that since every human soul is unique the light that it sees and the light that it shines have never been seen or shone before. Each of us may see, and reflect, a glimmer of the same Great Light, but every glimmer is a little different from all the others. This is the great wonder of the Equality of Souls.

———— * ————

The third volume of Lois's work is promised on the flyleaves of the other two; but when I asked about it in the Monmouth library they said that an earlier enquirer had been told by the publisher that 'there hadn't been enough interest to justify its publication'. I felt both furious with the stupid 'world' and bitterly sorry on her behalf. I know from Sister Paula that Lois L-S once stayed at the convent, so I shall get her address and write her a letter of angry commiseration – and fellow-feeling. (For are we not both the victims of benighted publishers!)

Yesterday was another of those harsh, jaw-clamping days. Endure! Endure! It's not much good saying anything else – reminding oneself, for example, that the pain is not useless; may even be fruitful. For here is another of those famous divine catches: if you can persuade yourself that the pain is doing you good then the pain will be alleviated. But the pain will do you good only if it is unalleviated: only if it seems utterly useless, and worse than useless: depleting: corrosive: crushing the spirit under a weight of darkness (Catch 2).

——— * ———

Laura was caught out again in a piece of petty pilfering. I delivered a little homily about sins against property being of very little importance, but sins against *trust* being much more serious... Later all this seemed odiously heavy-handed and mis-applied. I was talking from where I am – more likely from where I'd like to be – and she is simply in a different space (as they say), and speaking a different language.

Opening Lois's book I came almost at once on this passage:

'A child, faced with a contradiction with which it feels unable to deal, becomes guileful to a degree which outrages the susceptibilities of the normal adult, whose own dis-honesties have been buried out of sight beneath a vast rubbish-heap of conventional self-righteousness.'

Another quotation from the same source:

'Now I intended to catch the sun in the moment of his coming and watch how he made his entrance. What I saw was a very strange thing. There was no flash of light, no startling appearance. The change was neither gradual nor sudden, but imperceptible as that change which is wrought by the descent of the Holy Spirit in the moment when the human soul performs an act of pure choice in the direction of the good. The light was not. The light was.'

This might have been written by Simone Weil; and indeed

there is a curious resemblance between the two – as well as some very sharp differences. I might have contrived that description of the sunrise, but I could never have imagined – imaged forth – the comparison with the descent of the Spirit. I simply haven't the knowledge for that kind of illumination: thank God I can at least recognize its truth when someone else presents it to me.

———— * ————

I have begun to be haunted by the fear that Lois may be dead. She describes many illnesses; indeed it seems that she's never in all her life been really well. What if the publisher's brutish refusal of her last volume led her into some ultimate discouragement. I don't mean suicide; just surrender. On the other hand she surely has much to live for, with so much talent and so much understanding. When I get her address I'll ask her if I can see the typescript of the third volume.

———— * ————

Wilson* tells me that the OUP are the biggest publishers *in the world*; so the rejection acquires a sort of magisterial authority. I think of that great classical portico in Walton Street, and somehow the sheer grandeur of their decision against me makes me feel a great deal better.

> 'Come the three corners of the world in arms,
> And we shall shock them.'

———— * ————

So strong a craving to meet this unknown lady. When and if I'm able to write her a letter I must try not to *burble*.

———— * ————

The delightful way we live now: even the trees round the house seem like sentinels keeping out all the blaring horrors of the modern world. So is it an ivory tower that we've made for ourselves above this valley? Or is it, as I hope, a watchtower? Can I see better from here, at least in certain directions,

* Wilson Plant – Monmouth neighbour and close friend.

than those who have to inhabit the urban nightmare? It should be so. We should be able to use this outer peace to let the peace of God grow quietly within us. Even to the point where we shall transfer this peace to others: become *infectious* with holy peace. (How far we are, as yet, from such a state!)

———— * ————

I was smugly reflecting on how much more time I make for myself now compared with my hectic and bustling twenties. But my twenty-year-old self briskly answered me, 'Yes, that's all very well; but don't forget how much of *my* time has to be devoted to politics, talk, intrigue, chasing girls and trying to climb ladders!' A just rebuke. So much of the 'wisdom of age' is due to enfeebled lust, diminished interest in other people and no more worldly advantages to be gained.

———— * ————

The idea of making a pilgrimage to Chartres; perhaps next summer. S, though so averse to walking, seemed to like the plan: but I must be very careful not to press it too hard on her.

14 March

We'd accepted an invitation to dinner from our neighbours, Jeffrey and Nasi Hammond, but by the time we were walking to their house I was in a wretched state of strain and irritation. Absurd; for they are gentle and delightful people; and very easy to be with. Then, almost on their doorstep, S told me that she thought Laura had begun to look for another boyfriend. I stopped in the drive, feeling almost sick with pity for Paul and horror at the prospect ahead of him. For I strangely associate myself with that young man, and vividly remember, whenever this terrible sadness threatens him, the many such losses I had to bear when I was young. Not that I blamed Laura – any more than I could ever blame those lovely, rejecting girls of long ago. But what anguish it is, to be turned away from by somebody one longs to possess forever! All very well to say that possessive love is the wrong sort; but if you have hoped to spend a lifetime of shared love with one particular person the loss of that person empties the whole future of happiness; even of meaning.

The first half of dinner was almost unbearable; particularly as this is the kind of occasion when my personal prohibition is supposed to be most sternly observed. (On caravan trips, for example, I now happily drink beer in pubs, knowing that no harm has ever come of this.) Suddenly I said that yes, I would have some wine after all. And the relief was instantaneous: the rest of the evening positively pleasurable. No excess, but the heart lifted, the tongue loosened, the company enjoyed.

'A good servant but ...' Such a *very* good servant and so *seldom* my bad master that it seems absurd to impose these rigid restrictions on him. (I foresee that they will become less and less rigid from now on.)

———— * ————

The argument that belief in God is suspect because it satisfies a need. But surely this should be turned on its head. It's true that the need is no *proof* that God exists; but it is at least a suggestive and interesting element in many people's composition. Strange creatures, if we felt so strong a need for something which was never there.

———— * ————

Dreams about Tony have suddenly begun again; and as usual he is not dead but in some desperate state of physical or mental affliction. And I can do nothing to help him. Two mornings ago I woke in tears, and then that stirred-up grief distracted me all through the morning.

In fact I seem to have suffered lately from increasing heaviness of heart; as if depression were hanging just above my head like a black cloud which might descend at any moment and envelop me again. Am I, in fact, any happier now than in those strange years of wildly varied activity which led up to my depression?

[143]

Hard to answer. (And perhaps the wrong question to ask.) When I think of beating down the Bristol Channel with Gwyn – seven years ago! – I know that in recent months I've never been so consciously happy as I was then. Or as I was on my bicycle, riding to visit churches with all my glittering camera equipment slung over my back in a blue canvas bag. Or as I was in the very earliest days of the community, winching out tree stumps from the orchard with Bim and Dave Rowson.

But I like to think that I've acquired something sturdier and more secure than happiness; perhaps the ability to accept un-happiness and *make do with it*. Sometimes I still catch myself demanding happiness, as I always used to do: the feeling that there's something sickly and demeaning about a doleful man. But now it seems wiser and better to think in terms of active submission to whatever mood one meets: an awareness that even the drabbest day has its use; its *substance*.

———— * ————

Faint melancholy at the departure today of Rush and her calf; the coming sale of Victoria and Luna. These cows have been pleasant neighbours, and the twice daily visits of Barn House milkers have been a very pleasant form of contact. But now there's nobody who will take responsibility for them; and this is a major step in the process by which BH is departing from its original intentions. Perhaps too far and too fast. Simon tells us that there is no longer any enthusiasm for getting the vegetables sown or planted – as indeed I'd guessed from the state of the fields.

It's fine, of course, to talk of creating a spiritual community; but except for true contemplatives the spirit needs something to work on; something to feed on. Even if it were economically possible there isn't one of us who is qualified to spend all day in worship and meditation. And although the spirit may come to a chosen few by prayer and fasting I'm sure that it comes to most of us, if at all, by attentive devotion to the ordinary business of living. (Helped, of course, by whatever we can manage in the way of prayer and fasting.)

[144]

There must be a hundred Marthas in the world to every Mary.

———— * ————

The photograph of my father on the cupboard. He is standing with hands on hips, laughing into the light with hardly a hint of that extreme self-consciousness which usually made him such a difficult subject for photographers. Happiness; strength; the confidence that comes from achievement and its recognition. He must have been about seventy when it was taken, and still in his prime, dashing around the world and being adored on many a campus. I love him in that state of simple, totally un-arrogant happiness.

But when I look at that photograph I can seldom avoid the memory of him as I saw him last, crouched in bed after his stroke, his voice a frantic burble, his face wild yet vacant. *But not vacant enough.* His mind had been violently twisted and shaken; but it was hard to doubt that he was still capable of dreadful suffering; terror; a raging anguish of frustration. 'Do not go gentle into that good night.' Dylan at his emptiest and most rhetorical. How much I prefer 'Be with us now and at the hour of our death'.

———— * ————

I have written to Lois at the four-year-old Hereford address which Sister Paula gave me on Sunday. So near! It seems either too good to be true or that 'a meeting has been arranged'.

———— * ————

Laura was in such a state of nervous tension yesterday that I told S to watch out for poltergeist. Anorexia again, though let's hope in a much milder form. But what I notice most is that desperate *refusal* of the present moment which surely comes from her father. 'Hurry up and be gone! Hurry up, hurry up and go!' For it's unbearable to stay where one is; like running at top speed across a hot plate, and screaming at each step. (And when gurus stroll unharmed across live coals is it because of some supernatural patience: so total an acceptance of the present moment that nothing in present time can harm them.)

A bit implausible; but I spend much of my thinking time, now, in realms of provisional implausibility: 'Let's suppose ...' 'And what if *this* were so?'

And as for Laura the marvel is not that she has these occasional relapses, but that she has gained so wonderfully over the past six months in strength and independence. A year ago we had to constantly reassure her that she could go on living with us as long as she wanted to; all her life if she wanted to. Her dependence on us seemed so absolute that it was hard to imagine how it could ever diminish.

Now she spends much of her time in Gloucester; seems to be on equal terms with Paul; has become a person in her own right. Another reminder that the first thing a human being must do is to get himself a positive and self-defending ego. And if Laura wants to dissolve or reduce her ego later on this will be anything but a return to her former state of amorphous insecurity.

Per Ego ad Astra – and perhaps this is the only way.

20 March

St Teresa's four mystical stages: Recollection: Meditation: Contemplation: Union. I think I may have made some advance across the vast expanse of the first stage; even caught a rare glimpse of the second. At least I now settle down on the floor each evening with real pleasure; the expectation of a calming procedure ahead; even, with luck, an enlivening one as well.

——— * ———

'Almighty God, Son of God, Lord of the Dance, is thus the principal dancer, and He is at one and the same time perfectly still and perpetually in motion; He abides at the centre of the Dance and is, at the same time, active in every part of it ... The whole creation dances in eternal Joy, and the Ecstasy of Love moves from climax to climax according to the Rhythm of the Dance; and thus it is that

[146]

this Rhythm finds expression in the cycle of birth, growth, decline and death; and from this death, rebirth again ...'

This from a much-praised little book, Anthony Duncan's *The Lord of the Dance*. Alas, such rhapsodies are meaningless to me: worse than meaningless – self-indulgent falsifications. For it is not *true* that the whole creation dances in eternal joy: ask the mouse as the owl's talons clutch it: ask the child dying alone after the earthquake: ask my father at any time during the last fourteen months of his life.

There is such a thing, of course, as poetic truth; a truth which deepens and enlivens the literal facts. But if a high flight of words directly contradicts the truths we tell each other in sober prose then it's no sort of truth at all but a dangerous and foolish fancy.

———— * ————

So I turned with relief to a prosaic theological work by John Hick, in which he sets out to argue against the modern philosophical claim that religious language cannot be cognitive. Hick does this very well; but alas, he soon gets himself deep into Christian apologetics. I began to feel as frustrated as I had been by Duncan's windy poetics. Is there *any* available language at this time for trying to describe sacred reality? Perhaps there is not. (Why, for example, is there a virtual compulsion to use 'within' instead of 'inside'? 'The God inside me' sounds like an intestine or a kidney.)

25 *March*

On Friday morning the editor telephoned to ask me to write an Easter article for *The Observer*; as I'd done last year, and on several other holy occasions. (When John Bury and I used to roam the night-town of wartime Brussels disguised as army padres in black bibs and dog collars, I little dreamed that I would become, within thirty years, the unordained chaplain to a Sunday newspaper.) I accepted gladly, of course, and de-

[147]

cided that this time I would write a personal account of my own hesitant, badly bungled, half-achieved rebirth.

What I had in mind was a serious religious article which would also be gently self-ridiculing. And as S and I were leaving on Saturday morning for a DA working party I decided to get the article done before lunch on Friday. It seemed, as the airmen used to say, a piece of cake.

I was still typing and tearing up pages at five o'clock; when I realized at last that I couldn't do it.

So far as I can remember this is the first time such a thing has ever happened to me: I am, after all, a deft and seasoned journalist, and have always had a fluency which is invigorated rather than stultified by a tight dateline. But I like to think it a small sign of grace that I failed so totally; had to ring up Donald and tell him, with many apologies, that he must find some other way of filling that space.

In fact the assignment I'd given myself had become more and more grotesque – nothing less than to describe the damnation and salvation of the modern world in 1200 words or less.

The lead itself had seemed obvious enough; that murdered bodyguard lying in a Rome gutter after the kidnapping of Aldo Moro. Millions of men have been killed in the last few years, but it was this particular murdered man who penetrated all my usual defences and filled me with a sick horror; a desolated pity. I felt more strongly than ever before that we are living in a period of absolute social disintegration; that future historians, if there are to be any, will look back on the whole twentieth century as modern historians look back on the fifth; that this process is now gathering speed, a fearful crescendo of hatred, fury and contempt ... so many lives made murderous by emptiness ... Moro as much a murderer by gross default as the savage men who seized him ...

'Square my trial to my proportioned strength.' If real social collapse comes in this country before I die I pray that I shall be able to meet it with the calmness, courage and love which I so notably failed to show in 1939–45. I hope that by then I shall be able to give refuge here to those who need it; and have

[148]

the strength to support them if they need that as well. I pray that by then the love of God will be flowing through me without constraint ...

I can't even find the words to write it here: and how absurd to imagine that such an outpouring of private fear and hope could ever have appeared on the leader page! Besides, I begin to doubt whether this self-tormented prophet's stance would be of the slightest use to anybody. A thousand barefoot friars might well do better, not preaching damnation but practising love and humility wherever they go.

———— * ————

Our caravan expedition to Cambridge was certainly useful, and mostly enjoyable as well. Much affection, good sense and good humour from one and all: it now seems that we shall try to expand our activities cautiously and methodically. I restrained my natural impatience as best I could, for it's surely true that we shall do more harm than good – leaving so many poor depressives in the lurch – if we move too fast and without a stable organization to make our promises good. In other words all the old rules apply just as stringently to these 'alternative' activities as to any other. Order and method are needed if we are to supplement the sometimes heartless and undiscriminating order of the Health Service.

This is the very opposite way of loosening the hold of the state to those right-wing cries for a return to jungle law; and therefore to even greater power for the tigers. Not a free-for-all to make as much money, win as much power as we can: a freedom for all to use that holy love for one another which Merton rightly believes to be a natural part of us. Here he is again:

'Hence faith is by no means a mere act of choice, an option for a special solution to the problems of existence. It is birth to a higher life by obedience to the Source of Life: to believe is thus to consent to hear and to obey a creative command that raises us from the dead. And what can be a deeper motive for belief?

[149]

'We believe, not because we want to *know*, but because we want to *be*. And supernatural faith responds to the mystery of that natural faith which is the core and centre of our personal being, the will to be ourselves that is the heart of our natural identity.'

———— * ————

How delightful it is to be driving through England and stopping at likely-looking pubs for beer and a bar lunch! Because of my general restraint – which still survives certain cautious relaxations – this ancient pleasure has been much enhanced. And how much of the country, after all, is still un-spoiled! How great the pleasure of finding a church lurking down some budding lane from the village street: the awed excitement of opening the door *and always seeing something both utterly familiar and utterly unexpected.* Indeed I have become a regular Betjeman in my love of the English parish church. To me it is a perfect art; anonymously created; with a purpose which is both communal and holy; in a form which imposes rules yet leaves a wide freedom of creative choice within them. And also, of course, 'You are here to kneel Where prayer has been valid ...'

Yet there was one strange and shocking episode on our Cambridge journey. We had parked the caravan in a pub car park a few miles west of the city, and when we came back there after the DA meeting on Sunday we found three police cars assembled in the dark outside the pub, with winking blue lights. There was a wrecked motor bike against the wall, blood on the road and a stove-in crash helmet lying ten yards away. We were told that a boy had hit the side of a van and ricocheted into the corner of the porch only half an hour before we'd got back. His body had just been taken away and the police were now busy with flash bulbs in the rainy darkness.

But inside the pub it would have been impossible to guess that anything unusual had happened. There was loud jukebox music, loud laughter, rattling tills – that peculiar kind of hectic din which is heard only in English pubs late on a weekend evening. Nobody was talking about the young man who had just been killed on the other side of the very wall where the jukebox was beating and blaring.

Shock? A stiff upper lip? Or just a rabid determination that nothing should spoil the fun? I don't know which of these was the cause of that astonishing appearance of total indifference, but it looked and sounded to us more like the last than either of the others. There seemed to be nothing contrived or nervous about the general hilarity. (When the news of Swann's death was brought to the Duc and Duchesse de Guermantes, just as they were leaving their house for a party, they refused to hear or believe it. For if they had allowed themselves to hear the message convention would have compelled them to stay at home.)

Nor did the memory of that Sunday night tragedy disturb our own pleasure as we drove home yesterday through suddenly spring-like weather. (But the snow still lying in high pockets of the Cotswolds.)

27 March

To my great joy and excitement a letter from Lois Lang-Sims this morning. After reading those two tremendous volumes of autobiography I felt that I already knew her better than many of the people I 'know'. But I was pleased that her letter seemed to confirm that vivid personality; the same mixture of toughness and tenderness; hope and prophetic anger.

She is no longer in Hereford but back in her 'beloved' Canterbury; beloved still, in spite of the cathedral's 'desecration by "gift-shops" and similar horrors'. (Reverend Mother told me of a wan canon of Canterbury who had bewailed the ferocity of Lois's campaign against the Dean and chapter. Better, she'd told them, to let the cathedral fall down than to preserve it by such means. Christ and the money-changers! Yes, but I see their point as well.)

I wrote back at once, and with almost extravagant warmth, enclosing the letter in a copy of *Friends Apart*.*

———— * ————

Another quotation from Lois's books: 'The holy man, noticing me for the first time, turned upon me a gaze in which, as I met it, I seemed to see vast depths of spirit existing in a state of utter mindlessness. The black eyes, half-animal, half-angel, rested upon mine, imposing nothing, demanding no response.'

She sees, and vividly describes, all the horrors of modern India. But out of the horror shines this dark but holy splendour. She would be quite incapable of that evil and degrading despair which has been so widely dispensed in the arts over the last thirty years. Beckett and Bacon.

———— * ————

A nostalgic TV play about the thirties made me recognize again how much I belong to that period of my growing-up. Rugby 1930; Oxford 1935; married 1939; joined the army 1940. It was an appalling decade – fascism in Europe; savage poverty here – but though I knew about these things all the time, and even tried, in my ignorant but passionate way, to do something about them, I was hungry for experience with a kind of rapture which has certainly never been recaptured. And though I paid scarcely any attention to the beauty of the country I lived in I *now* see that it was still, from that point of view, a place of almost magical charm and grace. The little market towns; cathedral cities like Gloucester still almost as they were meant to be; quiet roads and country pubs which had stayed unchanged for two hundred years ...

Beware of nostalgia, that ever-distorting emotion: beware of the ageing man's hatred of a new age which he cannot understand. But surely England *is* horrible now in ways undreamed of forty years ago. And it's my very awareness of

* A memoir of two friends of PT's killed in the last war (second edition 1980, Sidgwick and Jackson, London).

these horrors which makes me so keenly aware of the surviving graces.

———— * ————

Characteristically I cut down my intake of Ativan (nightly tranquillizer) much too fast, in sudden disgust at my dependence. I suffered several bad nights as a result, and bad days as a result of the bad nights.

How often I have to *drag* myself back into that way of attention and prudence which I want to follow all the time. Prudence is a subtle and beautiful Christian virtue: the wisdom of not maltreating oneself: of attending to one's real needs so as to make oneself the best possible medium for the grace of God. (And what could serve it worse than my current relapse into self-poisoning by tobacco?)

———— * ————

At the Cambridge DA meeting a little old lady with a sad and gentle face sidled up to me and said: 'I knew Tony in Peking.' So we talked about his time there; the camel races; his near death from scarlet fever; what had happened to the other young consular officials of his posting ... More than forty years ago; breaking so suddenly and strangely into an occasion so different from anything he knew. I felt no melancholy, but gratitude to her for confirming that distant and, by now, almost private memory.

'The poor boy!' she said; and I felt that she perfectly understood the reasons for his suicide.

———— * ————

The Christian Year. There is something very attractive about traditional devotions changing with the seasons. Easter at Tymawr has made me wonder whether I shouldn't know more about all this.

———— * ————

Four qualities which must be cultivated before love can be effective in action: Calmness; Courage; Perseverance; Humility. None of these, not even the last, is a virtue in itself; many

[153]

enthusiastic members of the German army during the last war must have been well-equipped with all four; calm, brave, persevering fighters, well aware of their own limitations. But this doesn't alter the fact that nobody can love effectively if he is agitated; or cowardly; or easily discouraged; or proud. (As for me, my life of constant humiliation has kept me fairly humble, and I have a good deal of tenacity when I set my heart on achieving something. But I am neither calm nor brave: fear and anxiety are still my worst disablements for making this journey.)

———— * ————

Digging the garden yesterday, with unusual zest and attention, the word 'businesslike' suddenly came into my mind. Who would associate such a word with the religious quest; yet that kind of no-nonsense practicality seems to be another of the necessary qualities.

———— * ————

Running all round our loop-road in the rain, even up the steep hill to The Cherries, I felt that old ecstasy of the body being fully extended. (But when I stopped the car outside Monmouth a few weeks ago and watched the boys playing rugby below me I felt sharp pangs of regret. Playing well for school or college is certainly one among the memories of pure joy.)

———— * ————

Some are naturally talented for religion just as some are naturally talented for music. But there is this great difference: a man without talent who devoted his whole life to writing worthless music would be a sad figure of fun; but devotion to the way of God is as right and proper for the most unspiritual man as it is for St Francis or St Teresa.

In fact to do one's inadequate best on this way is wiser than to do superbly well on any other.

(Do I really believe this? Would Berlioz, a sardonic non-believer, have done 'better' if he had been converted, abandoned music and become a Trappist monk? I think the answers to such questions can be known only in Heaven.)

—— * ——

Was it a small sign of grace that I was *sorry* for the Cambridge crew when they sank on Saturday? Not so long ago I would have taken a nasty pleasure in their discomfiture.

—— * ——

Easter. At mass I *did* have a sense of unusual joy, caught, no doubt, from the extra radiance of the sisters. But as I read the Easter cards which several of them had left on our breakfast table I realized how *unleavened* my heart is still, compared with theirs. 'To Philip and Sally. With love and prayers for a peaceful and joyous Easter. Alleluia!' 'Philip and Sally with joy and love in our Risen Lord.'

3 April

S was feeling very oppressed and empty, and I dared to suggest that she should see the Reverend Mother, whom she knows well enough now to trust and honour as I do. At first she resisted this, not wanting to impose herself, but at last she agreed and I drove her over to Tymawr.

I felt nervous about putting so much pressure on her at such a time; but when she came back to me in the library I could tell at once that she was in a much happier state.

Mother had talked to her about submission to the will of God and trust in God's power to help her. These traditional words of Christian comfort would once have seemed to me stale and useless with too many vain repetitions: embarrassing in their naive, even crude, simplicity. Now I rejoice with my dear wife that these true and loving words have been spoken to her by someone with the authority to speak them. (If I had spoken them myself they would indeed have sounded unctuous and empty.)

—— * ——

Blessed peace and comfort when we were at Tymawr again

yesterday for mass. This has been, in a sense, *my* place rather than S's. She has seldom come to mass with me and never to evensong and compline; the sisters have inevitably been more my friends than hers. And now I thank God that I scarcely ever suggested that she should come with me, for now she makes her own approach, establishing, for instance, her own close and special relationship with Mother. (I call her this by right, as an associate; but also with a happy sense of her maternal reality for me.)

Meanwhile we have been reading and praying together rather more than we did before. I believe we shall grow even closer together in the love of God, which would certainly have seemed a most improbable development during the angry, embittering years from about 1962 to 1975. (So they seem as I look back on them; though I would never have admitted then that things were as bad as that between us.)

———— * ————

From Simone Weil's *Notebook*:

'Suppose one says to oneself: even though the moment of death brings nothing new but only puts an end to life here below without being the prelude to another life; and even though this world should be completely abandoned by God; and even though this word God corresponds to absolutely nothing real but only to childish illusions – even though this is how it is, I still prefer, even in this case, to perform what seems to me to be commanded by God, even though it leads to the most fearful troubles, rather than do anything else at all. Only a madman can think in this way. But if one has caught this madness one can be perfectly sure of never regretting any action accomplished with the above thought.'

As so often she expresses herself in the most violent and contorted way she can devise. What I would now say is that if it were irrefutably demonstrated to me that there is no God, and no reality above or distinct from the material world, then I would consider that human life is too terrible to be endured.

Fear, and some regard for the feelings of others, might prevent me from killing myself; but I would live out my life as a prisoner lives out his sentence.

But the fact is that I can no more conceive of such a demonstration being possible than Freddie, for example, can conceive of having a personal experience of God. In that important sense my faith is now absolute and unshakeable. I think of the gentle, strong and loving face of the Reverend Mother. I think of all those saints whose lives I have read and who seem to me to have lived, not just better lives than others but *more truly*. More *truthfully* in the most literal sense of the word: they were more full of truth than we are. How absurd to suppose that a ridiculous, humanly-invented *contraption* was their only enabling force!

8 April

Yes. But even if the faith really is unshakeable at some deep level of the heart and mind, the upper levels can be terribly lacerated by doubt, and worse.

In bed two nights ago I was beset by the suspicion that there may simply be nothing really true and serious in me at all. What if I belong to an appalling category of human beings who are condemned to be in constant search of a serious role to play, trying on one function or belief after another, but always coming back to the knowledge that

> Those who have crossed
> With direct eyes, to death's other Kingdom
> Remember us – if at all – not as lost
> Violent souls, but only
> As the hollow men,
> The stuffed men.

This expresses it very well, very exactly, for the dead do indeed seem real and serious by the very fact of having seriously died: and the living who are lost and violent are also real because of the real hellishness of their condition. We, on the other hand, are too frivolous ever to die; too vacuous ever to fill our lives even with serious pain. We are the survivors of the shipwreck, left bobbing absurdly on the surface when all the weighty men have sunk to the bottom of the sea.

Still under the influence of this painful self-doubt I found next morning that S's talk of God's will for her and so on (she very seldom talks in these terms) not only meant nothing to me but almost disgusted me. And when we went to the convent for evensong and a special healing service afterwards I still had to conceal a nagging self-disgust which swelled into a gloomy rejection of everything I saw and heard. We were seated, most unusually, in the front row of the visitors' pews, where I felt not only embarrassingly exposed but also in the false position of appearing to be wholly and closely involved in all that was going on. 'What the hell am I doing in this *galère!*' I wondered, as the rich, over-ripe, all-too-familiar, *meaningless* words came rolling out. And what the hell do they all think they're doing, these ladies dressed up so absurdly and going through their absurd motions for the ten thousandth time? (For it is a quality of hollow men that in the end they see everyone else as equally hollow.)

I knew that this is what many Christians would call an assault by the devil. I also knew that it was a mood which would certainly pass before long. But this knowledge took the unpleasant form of making me conclude that even the mood itself was not to be taken seriously: something to be toyed with; relished for its interesting taste. 'He can't even seriously persevere in his inability to seriously persevere.' An infinite recession of frivolity.

9 April

But I woke after a good night in a much more pleasant state. I've reminded myself this morning that I was always an earnest self-improver: even at the worst periods of my ostensibly clownish degradation. Tumbling and tumbling I aspired to heaven.

——— * ———

Chuang Tsu's *Inner Chapters*, the *Tao Teh Ching*, which is ascribed to Laotzu, and the *Dhammapada*, which is ascribed to Buddha. Lately I have been using these three for the main part of my meditational reading. To my ears there is a sort of melodious blandness about much of these Eastern classics; the sweet saga-city of platitude, and even of tautology. This, for example, from the *Dhammapada*: 'Men who are foolish and ignorant are careless and never watchful: but the man who lives in watchfulness considers it his greatest treasure.' The *Inner Chapters* are much more idiosyncratic; and often give me the feeling that something true and important is being said which I can nearly, but not quite, understand.

But I find the *Tao Teh Ching* far the most accessible of the three; a poetical good sense which sometimes reminds me of Cavafy:

> The sanest man
> Sets up no deed,
> Lays down no law,
> Takes everything that happens as it comes,
> As something to animate, not to appropriate,
> To earn, not to own,
> To accept naturally without self-importance.

12 April

Millenarianism – i.e. expectation of the imminent coming of the Kingdom – has had a very bad press both from historians and from nearly all religious writers. And it is true, of course, that every millenarian expectation, including that of Jesus himself, has been disproved by history. But surely anyone who believes in the loving activity of God in the world must also believe that the world might – could – one day contain a true

[159]

community of saints. Every organism moves towards its own completion; its own perfection. Fullness of life is the only proper goal for mankind, and the best of the saints show us what Jesus meant when he said that he had come to give us life, and to give it more abundantly.

'More life! More life!' Not enough Christians have made that their daily prayer.

13 April

Au delà du désespoir. Sartre at his most arrogant and melo-dramatic. For he does not mean, as a Christian would, that despair is transcended by the superior wisdom and maturity of *undeceived hope.* He means that after passing through the anguish of active despair one should reach a state of resignation to the absurdity of life; and to the exercise of human freedom only for the sake of avoiding bad faith (self-deception).

It even occurred to me, for a mad moment or two, to try to form A Fellowship of Hope. Not an organization of any kind, but simply a shared resolve to pause in quiet for one minute every day – if possible the same minute for everyone – and devote that time to an act of hope – that is, of trust in God and trust in Man under God. 'The glory of God is a living man; and the life of man consists in beholding God' (Irenaeus). An attempt to mitigate the many-symptomed modern disease – futile haste; activity for its own sake; unthinking greed; cruel and grasping indifference to the pain of others; refusal of honest self-examination; unconsidered and frivolous cynicism ...

———— * ————

I now see that I was foolish to treat humility as a mere pre-requisite to virtue, on a par with calmness and perseverance. Humility is much more than modesty; much more than the good sense of not having too high an opinion of oneself. Humility is close to truthfulness; much more than truthfulness in the usual sense of the word; an openness to as much of the truth as one is capable of receiving. 'Love rejoices in the truth.'

———— * ————

The Work. The crucial problem remains – how to relax, to let go, to move with the natural rhythm of things; yet also to hold tight, and tighter, to strive continually for amendment. I must learn to be at ease with myself; to relinquish all rigid postures. But there is also a bracing discipline, and this should grow stricter as time passes. The weekly fast: the meagre lunch; above all, unremitting attention.

I recognized the folly of my old ways when I went for a long walk last week and was dismayed, when I got home, to realize that I'd been away only an hour and three-quarters instead of the two hours I'd promised myself. This is that obsessive imposition of precise but meaningless tasks which has always been a folly of mine, and which needs to be *calmly* overcome. Just as I know that it is a strength, not a weakness, when I break off my meditation before the allotted hour is up – either because I want to do something else or simply because I've become aware that trying to meditate any longer would be useless: therefore worse than useless.

———— * ————

The Tea Ceremony. It continues to fascinate me. I suspect that for many Japanese it has now become elegantly and artificially archaic; fossilized; even effete. Yet if I were to try it – but with whom, now that Barn House is crumbling? – and if I adjusted the ritual to our own circumstances, perhaps I would benefit from that extreme formality and studied courtesy.

(But I must admit that my inclinations in this direction have recently taken a bit of a knock. I bought ten different kinds of tea in Monmouth; but found that the only distinction my ruined palate could (just) make was between Indian and China. Not that a nice discrimination of this kind is a necessary part of the ceremony; but it wouldn't be quite the thing to do it with teabags.)

[161]

17 April

Hearing of yet another friend's marriage troubles I thought that life – what we are born with, what we are nurtured into, what we make of ourselves – gives each one of us a unique and almost impossible task. A few simply refuse it; opt out and become lookers-on. But most of us are caught in the terrible machine of living with ourselves and living with others; tussling and blundering; shouting with pain and anger; sweating, regretting; failing again and again.

So there must be a pause at some point; a taking stock; a deep reflection. And this must lead to a recognition of the true work which has to be done, and a resolve to do it at any cost. To do, that is, as much of it as we can, bearing in mind the mangled state we are in after so many years in the life-machine. Before the pause we drag this increasingly lacerated self about with us; defending it against all-comers – and most of all against our wives, our husbands, our children. After the pause ... but the pause, of course, should never end. Recollection means cutting our 'true' selves loose from the selves we believed to be ours.

Of course there is a sense in which the existing self is more true than the other: it is perceptibly *there*, for us to know and hate, for others to see and smell. But religious believers – it is this which defines them – trust that the hidden, divine self (the soul) is a colony of that higher reality which is *more real* than the wounded and wounding persons who have been forced into existence by the material world.

21 April

After such high thoughts the inevitable thump-down. S was attacked by some bug last week; stomach pains, headaches, exhaustion. I showed frequent 'sympathy'; often remembered to ask how she was feeling; made her coffee and brought it up to her bedroom ...

A day or two later I began to suffer from the same afflic-tion; and *God*, the difference in the attention I paid to it!

———— * ————

'Is it possible,' asks Krishnamurti, 'to end all memories – not the memory of facts, the way to your house and so on, but the inward attachment through memory to psychological security ...?' But this makes no sense to me at all: or rather, a metaphorical sense only, which is obviously not what he intends. To remember the way to my house is part, and a very important part, of my inward attachment to psychological security. There is a sort of nonsense about being told to forget this, but remember that; as if what should and what shouldn't be remembered are two separable orders of facts and events.

———— * ————

'One can only excuse men for evil by accusing God of it. If one accuses God one forgives because God is the Good ... Sin is an offence offered to God from resentment at the debts he owes and does not pay us. By forgiving God we cut the root of sin in ourselves. At the bottom of every sin there is anger against God' (Simone Weil).

To me this is just as nonsensical as the passage from Krishnamurti. The Krishnamurti nonsense springs from getting lost in abstractions about man: the Simone nonsense from treating God as if he were another sort of man.

(Curious that I so often quote from her only to take issue with her. Yet she and Merton are the two religious writers of this century – of any century? – who speak to me most directly. But how different they are from each other; Merton essentially a wise man in the great tradition; she a brilliant urchin of the Spirit, biting and scratching at God and man.)

24 April

On Wednesday I did the longest meditation I have ever done; from one till four, with two little pauses to stretch my limbs. I can't say that it seemed to produce any better results than three separate hours would have done, except that it was harder on my legs and back. Harder, perhaps, on the mind as well. But is this kind of physical and mental endurance something that I really need just now?

Most of my meditation is hard on the mind; and in the case of someone with so many formidable blocks and distractions I think this is bound to be so. But sometimes I catch myself out in ridiculous self-inflictions. In a given breath-counting, which is still the basis of my meditation, I vow that I shall reach, say, fifty without letting the mind wander. And if I fail, even at 45, I send myself back to the beginning again, like punishing a naughty forgetful child. This is to become obsessed by achievement in the very field where all ideas of achievement should be dissolved. 'If I can do fifty without distraction I can add that to my credit account.' Whereas, as all the good books tell us, true benefit comes simply from accepting the fact of distraction and gently bringing the mind back to its lost concentration. Correction and punishment only magnify the distraction, instead of passing gently over it.

———— * ————

Reviewing a book on Tennyson last month, and this week Basil Bunting's *Collected Poems*, took me back to those old pastures where I used to spend so much of my time. Back, and down from the high mountains of spiritual reading where I have been slithering about for most of the last two years. A great relief.

In fact I have tried several times to break myself of this obsessive involvement with devotional and theological works; for I know perfectly well that this is another case of my foolish penchant for excess. But though I've tried every kind of reading which I used to enjoy so much, from thrillers to history, I find that these diversions soon become intolerably boring. So I return with relief, but a certain sense of imprisonment, to books with such alluring titles as *How to Know God* or *The Soul, and Where To Find It.*

(But when I can find a good life of a good saint – not easy
– this is by far the best reading of all. It takes one away from
all the terrible abstractions of religious discourse and shows
what faith can really mean; can really do.)

———— * ————

Laura now spends more time than ever with Paul in
Gloucester. This is a very good thing, of course, but there is
also a certain pain in watching our last fledgeling beginning
to flutter away from the nest.

———— * ————

It won't do, of course, that casual and moralistic dismissal
of Beckett and Bacon which I threw off here a few weeks ago.
It seems that I am constantly looking for simplicities of judgement even where I know, after so many years, that simple
judgements always miss the point.

Yet my almost lifelong attitude – that art and morals have
very little to do with each other – was another evasive
simplification. I see this huge, ancient, heavily-encrusted
problem rolling towards me like a stone of Sisyphus. Some time,
and perhaps quite soon, I shall have to start trying to push
it up the hill. But not yet.

———— * ————

Communion at BH on Sunday was particularly good. Phil
was directing things, and soon had us divided up into pairs
with instructions to do nothing but stare into our partner's eyes.
I was paired with Simon, and the first half-minute was a hellish
embarrassment to both of us, not without giggling and much
frenzied blinking. But once we were through those preliminaries
I think we both felt that trust between us was strangely
increasing the more deeply and unwaveringly we stared. By
the end – six or seven minutes – I could readily have taken
that lanky young man in my arms and held him tight. (And
did just that, of course, a little later, when we gave the hug
of peace all round.)

On the whole they steer clear of this kind of encounter group technique; wisely, I think, for God knows the atmosphere is already charged enough. But when I hear people speak ill of encounter groups I always remember the one we attended in 1973, and how deeply it affected me. I began it in a fury of resistance; and ended in a flood of public tears. What's more the tears flowed freely for at least four weeks afterwards whenever I thought of the people I had known *and loved* at that extraordinary event. And I think the effect has been permanent; a permanent opening of the heart and mind; not fully, of course, but enough to make many good things possible for me which were quite impossible before. (Lucy has told me that I use the word 'phoney' much less than I used to – this exclamation of defensive derision which was so habitual in the world I belonged to in Oxford and London long ago.)

—— * ——

Simon came to Tymawr with us for mass, and talked to Sister Benedicta about some pots they want him to make for the altar flowers. And I felt again the delight I've always felt when these two communities come together. Some hope even stirred, however illogically, that BH might be reborn, even at this late hour of its apparent disintegration.

We talked with Sister Paula about Schumacher's *Small is Beautiful*. 'There should be a big movement,' she said, 'to get things going in that direction.' But I suggested that the movement couldn't be big, in the ordinary sense, without contradicting itself. If there's ever to be a *widespread* movement it will have to spring from small independent activities, connected with each other only by strictly fraternal links. Any sort of centrally-directed administration would be disastrous.

Jason's little building co-operative in Coventry. This is absolutely on the right lines; the same lines, fundamentally, as DA; mutual help in work, mutual help in therapy, and the greatest possible independence of the state machine. (But what a task he has set himself! And nearly all his eggs in that one basket! I applaud as a citizen, but as a parent I tremble at the prospect of a devastating disappointment.)

—— * ——

[166]

Fear for the children. When Lucy came over yesterday evening I felt almost physically sick with the apprehension of something frightful awaiting her. *Not* premonition; just a very acute awareness of the dragon pits into which so many of my friends have fallen. (I have fallen into them too, but have always managed to clamber out again, however scorched and muddy.)

———— * ————

To S, facetiously, this morning:
'Grow old along with me; the best is yet to be –
The last of life for which the first was made.'

But then I cut out the sententious voice, and told her that this says just what I feel; and says it well. I kissed her; she bravely overcame her embarrassment, and kissed me warmly back.

———— * ————

'Square my trial to my proportioned strength.'

Milton wrote this somewhere – I've never bothered to find out where – and it has always seemed to me the best possible petitionary prayer. Of all my fears for myself – and that means most of my fears – the worst has been that some horror will fall on me which will be so much beyond my strength to bear that I shall disintegrate into utter, screaming helplessness. That just when my strength will be needed to support others my weakness will add me to their burden.

27 April

My grandfather used to quote approvingly from the beginning of a treatise by Cicero; something like this: 'The basis of all civilized life is the observance of contract.' He would contrast this, greatly to its advantage, with the opening words of the Sermon on the Mount: 'Blessed are the poor in spirit: for theirs is the Kingdom of Heaven.' The Cicero, he said, was a dry, but solid and useful statement about something real; while Jesus was just uttering vapid words to which anyone can attach any meaning he chooses.

But I always felt that this is a false comparison – something like the comparison of prose with poetry. To my mind what Jesus was saying transcends what Cicero was saying, but without in any way denying it, or even questioning its importance.

This has arisen because I found myself using the Cicero quotation at BH yesterday in answer to the maddening refusal of almost all the communards to commit themselves to any kind of future action. S and I were trying to find out how many of them were reasonably sure that they would still be here in twelve months' time ... six months' time ... *three* months' time. But the usual answer was that he/she could make no promises at all, for who could tell that he/she wouldn't be directed to do something else. In other words – though they didn't use them – the Spirit bloweth where it listeth.

This has to be respected, of course: at the very least their honesty must be respected. But how is it possible, in real life, to do anything with other people – to undertake any form of co-operative action – unless agreements are made about future action? The fields are still a mess: who will weed them? rotovate them? rake them? sow them? And when? 'Don't *worry* so much, Philip! It will all get done if it's meant to be done.' Inside my head I tear my hair: outside it I heave a heavy sigh.

And so, for the first time, S and I asked them at least to consider the possibility that this community may have run its course: may have reached its natural ending. 'Perhaps,' I couldn't help saying, 'this is how it is meant to be.'

At first Kerry – who has the misfortune to be both the most committed surviving member and also the least inclined to the others' jolly fatalism – was appalled and very angry. He thought we were charging BH with indulging in 'too much spirituality' and he repeated the phrase with bitter emphasis – '*Too much spirituality!*' And so we were off again on the true nature of the spirit, and what it demands of us according to our various situations. A swampy and foggy field indeed, where every practical issue is vaporized as soon as raised.

But I suppose the very vagueness of that topic helped to slacken the tension between us; and soon we were our usual friendly selves again. Or so it seemed. But I couldn't help being aware (and nor, I'm sure, could anyone else) that S and I had bared our teeth at them for the first time: brought out into the open, for the first time, the hard fact of ownership; the hard fact of who pays the piper. We have been so scrupulous, over these four years, never to pull that on any of them; always to present ourselves as simple members of the community. Not even so much as that for most of the time, being only associate members, living outside the house and therefore having *less* right than anyone else to make decisions.

It is easy to say that this was always a false situation; and that false situations are always exposed in the end. But it was the only way we could possibly have acted, since we were both equally determined from the very start that this would be a community without a boss or bosses; that it must find its way forward not by anyone's direction but by its own inner laws of development.

At the beginning, when the community consisted only of Bim, the Rowsons and us, we said that after five years we would turn BH into a trust and completely resign all special (property) rights in it. But at that time we were envisaging a stability which has never, in fact, been realized. True, there was the period of two very good years; but Robin, a key figure, left at an early stage in it to start a community of his own; Dave and Fiona (Rowson) found family life impossible at Barn House and moved to the other side of the county; Steve went off with Adima to her native Brazil ...

Last September, with all these good and valuable people gone, we made that great resolve to start again, accepting a change of direction and hoping that new members would come in response to the proclamation we sent around 'the network'. Phil came, but has now left for his hermit's cottage on Mull. The three Antipodeans – Richard, Mary and Shish – came, and stayed for several months, supplying a powerful driving force. But alas, there was constant and growing tension between them and our own Antipodean – Kerry. Kerry accused them of being insufficiently spiritual: they said – and Mary with Australian bluntness – that Kerry was putting too much pressure on everyone else to conform to his own ideas of what the spiritual life should be.

Now Richard, Mary and Shish have all gone, and nobody has come to replace them. Of course we could once again put notices in the 'alternative' press (I'm glad that word has been almost entirely dropped; I much prefer the present self-mocking 'freaks') but what exactly have we to offer potential applicants? The whole atmosphere of the place has changed; and where visitors used to feel a strong sense of true communion and true purpose they now find – as (ex-Buddhist monk) Stephen more than hinted – an amiable aimlessness; a distracted confusion of good intentions. It would now need four or five new people of the quality of those dear departed, Robin, Steve, Bim and the Rowsons, to save BH from dissolving into an irredeemable mess.

How much are we influenced in this by the prospect of selling the house and getting a nice fat sum into the bank? When S and I discuss this we admit that it can't be kept out of our thoughts, but assure ourselves that it wouldn't prevent us from encouraging the community to resurrect itself if that seemed a real possibility. We also remind each other that Jason and Lucy are badly in need of money; and that Laura may very soon be in the same condition. (When this particular discussion becomes heated – the community has always been delicate ground – S says that she *always* resented giving advantages to strangers which might have been given, in a different form, to our own children.)

I hope, in any case, that we are right in believing that we would again help to save BH if there seemed any chance of it saving itself. But I must confess that once the idea of that large sum in the bank had entered my mind I've found it very hard to push it out again. Ah, Mammon, if only God were as manifest as you are!

———— * ————

Yesterday we were planting onion sets with Kerry and Rose, and I think all four of us had the melancholy feeling that this was activity only for its own sake, rather than a practical contribution to the BH food supply. (Apart from anything else the ground was unfertilized and still full of barely submerged tufts of grass. Yet to have pointed this out to Kerry, who still has little understanding of vegetable growing, would have depressed him without doing anyone any good. The truth is that there simply isn't enough willing labour in the community now to get these fields properly sown and planted.)

———— * ————

If you *must* lapse into smoking a cigarette try to choose a strong one, and *smoke it with the utmost relish.*

29 April

Drove to Leominster on Saturday to meet Gerry Richards, who came half-way to meet me from Shrewsbury. His main religious interest is in trying to show that George Fox was no Christian, and that Quakerism shouldn't be regarded as a Christian sect. I can't contribute anything on this; and not much on Buddhism, which was our other main topic of conversation in that delightful hotel bar. Gerry believes that where Buddhism is superior to Christianity is in its strong emphasis on the need for *understanding*; its conviction that ignorance is the enemy which most needs to be attacked. I agreed with him that Christians make too little of this, though I said that the understanding we were talking about shouldn't be thought of as an intellectual exercise.

———— * ————

S and I are now reading de Caussade to each other in the evenings (Dom Chapman in the mornings). One of the greatest

[171]

of all spiritual directors. If I'm feeling a little low before our reading I often find that he has an immediate and animating effect on me.

———— * ————

Broke a rear window of the caravan, just after bringing it back from its refitting at Parkend. I held my temper down for about ten minutes, and was just on the point of self-congratulation when S made some quite innocuous remark upon which I instantly fell with all my claws exposed. So an old-style row followed.

But at least we cleared it up much sooner than we used to do: and at least I managed to gulp down my guilt once-and-for-all, instead of regurgitating it for hours like a cow chewing its cud.

———— * ————

Visiting Emily at Coney Hill. That great roomful of senile men and women. Em spoke so sensibly nearly all the time, and always bravely, though without the faintest awareness of her own courage. But how sad and shrunken her face is now. At her worst, in her heyday of doing housework for us at Barn House and looking after the children, she was almost *too* upstanding. In fact she was sometimes a tartar; though usually sweet, funny and kind. This makes her sad resignation in that place all the more poignant. But this is a holy resignation; though that too is something she's quite unaware of. An intelligent but uneducated woman she has never learned the terrible lesson of self-consciousness – which, once learned, can never be forgotten.

30 April

This from the *Dhammapada*, neatly confirming what Gerry said about Buddhism: 'But the greatest of all sins is indeed the sin of ignorance. Throw this sin away, O man, and become pure from sin.'

But this, from the same source, is just what I like least in that religion: 'Let a man be free from pleasure and let a man be free from pain; for to have pleasure is sorrow and to have pain is also sorrow.' In fact to have pleasure is also to have pleasure, and not at all to be despised on that account. But the implication of this passage is that sorrow is the worst of evils; to be avoided at any price. But Christians know that sorrow can be avoided in this life only by a terrible hardening of the heart; a cultivated indifference; or an apathy which is a kind of death-in-life. And sorrow is not only inevitable in the life of a living man; it is also a blessing, though often in the most desolating disguise. For, at the very least, sorrow is a way of diminishing our ignorance: we *learn* from sorrow as from nothing else. (Except, perhaps, from joy: but real joy, holy joy, is as rare a state as sorrow is a common one.)

———— * ————

Zen opposes all striving on the grounds that 'it is always a striving for *my* spiritual progress, etc., and therefore a selfish striving. It is simply another form of acquisitiveness, and will thus achieve exactly the opposite of what is aimed at; instead of losing the ego we are strengthening the "me" at its roots.' This – from Robert Powell's *Zen and Reality* – seems plausible at first; but I believe that it's only a cunning play on words. Of course we have to be conscious – extra-conscious – of the self in order to locate it properly; to become fully aware of its strength and its cancerous ramifications. But no evil can be got rid of until it has been observed: and even studied.

And here is the *Dhammapada* again, contradicting both Powell and itself: 'The man whose mind, filled with determination, is longing for the infinite Nirvana, and who is free from sensuous pleasures, is called *uddhamsoto*, "He who goes up-stream", for against the current of passions and worldly life he is bound for the infinite.' That's more like it.

———— * ————

Simone Weil on sex: 'Human sexual energy is not seasonal. This is the best indication that it is not destined for a natural purpose, but for the love of God.' Splendid – particularly from her.

———— * ————

X's autobiography, which was sent me for review. As I read the usual dreary anecdotes about the Sitwells, Evelyn Waugh, Nancy Cunard, etc., the terrible word 'vacuous' came into my mind. Since I now find it unbearable to devote a whole review to attacking a book, I rang up Terry and asked for something else.

(Yet when I was a young reviewer on the *New Statesman* how I revelled in setting up five bad novels simply to knock them down like ninepins.)

———— * ————

Music. It sometimes exasperates me as I try to listen – this knowledge that I am hearing only about half of all there is to hear.

1 May

Yesterday's review was of Julia's (Strachey) two novels, which Penguin have brought out together in a single volume.* Her life-work, in under 300 pages. They are both very good books, but who that knows her as I do could feel that such a life was in any way justified, atoned for, by such an offering?

She must be nearly eighty now, but has been demented and in hospital for the last two or three years. A fitting conclusion to a life of almost unmitigated wretchedness and bitterness.

Julia was my *femme-de-trente-ans* during my last year at Oxford; or rather my *femme-de-trente-sept-ans*. I admired her greatly as a woman of wit and sophistication; and for her aura of Bloomsbury and the twenties. But already there was something disturbingly mordant about her, perhaps the burden of her frightful first marriage and equally frightful widowing. But the long calamity of her life had begun with her desertion by

* *Cheerful Weather for the Wedding* and *An Integrated Man* (Penguin, London).

her mother before Julia was old enough to remember her; and it was to continue, with one interval of happiness, until her final collapse from slow self-poisoning by pills and alcohol.

She was the most acidulous disbeliever that I've ever known; and during all the years I knew her she scarcely wavered in her attitude of angry desperation; frantic but hopeless resentment.

Once, after one of the later and more savage blows, I dared to write something to her about the possibility of faith. She never answered; and my letter was almost certainly an idiotic mistake.

And so she will die, before long, alienated in every conceivable sense of the word. What could it possibly mean to pray for Julia now? To me it would be nothing but a sloppy, even corrupt form of self-indulgence: the pious pretence that she is still, even in her senility, accessible to the mercy and the love of God.

2 May

Ben came for the weekend; alas, a rarer visitor during the last four years. He had begun to feel, in that vague but powerful way of his, that Woodroyd is a place of depression, piety and teetotalism. Since he is my dearest friend, and since he has been visiting me in the country from London about four times a year over the last thirty-two years – first in the Isle of Wight with Anne; then with S in Suffolk and at Barn House – his awkward refusals of our invitations have caused me some pain. A fair-weather friend? Yes, I suppose so; but it is in the strange nature of his innocence that I accept this without resentment. He is a great lover of pleasure, and is drawn towards pleasure, and away from pain, like some migrating animal.

It was a splendid, old-time visit. Mellowed, but never worsened by drink the three of us talked with cheerful melancholy about all the good times we've shared in the past; all the comic episodes in London (comic *afterwards*); all our journeys in Europe together, stretching back to Venice in 1952.

Our old friend Wilson Plant and new friend David Jenkins*
came to dinner on Saturday and didn't leave till 3: an evening
of richly familiar argument, and never a cross word spoken.
(But what a shock to realize how much Wilson, too, has faded
out of our lives: and this entirely because of our own – *my* own?
– growing unsociability. He used to dine with us, or we with him,
at least as often as Ben came to stay. Now we see him only
on Monmouth Thursdays, in the boozy and often crowded
garrulity of the Beaufort bar.)

Ben was delighted, of course, to hear that we've now definitely
decided to bring the community to an end. Like nearly all our
old friends, he always thought the whole project quite insane:
and now he has vigorously encouraged us to 'send the whole
lot packing; sell the house; and come to Sicily with me next
summer for a proper holiday' (from his thank-you letter).

So the weekend took on a certain symbolic air: a sign of our
returning to old ways of life, with an implied rejection of all
that the community has represented. And yet – I tell myself
with a certain stridency – there can be no return to the same
place, for S and I have both been changed forever by the
experience of the last four years. (She would not put it nearly
so strongly.) And however I try to define the change it is
certainly not of a kind which would prevent us from enjoying
a holiday in Sicily with Ben. If anything my own enjoyment
should be all the greater, considering how much the word
'attention' seems to emerge as the primary lesson of those years;
and how lamentably inattentive I have always been when sightseeing with Ben in the past.

———— * ————

The decisive meeting at BH was even more painful than we'd
feared.

A young man called John had made a dramatic entrance
just as we were beginning last Sunday's communion. We heard
Kerry greeting someone effusively at the dark front door. Then

*Sixth-form classics master at Monmouth Grammar School.

we were aware only of a rather mysterious, bearded presence, as we made a place for him in our circle and he sat impassively through all our goings-on.

But when he came over here with the milkers he revealed himself to be a fundamentalist and revivalist Christian, a quiet, unquestioning fanatic of the most alarming kind. His bright blue eyes stare unblinkingly into one's own, forcing one into irritated embarrassment and a desperate search for something else to look at. He likes to be an enigma; will tell us very little about his background, except that he was once an actor and a sinner, but suddenly saw the light in South Africa. Since then he has lived in total poverty, preaching the word, relying on God to look after his bare material needs.

We quickly discovered that any sort of religious discussion was quite impossible: his only method of argument is to quote from the New Testament; or to say that he *knows* the truth because Christ is always with him. An impressive, infuriating, deeply worrying young man.

The point is that he has had a galvanic and confusing effect on the whole community. Kerry and Michele have become outright disciples: 'I knew that someone was coming to show me the way,' said Michele, 'and now John has come and has brought me back to Christ.' Kerry was a little more circumspect; even disagreed with John on his fundamentalism, but has plainly been carried away all the same. And although none of the others has gone overboard to the same extent – Simon and Rose are much too wedded to Sufi and Buddhist ideas – John's all-too-charismatic presence has startled even those two into a state of rather hectic spiritual excitement.

When John calmly sat down at the table to join in our discussion S and I protested that the meeting should be limited to those with some claim to being members of the community. But everyone insisted that John should stay – so there he sat, throughout the whole distressing business, saying nothing but exuding a great deal.

The point they were all now agreed on was that John's arrival had made them aware of how much BH meant to them; they had never felt so confident in the community's spiritual future as they did now: *this* was the regeneration we had all been waiting and hoping for ...

Naturally this made our task harder, but nothing that anybody said could convince either S or me that we should change our minds again. Either John would convert them all – and the community would be set on a religious path which we would dislike and disapprove of, or he would be a strong divisive force – after the first vague impulse of unconsidered enthusiasm – and the community would be split into ecstatic revivalist Christians and old-fashioned Barn House Eclectics. Perhaps John has 'been sent', I suggested – once again turning their own weapon against them – precisely in order to hasten the process of disintegration: a catalyst who will effect that chemical separation which we'd all been half-consciously anticipating. A Bailiff of the Lord.

I felt basely materialist when I also reminded them of the present economic situation: no money in the kitty; the pick-up a wreck, and quite incapable of passing its MOT; the fields still a mess; the house itself in desperate need of renovation ...

In the end they took our decision wonderfully well, as we should have known they would. All were disappointed, but none showed the least sign of bitterness. And when Simon came over to milk this morning he told us that they were still going to fell the area of wood they'd bought from the Forestry Commission, but would bring the logs to us instead of storing them at BH. It was far from his intention to make us feel guilty – Simon is incapable of such a ploy – but certainly he left S and me in a state of melancholy and sharp regret.

For all the difference of age and social background – perhaps partly because of them – these communards have taught us a great deal during the last four years. The bargain has been a very fair one: we provided them with the physical means of living and growing together; but I doubt if they learned half so much from us as we have learned from them. In fact I doubt whether they learned anything at all from me, for what did I have to teach? Whereas they, for all the rich confusion of their ideas, taught me a great deal about openness of heart and mind. (The more tragic if they should fall into the aridities of dogmatic fundamentalism. 'Ah,' said Sister Paula, 'the hotline to God. A dreadful danger.')

2 May

And now, to add absurdity to sadness, my celestial relationship with Lois ends in abrupt fiasco.

Several letters passed between us: she greatly appreciated *Friends Apart*: I found the typed third volume of her autobiography every bit as good as the two published volumes: she commiserated with me about *Pantaloon*: it seemed, increasingly, that we were deeply agreed on everything that really mattered. S and I were to visit her in Canterbury: a date was fixed, to which I was looking forward with the keenest possible expectation of a noble and fruitful meeting of minds.

Then, alas, she told me that she had also written a novel, which had been refused by a dozen publishers. I asked her to send it. I found it very, very bad. I wrote an evasive letter. She insisted on hearing my full opinion. I wrote that I thought it a melodramatic trivialization of religion, after the worst manner of the nineties: I hoped she would put it firmly behind her and concentrate on where her real talent lay. She was violently angry: could no longer see any point in the Canterbury visit, since we clearly had so little in common after all.

I feel wry about all this, to put it mildly. Real regret that this remarkable woman is not to be our friend; but also a strong sense of dire familiarity with situations of this kind. How many times in my life have I rushed into something with extravagant and unconsidered enthusiasm, only to come a cropper as a result. How many times I've leaped without looking, and found that I've leaped into a ditch full of mud and stones.

Many years ago that sensible wartime boss of mine, Colonel Geoffrey Vickers VC, warned me, after some calamitous escapade, that I was the kind of person who is always tempted to bite off more than he can chew. If I'd listened to his wise warning how many fiascos I would have avoided. (Even Lois herself seemed to discourage the effusiveness of my early letters.)

Yes: but if I had been more cautious in my life I would also have avoided a great deal of vital and animating experience. What could have been blinder than the leap which landed me in my present marriage! (Or was that a guided leap? Did my guardian angel give me a shove towards S? It can't have been quite as simple as that, since I was proposing, at that time, to almost every girl I met. But perhaps the angel ensured that only S would accept me.)

———— * ————

This deeply embittered correspondent of many years has taken, during the last few weeks, to telephoning almost every evening. He is clipped, authoritative, enigmatic; at times preposterous in the angry tributes which he pays me. A clever man, but with some deep inner sickness which he will not allow to be discussed.

I began to find these conversations an agony of embarrassment; and handed W on to S. Now she always answers when we believe it will be him; talks to him with her usual gentleness, shrewdness, wisdom and unfailing patience. And now if I answer the telephone by mistake it is her he asks for.

———— * ————

Dhammapada: 'The wise do not call strong a fetter which is made of iron, of wood or of rope; much stronger is the fetter of passion for gold and for jewels, for sons or for wives.' A very deliberate refusal to make any distinction between attachments. And Jesus also seems to have had little use for family ties; not even for filial and maternal love. But to me it would seem absurd and odious to put my material greed on the same level as my love for S and the children.

But here is the *Dhammapada* at its best: 'By day the sun shines, and by night shines the moon. The warrior shines in his armour, and the Brahmin priest in his meditation. But the

Buddha shines by day and by night – in the brightness of his glory *shines the man who is awake.*'

——— * ———

Simone W:

'Doubt is a virtue of the intelligence, and consequently there is a doubt which is not incompatible with faith; and faith is not belief.'

And this:

'The great obstacle to the loss of personality is the feeling of guilt. *One must lose it.*'

——— * ———

Now, as I'd anticipated, the dead elms begin to distinguish themselves much more sharply from the living trees. Yet they, too, are objects of great power; very strange colours and forms.

——— * ———

Ad Majoram Dei Gloriam? I used to find the notion of *praising* God very absurd; as if God could possibly take pleasure from that kind of flattery. But I now see that this praising is not done to satisfy the vanity of some emperor in the sky, but to spread the radiance of the Spirit more widely through the world.

I wish I could believe that I am keeping this journal *Ad Majoram Dei Gloriam*, and not *Ad Majoram Gloriam* PT.

——— * ———

Another of the prerequisites to virtue – *temperance*, alas!

——— * ———

De Caussade's great message could be expressed like this: 'God sends every moment, even the worst, in order that we may live it fully and use it for our own hallowing.' I would emend this and say: 'Every moment, even the worst, should be fully lived and used for our hallowing, since God makes it possible for us to use it so.' Briefly, not 'Every moment is sent by God' but 'Every moment can be used by God'.

[181]

It isn't God who makes us feel at home in the world: it is he who makes us partial strangers here by infusing us with the light of heaven. Yet it is also true that we can use this infused light to see certain material objects as illuminations of heavenly reality.

———— * ————

Here is a passage from the *Dhammapada* which makes me acutely aware of how alien Eastern thought can be:

'For it were better for an evil man to swallow a ball of red-hot iron rather than he should eat offerings of food offered him by good people.' Weird!

———— * ————

In Simone Weil's *Notebooks* there are many excited passages about her own interpretations of various myths: I'm convinced that she was preparing to make a great book out of these notes. Yet they were written within less than a year of her virtual suicide. (Certainly a death which she *permitted herself* – with great deliberation.)

Thank God, in any case, that she left so many treasures behind: e.g. 'Sanctity is the only way out from time ... In this world we live in a mixture of time and eternity. Hell would be pure time.'

4 May

As for theology the ideas about God and Man which are gradually emerging as I keep this journal should never be clearly stated; never be formulated. They should constantly move just ahead of me as I constantly reach out and try to seize them. Much better to leave them in that elusive state. Yet because of my congenital urge to express myself (the unassuaged wound of my 'inordinate self-expression') I know that I shall eventually write out these ideas as precisely as I can. So much for the renunciation I thought I'd made when I gave up trying to write *A Marriage of Heaven and Earth*!

———— * ————

[182]

Getting up too quickly from my chair I had one of those moments of near-fainting. A trivial physical episode, but it filled me with sudden terror of the abyss: I seemed to hover on the very edge of total and everlasting annihilation.

—— * ——

Just because daffodils are more conventional objects of aesthetic respect than winter trees I find them all the more recalcitrant. I must try to look through the conventional image – until suddenly the real object appears in all its extraordinary selfhood. The beauty is shed, and without that encumbrance the object is far more clearly *and revealingly* seen than ever before.

Same with that horse in the field above Copwell. In fact he became *grotesque* as I stared him out of his beauty: but he passed through that stage too, and became the most horsey horse I've ever seen.

—— * ——

At Tymawr yesterday I felt that I was indeed in a rare state of joyful truthfulness. As it seemed to me that I could never have reached – never have been given – this blessed state unless I'd gone through that painful afternoon of revulsion, when even the smiles of the sisters seemed false and silly.

—— * ——

I've just read a life of Chesterton, and I'm amazed by the affection and respect which I feel for him. A very good and very clever man, in spite of his follies – and worse. The clear perception that the Socialist makes the mistake of always starting with legislation, instead of with himself. But Chesterton, of course, was everything that we despised when we were young, arrogant, intolerant – and ignorant.

—— * ——

Gerry had sent me a splendid pamphlet by Kenneth Leech called *Contemplation and Resistance*. This reminds me of how closely Merton associated the two; and how dangerous it is to write so slightingly about 'legislation' – which stands, in the passage above, for all forms of political action. Leech quotes from that brave and revolutionary priest, Daniel Berrigan: 'In the derangement of our culture we see people move towards contemplation in despair, even though unrecognized. They meditate as a way of becoming neutral – to put a ground between themselves and the horror around them ... We have a terrible new drug called contemplation.' Such contemplatives, he says, are cut off from 'social prophecy. They become another resource of the present culture instead of a resource against it ... Capitalist culture can make contemplation itself a commodity.'

Yes indeed: TM to pep up weary business men: Zen as a training for kamikaze pilots ... 'Prophesy' is a fine word. We must have our true and brave prophets, who will be persecuted for their denunciations. (And yet those prophets will become arid, embittered and self-righteous unless they constantly refresh themselves by prayer, silence and contemplation.)

———— * ————

Dhammapada: 'It is sweet to have friends in need; and to share enjoyment is sweet. It is sweet to have done good before death; and to surrender all pain is sweet.' Again, the deep contradiction at the heart of Buddhism: if you have friends who suffer you will and you should suffer with them. Therefore to surrender all pain is incompatible with true friendship.

Christianity, for all its past and current failings, has had to submit to much healthy criticism in the light of modern evolutionary and genetic knowledge. Perhaps the attraction of Buddhism to many Western minds is that it still exists in a state of pre-scientific confidence – and innocence. It has not had to go through the tortuous adjustments which have distracted so many modern Christians.

How, for example, would the doctrine of reincarnation stand up to the facts of evolution?

———— * ————

I am sometimes disturbed by the story of the eighteenth camel. A certain Arab died and left seventeen camels, which he bequeathed to his three sons in the following proportions: to the eldest a half; to the second a third; to the youngest a ninth. The three sons were disputing violently about the proper division of the camels when a stranger rode up to them from the desert and asked them the cause of their anger. When they had explained it to him he said: 'But this is very simple. I shall give you my camel; so now you have eighteen instead of seventeen, and the sum is easily done. The eldest will take nine, the second six and the youngest two.' When the three sons had each taken the camels allotted to him, they found that one was left over. 'And therefore,' said the stranger, 'I can now take my own camel back again, and yet leave you with no further cause for dispute.'

The bequest made sense only if the sons assumed the presence of a camel *which didn't even need to exist*. I find that the world makes sense only if we assume the existence of a loving God. But what if God were the eighteenth camel?

------ * ------

A very good Thursday in Monmouth. As I was shopping I had the strongest sense of how much we have come to belong to this beautiful and lively little town. How pleasant to walk down Monnow Street, or across Agincourt Square, saying good morning to so many acquaintances – some of the shop girls we knew eighteen years ago are now middle-aged women with almost grown-up children.

After shopping I spend about twenty minutes in the library; then ten minutes' prayer in the little Catholic church; to The Swan by half past eleven for a talk – and a Coke – with Father Philip. We talk about ourselves and our beliefs, with warmth and freedom. Then to the Punch-House at midday to meet Bill (Bayley) – and Lucy if she's off duty. Bill and I never talk about ourselves; never, at least, with the intimacy which Father P and I have so easily and naturally accepted, as if it were a gift. I discuss history and literature with Bill, and I wouldn't say that our intimacy is any less for the fact that our topics are not ostensibly intimate. So far as religion goes there is a constant pretence that I am out to convert him, and that he is deftly warding off my assaults. But we both know very well that he is quite impervious: indeed, as I've told him, what he suffers from is *too much* tolerance, good sense and general benignity. It would need more than a bow of burning gold to pierce *that* armour.

Finally Wilson and other old friends in The Beaufort, where the conversation is vigorously topical; often political; sometimes fierce. Wilson's views can be hair-raising, but nothing he says could stop us loving him. Such charm as his is always the product of real respect and affection for others.

Lately we have made a new friend in Jean Mackie; a woman who has suffered a great deal, and with wonderful fortitude. She is a believer; a rather wayward Catholic, but not at all a tepid one. An immediate sense of extraordinary closeness; and a conversation followed which would have been intolerable to Wilson, embarrassing to Bill. The bare fact of a shared faith is certainly not enough to produce this deep and immediate understanding. But it is a necessary condition for that joyful sense of being able to say the strange things which are closest to one's heart and mind. And to receive from the other person confidences to match one's own in strangeness – so that what had seemed altogether *too* strange becomes, by this sharing, quite natural and acceptable; even alight with truth.

5 May

The rich man and the needle's eye. But think of an all-too-common scene of the last two hundred years. A well-fed European or American is being pulled in a rickshaw through a Calcutta street where hundreds lie half-starving in the gutter. It is a Christian commonplace that the man in the rickshaw has far less chance of salvation than the people in the gutter. But is this really so obvious? True, the rich man is likely to have encrusted himself with greed, and with protective insensitivity to the sufferings of others. But in this case those others are in a condition of such deprivation, such continuous affliction, that the great majority can think of nothing except how to get their next crust. This enforced poverty has reduced them to the condition of starving animals; just as many concentration camp victims became as bestial as their guards.

The passing tourist, on the other hand, may be suddenly pierced by compassion: he may decide to give most of his wealth to help the starving, while – very reasonably – keeping enough to prevent himself from joining their ranks. And now, living by Western standards in very modest circumstances, he has leisure and energy left for prayer and meditation. He is free to think and to feel without his whole mental and emotional life being impoverished, perhaps poisoned, by the obsessing condition of his body.

Voluntary poverty is a royal road to the Kingdom of Heaven. Unchosen and unwanted affliction nearly always depletes and deadens the spirit as much as it lacerates the body. And so the injustice of the world is terribly compounded.

The traditional Christian device for evading this appalling fact is to say that the greatly afflicted (Lazarus) will be rewarded after death; while the unregenerate rich (Dives) will be equivalently punished. But this only replaces one injustice by another, and an even greater one. For the ordinary rich man, who has been desensitized by his wealth, and for whom, according to Jesus, salvation is virtually impossible, is to suffer eternally for an earthly incapacity which he had no more chosen than the destitute have chosen their destitution. (He may have chosen the wealth, but he never willed it to corrupt him.)

The Buddhist/Hindu device is even more brutal; for the logic of reincarnation insists that the Calcutta beggars are in that condition because their previous lives have been evil. Therefore they are not even deserving of sympathy; let alone of material help. What's more, and worse, they can escape to a higher level of existence next time only by leading 'good' lives this time. Yet – see above – to be good in these conditions – i.e. to achieve a self-sacrificing love of others – is even harder for the starving than it is for the rich man to pierce the carapace of his selfish greed.

What it amounts to is that the search for justice is hopeless, either in the Christian or in the Eastern terms of survival. The only conceivable justice would lie in the instant blessedness of *every* soul at the moment of death; for nearly everyone has suffered on earth from *some* form of stunting deprivation; of harsh conditioning against salvation. So if it is within God's power to correct this almost universal insufficiency – physical, spiritual or both – then he must, in his mercy, give in abundance what nearly all of us have so signally lacked on earth.

For the mercy of God and the justice of God are not two different, and perhaps conflicting, aspects of his nature – as some Christians have so curiously imagined. Nor is it true that because we are miserable sinners we have forfeited all claim on God's justice, and can only beg for the utterly gratuitous gift of his mercy. We are *miserable* sinners, and have earned the mercy/justice of God by the miserable deprivation imposed on us by our sinning. I've no doubt at all that he gives us his grace and merciful love, both here and hereafter, *to the very limit of his power*.

10 May

A grotesque and painful episode at BH. During communion on Sunday evening Phil (back from his Western Isle) was reading from one of the Upanishads when John (the prophet) interrupted to condemn the reading and to inform us that before the coming of Christ man had worshipped nothing but sticks and stones. When this sermon was over – for it amounted to that – Phil mildly asked whether he might go on reading. We all said yes of course, except for John; but when Phil began again John got up, left the room and left the house – for we heard the front door slam behind him. A minute or two later Michele followed him.

Most of them wanted to go on as if nothing had happened, and Phil insisted that he wasn't the least offended; that John and Michele had a perfect right to do their own thing ... But

S and I were furious, and made no attempt to hide it. So, for the moment, was Simon. We pointed out that the whole generous and receptive spirit of our community had been harshly rejected by John's action – and by poor Michele's almost zombie-like obedience to her master's implied command. (Michele! One of the most gentle and loving spirits among us!)

Kerry had been upstairs suffering from a headache which may well have been diplomatic: he surely foresaw that something of this kind was bound to happen. But it seems that he is scarcely less under the spell of this misguided bigot than Michele. S and I are worried about what he may do to our two friends; and worried, too, by his capacity to poison the whole atmosphere of BH during its last few months. (We have asked them to be ready to leave by early September.)

This young man is utterly convinced of his inspired fitness to 'lead others to Christ'. He has no need, he tells us, to learn anything else from anyone, for the word of Christ is there for all to read and the spirit of Christ is within him, guiding him in all he does and all he says.

I suggested that his best course of action, after receiving that illumination in Africa, would have been to seek out a wise spiritual director and submit himself to *that* kind of guidance. He might have been shown that the light he had seen included the ancient message of humility; the need for a long period of silence in 'the wilderness'; perhaps for study; certainly for a deep chastening of the soul.

But the prophet *knows*. And just as the words that Phil was reading on Sunday were words of the devil so also was this attempt of mine to turn him aside from his holy path. His eyes cried 'Get thee behind me, Satan!' in our kitchen today, even if his words were a little less outspoken.

These thoughts tormented me in bed last night, especially as I knew that I was falling into a pit of hatred for this intruder. Mixed with indignation at so much spiritual pride was a jealous rage at his invasion of *our* Barn House; his taking possession of *our* good friends and comrades; his brutish disturbance of *our* community when we'd been hoping that it would come peacefully, even lovingly, to a close.

This unholy anger got mixed up in my restless mind with an equally unholy anxiety about the sale of our thirteen acres at St Briavels. Will we get *enough*? And will we get it before it becomes too late to let the fields for this year's grazing? Anger, greed and fear – a hideous trio of tormenting demons.

—— * ——

For several years I've been corresponding with Ann Horne, and her letters have always been filled with the warmest gratitude for my 'kindness'. In her last letter she even called me her 'angelic helper'. 'What a very nice person she must be,' said S when I showed her the letter; and I realized, with a fearful jolt, that I've given very little real thought to what this unmet sufferer is *like*. More than anything else she has been the pleasingly grateful recipient of my shrewd but abundant goodness of heart.

Real dismay that I could have been so blindly self-centred for so many years. And deep shame towards Ann Horne, who has been deceived, for all those years, into thinking the letters she was getting sprang only from my overflowing benevolence. Then gratitude to God for at last succeeding in showing me the wretched truth of the whole affair. (No doubt he's been trying to show me this ever since the correspondence began, but he couldn't pierce the horny skin of my self-approbation until he was able to speak through the mouth of my wife.)

—— * ——

I think I had a momentary glimpse last night of what real passivity and openness might mean. To silence the mind is not enough: it has to be a *listening* silence. Very hard to get there: harder still to stay there.

—— * ——

A new image of my latent depression. It seems like an animal lying curled-up inside me – on the left-hand side. Most of the time he's asleep, but sometimes he shudders and stirs in his sleep; sometimes he quakes all over, the fur rising on his back; sometimes he even opens his mouth wide in a huge snarling yawn ...

———— * ————

When Anne was here I told her that she, Phine (Josephine) and Bun (Lawrence) were the only people in the world – apart from S – with whom I feel justified in trying to share my faith. My first wife; my eldest daughter and my surviving brother. This is not only because I love them, but also because I detect in all three a possible openness to the grace of God. All three, in fact, could easily become more open than I have ever been.

But even here the greatest tact is needed. The word 'proselytize' has fully earned its ugly sound and reputation.

18 May

A splendid weekend visit from Robert and Cynthia (Kee). One of the many good turns which such old friends do for me is to restore me to that clown's role which this seclusion has almost dried out of me. (S and I sometimes clown together; but we both need the stimulus of such friends as these to give of our best. For they carry us back to so many jolly, and funny, times long ago.)

So why are these visits so rare?

Because the excitement leaves us both in a depleted state; or worse. Though I seldom get drunk on such occasions I drink a lot, and almost all day long: then find it hard to stop when the dear, drink-inciting guests are gone. The eventual withdrawal, after two or three days, is almost always followed by depression in some form or other; expense of spirit in a waste of shame ...

And S is sometimes disorientated, in her different way, as

a direct result of these rare treats. So the sad fact of the matter is that we love our friends and long to see them, but seldom invite them to our house. I pray that this wretched condition won't last for the rest of our lives.

———— * ————

Suddenly, listening to the evening news, the fact impinged on me that *The Observer* is in serious danger of folding up. Luckily I had just completed an hour of fairly potent meditation; so I was able to take this fearful threat without flinching. 'Be here now.' 'Take no heed of the morrow.' 'The peace of God.'

Fine! But what about sparing a few thoughts for all those others who would lose their jobs, and whose position would be far worse than ours. (So many traps on this journey: one might suspect that it had been deliberately planned as an obstacle course.)

19 May

Still, at least the fortitude was reinforced by reading the right book in bed last night (*He Leadeth Me*). It is the harrowing but inspiring (in-spiriting) account of a Polish-American priest's five years in the Lubianka; eighteen in arctic Siberia. He not only endured these hells; he never lost his love of God and man.

Perhaps it is part of *our* proper humility to recognize that we are not called to such heroic enterprises; that we are incorrigibly of the bourgeoisie; soft, domesticated, easy-living creatures. It seems that my own life and the life of that priest are on two quite different scales; mine a tiny model of his, in which to accept the prospect of losing my job with reasonable fortitude is the 'equivalent' of his refusal to abjure saying mass for his fellow-prisoners even under the threat of many years in solitary confinement.

A fortnight ago today I was working in the garden, under a benignant sun, when Laura came out of the house to say that Pinkie wanted me on the telephone. I went cheerfully indoors, hoping that this old and beloved friend might be suggesting herself and Martyn* for a visit. I can't now remember the words she used; only the horror in her quiet voice when she told me that Ben has died.

Darkness falls from the air. This is not a 'felicitous' quotation but a very accurate description of what it felt like. Coldness as well as darkness. Wild, uncontrollable sobbing as I tried to make sense of what Pinkie had told me. For a strong element in my reaction was the sense of Ben's *unsuitability* to this deep, grand business of mortality – crashing down, as it happened, from his great height, on the platform at Leicester Square, after a dinner at the Beefsteak Club.

The dear, long, clerical face, and the solemn voice which I knew so well that I perfected my imitation of it more than thirty years ago. (We first met at Oxford, in 1935; suddenly became close friends during the summer of 1939, setting out for debutante balls together from the modesty of our neighbouring Bloomsbury rooms.)

What will they make of him at Heaven's Gate: or he of them? Ben, for whom any notion of the spirit was not just alien but totally incomprehensible; never for a moment attracting even his hostile attention.

S and I try to console ourselves by thanking God for that last visit, when everything was again as it had always been until three years ago. But his death will be even more terrible for Anne, Pinkie and his other London friends, who saw him so constantly and valued his constant company so much.

We knew, of course, that he'd had a clot on his leg for the last eighteen months; but none of us had fully faced the

---

* Martyn and Pinkie Beckett – old and close friends.

implications. A nagging worry; and efforts to make him cut down his cigarettes ... But how he hated any sort of fuss about his health! How comically, almost ludicrously, he could remain unaware of his own illnesses, until someone else observed them and sometimes compelled him into bed, or to the doctor.

In a nightclub, just before the war, I told him that he had become my elder brother, a substitute for Tony who had died in the spring of that year. We were as different as two upper-middle-class, twentieth-century English intellectuals could well be, yet each of us knew that the other supplied exactly what he himself most lacked.

13 June

Ben's death rises to the surface again: the loss of him ... visits to London and never again to stay at Holland Park; never again to see him come stooping into Anne's drawing room, his solemn face aglow, for those who could read it, with the expectation of enjoyment ...

——— * ———

'It is of the greatest importance to understand that religious truth is not a special kind of truth, nor religious experience a queer, unnatural kind of experience belonging to some strange and other world. Religious experience is normal experience and we have religious experience every day, whether or not we recognize it as such. Religious truth is normal experience understood at full depth: what makes truth religious is not that it relates to some abnormal field of thought and feeling but that it goes to the roots of the experience which it interprets' (Professor Jeffreys ?).

This is a splendid passage; as apt to my own condition as any that I've written down in this journal. It helps to stop me bothering about the total absence, in my own life, of any special intimations or mystical raptures.

But it isn't the whole truth, of course, for there *are* such intimations and such raptures: there *have* been saints in ecstasy and curious 'signs'.

———— * ————

After a long DA expedition to King's Lynn last month, which included our first visit to Peterborough Cathedral, we met Goronwy Rees at a friend and neighbour's house. As one of the editors of *Encounter* he suggested that I should write something for their 25th anniversary number.

My impulse nowadays is always to refuse; a legacy of the depression years when every extra task seemed utterly beyond me. But my botched attempt at *A Marriage of Heaven and Earth* has left me with a strong sense of unfinished business; so I decided to see whether I could pack the central material of that mess into an article short enough for *Encounter* to print. The result, after much hard work, has been better than I'd expected.

EVENSONG AT PETERBOROUGH

On one of the wettest and foggiest days of early May my wife and I were driving from our house in the Wye valley to the house of a friend near King's Lynn. Neither of us had ever seen Peterborough Cathedral, so we started early enough to include it in our journey. We knew most of that cross-country route very well: – the road along the suddenly-narrowing Severn between Lydney and Minsterworth; the ring-road round Gloucester; the sharp rise into the Cotswolds; the gentle countryside of Oxfordshire and Buckinghamshire, ending so abruptly in the slashed soil, bulldozers and new urbanization of Milton Keynes. But this time we were travelling further north than usual, to skirt Northampton and Wellingborough; and we had just got a faint whiff of the fens when we were grabbed, so it seemed, by a great new highway which thrust us through the scattered industry, suburbs and railway-yards of Peterborough.

We got no more than a glimpse of the old inner city before we saw the long, low-slung cathedral in front of us and an open gate into the close. There is something in every cathedral to take the breath away, and at Peterborough this comes as soon as you set eyes on the amazing west front with its three huge and equal portals, early gothic in their perfect simplicity, and only slightly marred by a fussy little fifteenth-century porch stuck on to the base of the central arch. A notice on the porch-door told us that Evensong had already begun and would we please sit down until it was over. If we wished to join the service we could take our seats in the choir.

But to do this would have meant a rather ostentatious walk over the last, and pewless, section of the nave; so we compromised by sitting down on the foremost nave pew but one. The choir was half-way through a psalm as we sat down, the choirmaster, hunched at the western end of the first decani stall, conducting with a passionate, almost agitated fervour. Between this surpliced conductor and ourselves a congregation of some twenty or thirty faced each other in the remaining stalls of the choir, and each row was neatly terminated by two clerics in full canonicals – perhaps the dean and three of his canons.

Choir, congregation and priests seemed to be islanded there, between the nave to the west, the aisles to north and south, and an eastern space of crossing, chancel and apse which we had not yet been able to see but which seemed to stretch almost as far beyond the celebration as the splendid late Norman nave was stretching away behind our backs. As for us, although we were familiar with Anglican liturgies and have often attended Evensong in the chapel of a little convent across the valley from our house, it was impossible to feel that we were fully a part of those proceedings in the unknown cathedral.

This was not only due to our physical separation from the service, but also, I think, because a strange air of professionalism and remoteness enveloped those priests and choristers as they went so gracefully through the prescribed devotions for AD Saturday, 6 May 1978. Both the real professionals and the congregation seemed like figures on a stage, so isolated were they from the rest of the cathedral, so brightly lit in the surrounding gloom.

A long lesson from *Judges* was read by a priest on the decani side: we were reminded of how Gideon had been called by the angel to destroy the altar of Baal before attacking the hosts of Midian. After this an old hymn was sung, but to a difficult modern setting which needed even more passionate gestures from the choirmaster. A succession of prayers was then read aloud by a second priest, and when these were finished another of the celebrants read a lesson from the Epistle to the Hebrews.

The service came to an end with the *Nunc dimittis* and the *Creed*. Then the choir filed westward towards us, smallest choristers in the lead, then wheeled with excellent precision to their right and disappeared up the north aisle and into the transept. The priests followed them and finally the congregation began to break up with that air of informality too suddenly returning which always gives a certain awkwardness to the ending of a religious function.

So we also got up from our places, to make our circumambulation of the cathedral, guide-book in hand, much admiring, as we were told to do, 'the fifteenth-century retro-quire which envelops the apse in its lower stories'. We walked through the west porch again and found ourselves back in the quietly-undistinguished close. We drove out of that drizzling city and lost ourselves for many minutes on the great new ring-road before we found our way out at last towards Wisbech and the east.

———— * ————

By now this episode has compelled my imagination many days, and driven my mind in several different directions. Sometimes, when I think of Peterborough, the whole of that Evensong seems almost as unreal, even uncanny, as the famous eighteenth-century Versailles ball which those two English ladies claimed to have watched some eighty years ago. Entering a cathedral is often followed by at least a hesitant translation through time, and this little-remembered drama of traditional Evensong sometimes seems as remote in time from the England we had been passing through as it had immediately seemed remote in space. Yet there were elements in the celebration itself which showed very clearly that it belonged to our own age: a modern translation of the Bible had been used: that hymn had been sung in a thoroughly modern manner: there had been a merciful absence of any parsonical droning.

But the dominant impression which remains is of a gracious, holy but esoteric ceremony being performed in the choir at Peterborough, massively isolated from the modern city outside by the wider spaces of the cathedral; by the close; by the little market town which had already been long surrounded by an outer ring of railway-works and suburbs, and which was now being further enveloped by a new industrial sprawl.

And yet we had not been only spectators of that deft performance; so far as each of us had found it possible we had also been participants. And if we had arrived five minutes earlier we would certainly have accepted the invitation to take two of those vacant places in the choir stalls. For certainly we both belonged – wholly in spirit and largely in faith – with what was being celebrated in Peterborough Cathedral on that Saturday afternoon at the tail-end of the football season. And certainly we were saddened by the weird isolation of that Evensong: and certainly we were well aware of how strenuously the Churches have been trying to break through that isolation during the last fifty years.

But I doubt whether even the most fervent modernizer could believe that if only the choir had been singing rock-and-roll, if only the lessons had proclaimed God the True Integration of Self, then the whole nave would have been filled with cheerful and loud-voiced participants, greatly to the detriment of the takings that afternoon by Peterborough United Football Club. It is absurd to pretend any longer that a jazzed-up liturgy and a castrated faith will bring the multitude flocking back into our cathedrals and our parish churches.

And yet there seemed to be something serenely *resigned* about that celebration; as if to say, we've done our best to bring them in, but since they won't come at any price let's get back to doing it just the way *we* like. This drama is now being performed for the sake of the cast alone, and if the auditorium is empty all we can do is to keep the old play going in the hope that it may one day attract an audience again.

Perhaps this seems the only possible attitude for the Churches to adopt in an age when ninety per cent even of that minority who ever enter a cathedral do so only in order to admire the fifteenth-century retro-quire. 'Damn!' they mutter as they come through the great west door. 'There seems to be some sort of service going on. We'd better go out and have some tea and come back later.' But surely every practising member of a Christian church must hope that cathedral naves will be filled again for other ceremonies than a performance of *The Messiah* or Verdi's *Requiem*. So I began to ask myself again whether certain hesitant divinations of my own might, after all, make some small contribution to the rebirth of Christianity in England. What follows is the (almost desperate) compression of a much longer work called *A Marriage of Heaven and Earth* which I abandoned about six months ago.

———— * ————

1) The full array of orthodox Christianity has been a splendid and inspiriting body of doctrine. And if this faith is now dying to be born again the emergent phoenix must shine at least as brightly and transformingly as the old one used to do.

'Glory to glory, as by the spirit of the Lord.'

2) And like every new Christian exploration this one must turn back yet again to the New Testament and find in that undimmed constellation yet a new pattern of signs and proclamations.

3) Reading those too-familiar books again I have begun to think that I see something hinted at there, and nearly spoken aloud, which may have been missed by other readers, and which might, by one of those slight shifts of vision, reilluminate the word and give a new Christian message to our time.

4) The earliest recorded Israelites had understood God in the image of their Most Admired Man. At that time this meant any great king or emperor who had carved out a great dominion for himself; who ruled it with beneficence towards those who humbled themselves before him, but with terrible anger against all who resisted or denied him.

5) But a new kind of God had been gradually softening the harsh lines of the old one; and what Jesus nearly did, by his recorded words, his life and death, was to proclaim this new vision of God as a total transcendence of Jahweh, the tribal tyrant of Israel.

6) Yet what was left to the world, according to the traditional interpretation of the New Testament, is like a sublime statue half-emerging from a great block of rough-hewn granite. Because Jesus was himself a believing Jew; because he suffered from an anger which could distort his marvellous vision; perhaps because his words were misunderstood even by his closest disciples, the Christian Churches inherited a concept of God which is centaur-like in its weird inconsonance.*

7) The traditional God of Christianity has been that same old Emperor-Creator, but one who also loves his creature-

* All this may seem a blasphemous impertinence; but there is an old image of the pygmy who sits on a giant's shoulders and sees a few yards more of the great landscape discovered by the giant's mighty vision.

subjects as a father loves his children. Thus the Problem of Evil has bedevilled the Christian faith at least since the age of Augustine and Pelagius. This ancient conundrum of a God who is both all-powerful and all-loving has become even more acute both as men have learned more about the physical universe and also as they have come to regard cruelty as the worst of all human – and *a fortiori* of divine – abominations.

8) We have been told that an all-powerful, all-loving Creator-God has made a world of earthquakes and meningitis; of Belsen and Hiroshima; – a world which has reached its present state after the brutal, billion-year tale of the fittest so savagely surviving.

9) Almost every modern theologian has tried to solve this problem; but it can never be solved until one of the contradictory terms is removed. What was so nearly revealed in the New Testament, what can be seen there now in brilliant but elusive outline, is *a God who does not possess two distinct attributes called 'power' and 'love', but a God whose power lies only and wholly in his love.*

10) A believable God must always be an extrapolation from the most admired of men, for we see such men as true manifestations of God. In our own time all Christians, and all those non-believers who still live in the moral ambiance of Christianity, are agreed that Jesus is more to be admired than Augustus; St Francis than Genghiz Khan; the Curé d'Ars than Napoleon. Yet most Christians still try to worship a God who is half Genghiz Khan and half St Francis.

11) And even if the Jesus of the New Testament is not a sinless man – his terrible rages against all who would not accept him are all-too-human – the essential message of his words, his life and his death is that love triumphs not only over all physical power but even over death itself. (We have tended to treat St Paul's great passage in his First Letter to the Corinthians as the natural hyperbole

[201]

of a poet. But it is literally true, even in this world, that love is the only enduring power, since it is the only power which is not ultimately self-defeating.)

12) All Christians believe that God was made manifest in Jesus Christ: many Christians still believe that God *was* Jesus Christ. But Jesus not only exercised no physical or political power; he treated the offer of such power as a temptation by the devil. Can anyone believe that the Father revels in what the Son so scornfully rejected?

13) Every theology is a mythology and must have new stories to tell.

14) This story begins in that total ignorance of all origins which most physicists and astronomers now confess to. And the story itself is taken up where the scientists first begin to make persuasive guesses. The Earth is thrown off the sun: it cools: life begins in the ocean: life evolves on land and culminates – so far – in man.

15) But those who believe that this is a summary of the *whole* story are surely confronted by the exact converse of the problem which has tormented so many orthodox believers for so many centuries. Rationalists, materialists and atheists have never yet fully faced the *Problem of Good*.

16) If man had been the product of natural evolution alone he would indeed be a Naked Ape: all his superb intelligence would be directed only to the survival of his own species in a state of maximum pleasure and minimum pain. He would differ from the other animals *only* by the higher degree of his intelligence.

17) The best we could ever expect would be a society conforming to some old blueprint drawn up by Sidney and Beatrice Webb – a community organized with the maximum intelligence to provide the greatest possible physical and mental satisfaction for all its members.

18) There would be no art in such a society, for art always implies a dissatisfaction with given reality. There would

be no religion, for religion is always the yearning for an unachieved condition – of love, of wisdom, of illumination. Men and women would be united by bonds of enlightened self-interest, but there would be no love between them: for love leads to the pains of separation; to the ultimate anguish of bereavement.

19) Why, then, has such a 'utopia' never been achieved? Why would most human beings reject it with horror if it were offered them? Why do men hunger so irrepressibly for love, for beauty, for truth? At least *for struggle*? Why does the totally supererogatory goodness of Jesus or St Francis continue to captivate the imagination even of those who cannot believe in the God of Jesus and St Francis? *Where* did Jesus and the saints find that sublime love which would not only be superfluous in a Naked Ape but deeply destructive of his super-simian contentment?

20) 'Naturalistic' interpretations of Jesus or St Francis, of St John of the Cross or St Teresa do not seem blasphemous or even disrespectful. Such accounts of these figures never get near the reality of those extraordinary lives; they seem grotesque in their irrelevance. It is as if someone had given an account of a great picture by a careful description of all its shapes and colours.

21) So this theological story tells of something outside our universe, and of a different kind from it, which is constantly pressing in upon our domain of the senses and trying to introduce the freedom of the spirit into an order of rigorous material necessity.

22) When we think of this 'something other' as a force, a state or a domain we call it Heaven: when we think of it as a person we call it God. And just as physicists treat light either as waves or particles according to context, so we talk either of God or of Heaven as it suits us. Yet we are *always* fully aware that whatever words we use will be no better than pointing fingers; gestures of dumb joy; grimaces of bewildered love.

23) One model might be a black and hollow globe surrounded by radiant light: whenever the smallest chink appears in the surface of our globe the light *will* enter, of its very nature. Or we may think of a wise and loving father or mother who is constantly offering strange and inestimable gifts to sons and daughters who seldom even hear the parental voice, and still more rarely open their hearts and minds to receive what is being offered.

24) The present story tells us that as evolution proceeds, on this or any other planet, so God enters the expanding minds of thinking beings as best he can. (He may have other ways of entering our universe and influencing events here, but the only way we can hope to understand is the way he makes into our own minds.)

25) These divine gifts are prodigious and invaluable, for all of them are of heavenly origin and could not have been the products of any earthly process. The greatest gift is the gift of religious understanding, for this can enable us to receive as much of Heaven's Light as we are ever able to receive. Other gifts are inner freedom (for the natural world knows nothing but necessity); the knowledge of good and evil (for the natural world knows nothing but advantage and disadvantage); art; love; a joyful perception of beauty in the uncreated world around us; ardour for truth; redeeming pain ... When we see, or feel, these gifts in action surely they seem like mysterious colonists from some more splendid realm of being than our own?*

26) So the supreme function of men and women is to receive God's gifts, the light of Heaven, as fully as they can. Some people are congenitally better attuned to the will of God, more permeable to Heaven's light; but all of us can work continually to make ourselves more receptive – by encouraging whatever we can find in ourselves of faith and hope; by prayer and meditation; by reading; by self-

* Thus God is indeed the creator *of man*, in the sense that he has given man everything which is of the least value in him, and everything which enables him to value truly.

attrition; by alert attention to even the most familiar and everyday experiences. But, above all, by practising the art of love. 'I am come that ye might have life and that ye might have it more abundantly.'

27) If it is hard to reach this God it is not because he coyly, or pedagogically, withdraws himself from us, but because it is as hard for him to penetrate our world as it is for us to receive the radiance of his love. For most of us God is an endless journey.

28) The tragedy of this life is in no way diminished by discovering a God of Pure Love, but the tragedy is not due to God's obscure purposes in tormenting us but to the hard fact that we are truly the creature-victims of a world ruled by unfeeling necessity. Yet the tragedy is now truly redeemable by the accessibility of God's *unequivocal* love.

29) Stupidity, blindness, folly and wickedness form a thick impasto around us through which God can scarcely reach us, even though his effort to do so is never relaxed. (This is clearly a God to whom the phrase 'Forgive us our sins' cannot be addressed with any meaning whatever! Our sins are forgiven as soon as they are committed; *before* they are committed. The problem for us is to penetrate our carapace of sinful egotism and recognize God's love as something which is always there; which can never be withdrawn.)

30) Many modern theologians have mocked the idea of 'a God out there', and many of them have ended up with the man-centred parochialism of suggesting that 'God' is simply another term for 'our deepest concern' or 'the depth of our being'.

31) But the present story, while reluctant to use such huge and hollow words as 'infinite' and 'eternal', records that God/Heaven was there long before the arrival of man on Earth, and will be there long after man's departure. (God may be latent within us all, but he can be brought into loving activity only by our worship of a God whose existence is in no way dependent on our own.)

32) But it seems futile to speculate about the intrinsic nature of God, and it was the tormented efforts of early theologians to do this which led them to create their forbidding structures of creed, dogma and anathema. New Testament Christianity scarcely concerns itself at all with the inner nature of God and Heaven. The gospels, the Acts and most of the epistles, Pauline or otherwise, are intensely concerned with the mystery of God's dealings with man as revealed by the recorded words, life, death and resurrection of Jesus Christ.

33) The first two supplications of the supreme Christian prayer contain the heart of the whole proclamation. 'Thy kingdom come. Thy will be done in earth as it is in heaven.' For the kingdom is *not yet* come; God's will is *not yet* done on earth.

34) Indeed if we now read the New Testament in the light of the present story it is extraordinary how little needs to be surrendered; or even reinterpreted. And there are some great utterances which make *more* sense in the light of a God truly revealed by the life of Jesus; truly almighty in love alone. 'My grace is sufficient for you: my power is made perfect in weakness.' (If God were really a wielder of mighty physical power surely he would choose for his most favoured children those who most resemble him: not the weak, the poor and the humble but the great kings of the earth. But being himself a persistent suppliant on earth it is to the weak, the humble and the supplicating that he finds it easiest to come.)

35) The great Heaven-sent utterances of the New Testament surely sound all the louder and clearer once we have banished that Omnipotent Creator and Omniscient Predestinator. 'Abide in me and I in you.' 'Perfect love casteth out fear.' 'The truth shall make you free.' 'Except a man be born again he cannot see the Kingdom of God.' 'Rise, thou that sleepeth, and arise from the dead; and Christ shall enlighten thee.' 'The words I speak unto you, they

are spirit and they are life.' 'God is a spirit, and those that would come to him must come in spirit and in truth.' 'Where the spirit of the Lord is, there is liberty.' 'I am the Way, the Truth and the Life.' 'Seek and ye shall find.' 'Peace I leave with you, my peace I give unto you: not as the world giveth give I unto you.'

Under a new proclamation of God Almighty in Love Alone there would not have to be any new and outlandish words at Evensong, in Peterborough Cathedral. Not that a merely emended liturgy would bring the football fans crowding into the cathedral on a Saturday afternoon. But as I listened to the beautiful singing of the choir there a month ago I already felt the presence of that true Christian God among us; and I know very well that many of the celebrants felt his presence far more strongly than I have ever been able to do.

But how can one deny that the proclamation was muffled on that occasion, and not only by the bewildering intrusion of Gideon and his god of tribal vengeance? For how can we ever call clearly, out of our affliction, for the loving help of a God who is himself responsible for our affliction? Creatures of earth and necessity, sharing the bitterness of that condition, how much more clearly and truly we could sing to God if we knew him to be as urgently concerned to give us his unconditional love as we are to receive it. A song of true revival and of faith reborn in new simplicity might, after all, be heard beyond the cathedral walls, beyond the gates of the close, and even as far as the factories and the railway-yards. 'From glory to glory, as by the Spirit of the Lord.'

18 June

Laura finally left us yesterday to establish herself with Paul in Gloucester. Sorrow at her going, and some fears for how she will manage; but she seems to be gaining in strength every month.

And now we are alone together at last, an establishment of two for the first time since the birth of Jason in 1953. And how will *we* manage on our own?

———— * ————

My new device, when I find myself falling into some shameful fatuity of the mind, is to cry out 'Help!' – aloud or silently. This is partly a comic and deflating shout of dismay, but also a real cry to God to 'cleanse the thoughts of our hearts by the inspiration of thy holy spirit'.

———— * ————

'The deeper that sorrow carves into your being the more joy you can contain' (Kalil Gibran). Yes, but what if those caverns were deeply dug but no joy ever came? Then you must live till you die in Kierkegaard's *expectation* of faith. An aching hollow.

Ben's perpetual absence. So he is not to be with us, after all, during the last years. (I wish I could believe that he is now perusing possible Caravaggios in some celestial but dustily unexplored country house.)

———— * ————

Those Buddhists from Kent – Stephen, Christopher, Tina – have been running a two-week retreat in the Polish Boy Scout hostel at the very bottom of our hill. (In fact, though Stephen and Christopher were both monks in Thailand and India for six years, their community is not committed to any faith.)

I walked down several times to join their meditations. We usually sat scattered over the floor of the largest room (ferocious Polish symbols of war on the wall in front of us); sometimes we walked very, very slowly round a rectangle of rough grass; sometimes we stood quite still in the dappled light with blankets over our shoulders and eyes closed or gazing across meadows at the river.

I liked the people very much, and the whole atmosphere of

hard-won purity, austerity and discipline – but without a trace of puritanical repression. The day always ended with a talk – good, reasonable advice about the true value of our life on earth – and the talks always ended with the words, 'May there be love and clarity among us. May there be clarity and understanding in the world ...'

I felt, as I told Tina, that all this was like a marvellous preparation for something else: something richer and more committed. 'We don't want concepts to get in the way,' she said. But I need a few concepts; could never remain long in this cool antechamber with its bare walls and mild, sensible words.

One day I was down there from 2 till 9. A near-panic at the start, and such exhaustion at the end that I could hardly stagger up the hill again. But I felt a certain satisfaction in this achievement: inconceivable that in the old days I could have done even one hour of silent meditation; let alone seven hours – with a few pauses.

———— * ————

Anne came for the weekend, and the three of us talked with sad love about Ben. She also spoke very lovingly to S, whose spirits have again been low. How different they are, my first and my second wife, but what they have in common is a certain stoical strength, and a capacity to give a great deal without depleting themselves. (When I'm obliged to give I seem to be sucked dry in no time; I wilt like a flower which has had all its sap drained out.)

Oh Lord, how can I have love unless I have peace; how can I have peace unless I have strength and courage!

Walking through the wood to BH today, sometimes at a Buddhist pace, the trees were sparkling with sun and breeze. But I was in that all-too-usual state of self-distrust, fear, anxiety, dryness ... I prayed as best I could, but it wasn't until I'd done some hard digging in the garden that the bleak mood lifted.

The True Wilderness. We gave up reading de Caussade in the end, because of his ever-repeated theme that all that happens must be good, being willed by God. This seems as use-

less as Leibnitz's Best of All Possible Worlds, which Voltaire
played such havoc with. I will not regard Ben's death as in
any sense a blessing.

———— * ————

Great gusts of quenching rain at last on the parched garden.
I cannot thank God for this (unless I curse him for droughts
and earthquakes), but I can thank him for the delight I took
in it, dancing naked on the brown lawn and letting my cupped
hands fill with water.

27 June

The well-ordered day. How I love it and need it still.

But when R, of whom I'm very fond, appeared unexpectedly
on Saturday evening and set his plump form down on the sofa
between me and any chance of escape to my room, I was
suddenly back in the worst of the old days. I felt hemmed in;
speechless with embarrassment ... finally rigid with anxiety and
resentment.

Made up for this a little on Sunday when Dave and Michele
appeared, and I did succeed in praying my way to a peaceful
acceptance of their presence. At last I was even able to enjoy
it.

———— * ————

We took the caravan to the Wylie valley for two beautiful
days. Many memories of Wilton in 1941, when I was an intelligence officer at Southern Command. The bungalow in the
village where Anne and I first set up house together. The
double cube room where I used to lie in bed on my duty nights,
a telephone beside me and a quarter-bottle of rum under the
bed clothes; ready, in principle, for the first news of a German
landing on the South Coast. And those smooth chalk streams
which I used to fish on late summer evenings.

As for the house itself, which I scarcely noticed during the
six months I worked there, I felt my usual flicker of resentment
against all stately homes. But I knew it was absurd to let social

disapproval spoil my pleasure; and the pleasure was great as we walked through the classical gardens and past the Palladian bridge, where I once caught a two-pound trout.

In Salisbury Cathedral a voice suddenly blared out at us from a dozen loudspeakers, welcoming us as visitors but shouting at us to remember that 'THIS IS A HOUSE OF GOD – AND NOW – OUR FATHER WHO ART IN HEAVEN ...' So we all stood about in the nave, aisles and transepts, mumbling the Lord's Prayer a word or two behind our masterful clerical cheerleader and feeling, at least in the case of S and me, not only embarrassed but resentful.

This episode was made all the more absurd by the presence among us of several groups of Arab and Japanese tourists.

They would say, of course, that our great cathedrals mustn't be turned into mere museums, despite the bookshops and canteens in the cloisters; the canons offering themselves as guides ... But better, surely, to be frankly a museum between services than this bullying pretence to be a genuine house of prayer.

———— * ————

Ann Horne, my delightful correspondent from Beaconsfield, reminds me that we did indeed meet once. She it was who lent her London flat for the Romillys' farewell party when they left for America in 1939: she is Decca's* first cousin and childhood best friend. 'All I actually remember is you, thin, dark and furious, standing at the top of the stairs and shouting four-letter words.' Then she adds, in sweet mitigation: 'Not, after all, so desperately unreasonable, *and* forty years ago.'

But since reading her letter I've been mildly haunted by the vision of this drunken maniac on the stairs – particularly as drink nearly always makes me boringly silly rather than savage and alarming. What was in the mind of that young man? Who *was* he? Did he have more self-assurance, in his lunatic bad behaviour, than I have now in my painful struggle to undo the harm he did me; the frightful legacy he left me? Yet he

* Jessica Mitford – old and close friend.

was never consciously of the devil's party; always admired the good from a distance: and even made sporadic attempts to reach it.

28 June

Reading *Witness*, John Bennett's extraordinary autobiography.

The whole Gurdjieff-Ouspensky business fills me with sharply divided feelings. Those frightful masters with their brutal and imperious arrogance; their childish feuds; their mumbo jumbo! Yet Gurdjieff, at least, must have been a man of amazing mental and spiritual power. A monster, without a doubt, but also a true master who really helped others to find whatever deep truths they were capable of learning.

The mumbo jumbo makes me shudder, though. 'There are Seven Primary Lights and each of these is accompanied by its Dark Companion, and each pair breeds seven angel-attendants ...' Was it I who coined that phrase 'the misplaced concrete'?

But who could fail to be impressed by Bennett's personal story: forty years of indefatigable search, and nearly always in the wilderness; then, near the end of his life, the terrible, yet joyful, recognition that nearly all that time and energy had been wasted because of his own stultifying faults of character and temperament. There remains something crazy about him, which may be one of the marks of a true master. For I feel sure that he *was* a master in the end; and a humble one too, unlike his two great *monstres sacrés*.

Here is a *hadith* – whatever that may be – which Bennett quotes in *Intimations*: 'God says, whoever comes one step towards me, to him I come ten steps.' I believe this with all my mind and soul; but how desperately hard it is to take that single step.

——— * ———

'Plough the soil as one ploughs the earth to prepare it for the seed. Labour the soil of oneself' (Simone Weil).

Yesterday my worst depression for more than a year. Stirrings at lunchtime – always the worst of the day – carefully kept in order as we drove to Gloucester. But seeing Emily at Coney Hill, among those wrecks of old men and women, almost made me break down then and there: not at all the place for such a display. 'Who are these?' asked the black staff nurse. 'These are my old master and mistress,' said Em, proudly. 'Your *friends*, Em!' I said, knowing that this had to be said, but hearing the dreadful hollowness of those words. 'One of the family,' we used to say: and so did she. But also our hard-working paid servant: at the going rate.

By the time we got home I was weighed down by that heavy lassitude, that aching exhaustion which I used to know so well. I tried to meditate; but the effort was too great. I tried to pray, but all I could say was 'Lord, have mercy, Lord have mercy, lord have mercy, lord have mercy ...'

Because I left off my anti-depressant pills? Perhaps it's a foolish kind of pride to hate that dependence so much. Perhaps God also works through Ludomil. He certainly works through my wife, whose hand in mine is the only effective anti-depressant that I know.

———— * ————

I was thinking of Ben, and thinking it very odd that he had devoted most of his life to the study of holy pictures without having any notion of what the word 'holy' means. But then I saw the answer to this. For holy pictures are not pictures of certain unique religious events. They are pictures of peculiar depth because of their peculiar universality: a mother and child; a man in anguish; a mother lamenting over her dead son ... (When the iconography of the Old Masters became highly particularized – by the Mannerists – decadence had destroyed the earlier vision. We don't want the Virgin's face to be interestingly special, or the announcing angel to amaze us by the shape and colour of his wings.)

From *Observer* review of *The Dying Gaul and Other Writings* by David Jones (Faber & Faber, London).

I think David Jones was as true a prophet as Blake, but I think his major works, like Blake's prophetic books, were noble and fascinating failures. Jones writes here that '. . . in the case of written poetry, if the allusions are outside the comprehension of the reader or listener, clearly a sense of what is said is immeasurably blunted'. Blake blunted the comprehension of his readers by inventing a private mythology: Jones did so almost as effectively by the obscurity, and even quaintness, of his references. He was one of those modern writers who found it necessary to annotate his poetry, after the bad example of Eliot in *The Waste Land*.

The danger of Jones's moral, religious and artistic position was that he could too easily become idiosyncratic; at his worst he could be maddeningly puckish and fey.

But this very interesting collection of essays will surely show anyone who has never read David Jones that this was a major prophet of our time; one who recognized that small is beautiful long before it was being more generally said; but above all one who was an almost perfect example of the true conservative. Of course he hated and despised the whole great commercial and industrial complex which our own Conservative Party so ably represents; of course he recognized that there are many true modern values which most earlier periods have grossly disregarded. But he wanted the present to be a true continuation of the past – not a constant series of brutal and violent rejections. If he had lived to hear it how well he would have understood the phrase 'future shock' – that cruel assault inflicted on the human spirit by, for example, suddenly transferring people from horizontal slums into vertical ones.

But there are dangers even in the most thoughtful forms

of conservatism, just as there are dangers in the most spirited forms of social optimism. And these dangers are enhanced if the conservative is also a passionate sacramentalist. 'In contrast with some beliefs,' wrote Jones, 'that of the Catholic Church commits its adherents, in a most inescapable manner, to the body and the embodied; hence to history, to locality, to epoch and site, to sense-perception, to the contractual, the known, the felt, the seen, the handled, the cared for, the tended, the conserved; to the qualitative and the intimate.'

I would substitute 'Christianity' for 'Catholic Church'; and perhaps David Jones would also have done so if he had lived to make the change. But this seems to me an admirable statement of that sacramental faith which perceives that only what is real can be sacred, and that human artefacts may, according to their use and purpose, be valid signs of the Spirit. This is a view, of course, which shows the close connection between true art, true virtue and true religion, without ever allowing these three to be confused.

But the position which David Jones adopted required, like all exacting intellectual positions, that he should constantly keep his balance. And in one disastrous essay called *Art in Relation to War* he not only loses his balance but falls headlong into the pit. The essay is rambling, digressive, sometimes obscure; but one thing which seems to emerge is that Jones has almost wilfully confused art which is about war with what has so long, and so grotesquely, been called the Art of War.

We know from *In Parenthesis* that Jones found certain great and traditional virtues in men at war – though he managed to believe that the 'good' early war of 1915 turned into the bad (over-mechanized; dehumanized) war of 1916–18. (Did those who fought on the Somme really envy the joys of those who fought at Loos?) In the following passages he is even more explicit:

'It is undeniable that "the trenches" are objectively a "better" life than that to which vast numbers are condemned by their avocations in the "peace-time" world of today ...'

'When we see even the shoddier form of tommy-gun we recognize some sort of functional form, some sort of valid expression, and in consequence experience some measure and some kind of "delight"...'

'Not only the Preface for Christmas, not only Norman vaulting, not only Piero della Francesca's *Nativity*, but Rommel's desert tactic and Nelson's touch, are empty of all significance – "they need not have bothered" – unless form is good in itself.'

Surely the nervous inverted commas suggest that Jones was half-aware of how deeply he was betraying his deepest truths by these appalling – I would say blasphemous – paradoxes.

How then did this wise and good man land himself in such tragic folly? The vital clue is given a little later when he allows the Chesterbelloc to rear the silly side of its Janus-head by writing about the 'traditional virtue of the sword and the traditional baseness of money'. He then regrets that the two have become disastrously interlocked. Thus in his extraordinary desire to sanctify war Jones has betrayed both his devotion to historical reality and also his sacramental understanding that artefacts are holy or unholy signs according, not to how they look, but to the spirit in which they are made and the uses to which they are put. Fundamentally money is a means of exchanging useful goods: fundamentally the sword is a tool for hacking people to death. And as for the marriage of the two, did Jones know nothing of Edward III's deep indebtedness to Florentine bankers for the constant wielding of *his* noble sword in the foul brutalities of the Hundred Years' War?

It is sad and strange that a man who hated abstractions made such an abstraction of the word 'sword' that it enabled him to delight even in the hideous and unholy shape of a tommy-gun.

Here is a quotation from Bennett which expresses very fully
and powerfully a religious attitude which I now totally reject
and with immense relief: 'My own most intimate experiences
and my attempts at a universal synthesis agreed in assuring me
that God is the Supreme Will, manifested as the Reconciling
Power that harmonizes affirmation and denial everywhere and
in everything. I am convinced that to picture God as a Being is
an anthropomorphic fallacy no longer necessary at the present
stage of human development.'

He thought about God far longer and harder than I have
done, but all my limited experience teaches me that these
abstractions are no use to me at all. For me it must be I-and-
Thou, or nothing. I pray to *you*, O God of Love; O Heavenly
Mother; O Holy Spirit; O Guardian Angel! And all that you
are besides and beyond these simple aspects is no concern of
mine. (Or rather it is indeed my concern *that* you are so much
more than the words in which I address you; but I can't even
try to fathom *what* you are in those further depths.)

A new prayer: 'Heavenly Mother, lighten my heart with
love.' I like the two senses of 'lighten'.

But it seems that the writing of good prayers is almost
impossible in our time. To think of Cranmer reeling off those
collects with the glorious ease of his unquestioned (though
reconstituted) faith!

———— * ————

'It is by means of living our human lives in this world that
God is creating us' (H. A. Williams in *The True Wilderness*).
And this, whose source I have forgotten: 'The God who makes
us make ourselves.'

Two convergences with what I tried to say in *Evensong at
Peterborough*. And perhaps our age *may* see a new vision of God;
not as a creed, but as a hope by which each searcher can align

his path. For the old creeds really do seem worse than useless now.

———— * ————

'Those afflicted lovers of the Absolute who are lost in this world of relative things' (?). And earthbound though I am I must, I suppose, be one of these. Perhaps everybody is. Perhaps even those seemingly happy hedonists and materialists who disclaim any longing for anything beyond the good pleasures of this world. Perhaps even Norman Douglas was pricked, in the small hours, by some little jab of divine discontent; of yearning, of terror, of abasement. (Yet it would be a kind of moral imperialism to *assume* that this is so: just as the humanists are guilty of moral imperialism when they try to explain our faith in their own terms.)

10 July

John E has put me on a new pill – Norval – but it will take at least two weeks to lift me out of this depressive's 'refresher-course' which I'm now undergoing. One element in the dire disease which I'd almost forgotten is that each attack combines a frightening novelty with a sickening familiarity. 'Christ, it was never like *this* before!' 'Christ, *this* again!'

I think, 'There is always ECT to fall back on, if the worst comes to the worst. Oh yes, and God, of course!'

———— * ————

Jason and Chrissie for the weekend. Fought hard and well to hide the bad times. It is so important to S and me that all the children should associate this house with calmness and good order; not with tension; pain; emotional inundations.

———— * ————

I'd given Sister Paula a copy of *Evensong at Peterborough* last Sunday, asking her to show it to Mother after she'd read it herself. So I was a little apprehensive when we went to mass yesterday. Of course there was no need. Sister P had prepared quite a formidable document in answer to my wilder heresies, but all with the best will in the world. As for Mother, she amazed me by saying that she agreed with ninety per cent of what I'd written. When she, Sister P and S and I were talking in the library I realized how desperately concerned they are for our Church; how ardently they pray for a reawakening of faith in the wider, faithless community. The fact that they are an enclosed order gives them, perhaps, an even clearer and more painful view of the world outside.

———— * ————

Not so much a sinner as a *meagre* man. The smallness of my normal waking mind appals me. A stream of self-centred triviality.

(But this is true, perhaps, of most other people too.)

———— * ————

At her worst there is a really perverse ingenuity in Simone Weil's thought: the wilful pursuit of some embryonic idea to its most sensational extreme. 'God's great crime is to have created us; is the fact of our existence. And our existence is our great crime against God. When we forgive God for our existence, he forgives us for existing . . .'

A sort of mad rationality; a vicious game with words. Never was a great religious soul so tangled about by the tortuous ingenuities of an unappeasable mind.

18 July

The looming sale of Barn House has stimulated my greedy anxiety to an almost unequalled pitch. Have we asked enough from that very pleasant potter in St Briavels? Could we get more if we restored the house to its pre-community state? How much shall we give the children? How much should we give to a good cause? So how much will be left to protect me from my fears of destitution – a life without beer?

It is alarmingly like my father's almost pathological obsession with money. But unlike him I am not only fearful of ruin but also giddily extravagant. New speakers – again! – for the music centre; an electric lawn-mower; and now, at last, a colour television. This last has always been a symbol for us of the grossly unnecessary possession; so it was some relief when buying the set to learn that 70% of the population now own or rent them.

Anne had told us that the colours are often very beautiful; and once again a large part of *my* motive for this new acquisition was the naive but persistent belief that gadgets can help me towards the Truly Good Life. As I watch Cousteau's frogmen glide between shoals of brilliant, variegated fish I shall suddenly fall on my knees and praise God for what I have apprehended by means of those paradisal shoals. At only £270!

———— * ————

None of this put me in a very good position for our Grand Disputation at BH. I had arranged this in the hope that John would expose himself in all his narrow and bigoted self-righteousness. This happened, to a certain extent; and there were moments when he became very rattled indeed. But no more rattled than I was. In fact I lost my temper violently at one point and shouted 'Get out of that bloody pulpit, for God's sake, and listen *for one moment* to what other people are saying.'

A futile affair, except for the comedy.

———— * ————

Mixed reactions to *Evensong at Peterborough*, but enough real enthusiasm to make me feel it was well worth writing; well worth photocopying and sending out to so many friends.

———— * ————

Invited by Ben's brother Nigel I read the lesson at the memorial service in St James's, Piccadilly. Half the congregation were professional associates – art historians, curators, dealers, etc. – but the other half were old friends of Ben's and mostly of mine as well. Many, many familiar faces, though some of them much aged by the twenty years or more since last I saw them.

The passage which had been chosen for me to read was Rev 21:1–7. 'And I saw a new heaven and a new earth ...' Famous and very beautiful; but with no special relevance to the man we were honouring there. I was tempted to read all this in the proper way – mildly, clearly and as eloquently as I could without overdoing it – *then* to step forward with ferocious mien, finger of damnation thrown out at Freddie and all my other disbelieving friends, and shout *the next* verse at their startled faces. So I would have ended the chosen passage with words of great benignity and comfort: 'He that overcometh shall inherit all things; and I will be his God, and he shall be my son.' Pause for the thunderous sequel: '*But the fearful, and the unbelieving, and the abominable, and the murderers, and whore-mongers, and sorcerers, and idolaters, and all liars, shall have their part in the lake which burneth with fire and brimstone: which is the second death.*'

Ben would have greatly enjoyed this caper; and none of his old friends would have been offended. But alas, I hadn't the courage to do it; sat down meekly after verse 7 and handed the whole affair back to that unmitigated parson.

——— * ———

New pills seem to be working. Seven clear days without even a twinge.

——— * ———

We took the caravan to a big park outside Hemel Hempstead, and drove up from there to Sunday's D A working party meeting at Elizabeth K's flat in Tottenham. How blue the summer air, and the great July trees! Now as S drives I watch the trees most of the time, partly to name them if I can, but the naming is an aspect of the looking.

I was dismayed to notice – suddenly and rather belatedly – that almost every breed of cattle has disappeared except for the ubiquitous Friesians and Herefords. So glad to hear of a neighbour's farming friend who is defiantly starting a herd of longhorns.

The D A meeting was very good. We are becoming a cohesive

band of friends, more united in respect and affection every time we meet, and thus more capable of making progress in this wearisome business of giving ourselves a constitution in order to apply for charity status.

———— * ————

Talked too much at Martyn and Pinkie's, on the evening before the memorial service. Aggressive, self-assertive talking; inflamed not only by wine and whisky but also by such a long deprivation of all that good company. I miss them bitterly, as I realized most keenly at the lunch party which Anne gave after the service.

A painful reminder that though I seldom get drunk in the course of our 'normal' life that life has itself become wildly abnormal because of my fear of drink. So drink plays a perpetual and unremitting part in our lives: a sort of discreet warder at the gate who seldom finds it necessary to remind me that I can go out to those smiling friends only at the frightful cost of probable shame; the infliction of boredom; days, afterwards, of ill health and mental punishment.

———— * ————

Last Friday I caught myself hurrying with my digging; hurrying in and out of my bath; hurrying over my tea – *in order to get my meditation in*! (For custom insists that it must start at 5.30 and last till 6.15.)

———— * ————

A blazing row with Terry and Miriam over yet another postponed review. This is partly due to a decent professional pride: I'm paid as a weekly reviewer and I want to do my job properly. But I also detected the vanity in my anger over the telephone.

23 July

And then the mad extremity of self-disgust – disgust with the self for being so full of self-disgust. Fénelon is very good on this: 'As to speaking of oneself in condemnation I can say little. If a person does so in real simplicity, through a sense of abhorrence and contempt of self inspired by God, the results have been marvellous among saints. But ordinarily, for us who are not saints, the safest course is never to speak of oneself, either good or bad, needlessly. Self-love would rather find fault with itself than abide silent and ignored.'

Bennett, too, is good at distinguishing that self-inflicted pain which is only a mental and moral exercise from the unavoidable pain of love.

So much meditation seems to be a flexing of the muscles rather than a means of loving.

——— * ———

'Faith creates the truth to which it adheres. The certainty that a rite or ceremony gives spiritual regeneration confers that efficacy upon it' (Simone Weil).

There are great dangers in this thought; but a difficult truth is lurking here.

——— * ———

Something which stays in my mind from our last caravan trip. The simple and beautiful little church at Thame, where we stopped for lunch. Then my mounting discomfort as we were guided round Blenheim: culminating in a sense of surfeit and nausea. God and Mammon; how each of them chooses to live in the world. (But what about St Peter's!)

——— * ———

A fearful figure has come to haunt our lanes. This is Max, a Pole, an ex-London photographer; now an alcoholic and a depressive. He is staying at the bottom of the hill with the saintly Polish professor, but roams about the loop-road in ragged shirt and khaki shorts, looking deathly sad and ill.

S stopped at Birchfield the other day and took his confession for nearly forty minutes. I shuddered as I listened to her account, so menacing was the challenge to all that I've ever said or written about giving love and paying attention.

Yesterday afternoon, as we were both gardening, Max

stopped and leant over the fence, apologetic but even in his apologies remorseless. 'I have no right to bore you ... please tell me if you don't want to listen ...' So there we stood, Max just outside our boundary; S a few yards away, having walked across the garden towards him; I, scarcely moved from my work, half hiding behind my wife. Though twelve years younger than me his decay was almost as far advanced; and with his balding head, untidy grey hair, gap-toothed mouth, shorts and rough shirt he looked like my gruesome mirror image. But the enormous difference was that he was standing *outside* the hedge: he was doubly-exiled – from Poland and from his once-respectable job – while I was the English proprietor not only of this neat, small house and garden, but also of a large house down the valley. And I, though my life must have been at least as heavy as his with drunken offences, still hold a good job; and even a certain repute in the world. And I, when depression overcomes me, have a safe room to hide in and a good wife to comfort and look after me.

I did not think, 'There, but for the grace of God ...' for I don't in the least believe that God chose to salvage me from my many near-shipwrecks, but to let Max drown in his. There but for my good luck ... There but for the workings of blind necessity ...

And all the time that he and S were talking, with rare interjections from me (we established that he and I are both on Norval), I was painfully aware of what I ought to say: 'Look, Max, since you're so lonely treat this house as your own. Call in whenever you feel like a chat and cup of tea. Or a drink, for that matter. We'll talk about our troubles together and see if we can't help each other.'

Failing this I should at least have asked him in on this one occasion. Yet I felt no more capable of speaking those hospitable words than of rudely ordering him away.

Would S have invited him in if she hadn't known how appalled I would have been? When I asked her this afterwards she said no; but I think this was to spare me an exacerbation

[224]

of my guilt. Although she wouldn't have enjoyed the role of comforter to this miserable but relentless man, I'm sure she would at least have asked him in just this once.

So I'm not only responsible for my own lack of charity: I also prevent my wife from using hers. (Yet she also said that she was glad to be able to hide her own unwillingness behind my violent aversion. And there may be some truth in this as well.)

Anyway, the spectre moved away at last; after a full half-hour of his haunting. And I recovered quite quickly from my resentful guilt, thinking that God in his wisdom must know very well what each of us can and cannot do in his service. Tomorrow, I remind myself, I have a long letter to write to a young depressive from Newcastle, who has sent me a wodge of verse to criticize, as well as his anguish to assuage as best I can. And Lord, I shall do this thoroughly and well. Because of Max, Lord, I shall do it even more thoroughly than I would have done it without that fearful goad to compensatory virtue.

I get no answer to this, of course; but I strongly suspect that he doesn't find it good enough. 'Feed my sheep ...' 'In so far as you have done it unto one of these ...'

———— * ————

'There are three mysteries, three incomprehensible things in the world. Beauty, justice and truth.

'They are the three things recognized by all men as standards for everything in the world. The incomprehensible is the standard for the known.

'What wonder if terrestrial life is impossible' (Simone W).

Just so. There is nothing of which we are more certain, or less able to prove, than that it is better to love than to hate; and that all our feelings, words, actions *ought* to be ruled by this certitude (Max!).

———— * ————

One of the many problems is how to detect the self's ingenious devices for its own protection and display without falling into the pit of morbid introspection. To be a *jolly* huntsman: 'Aha! My foxy vanity again! Tally-ho!'

30 July

Terry came for a delightful weekend. But when we were talking about grave matters after supper I found – as I do more and more – that I became almost desperately inarticulate. This is not because of the ineffability of the Holy Spirit, etc., since what I'm trying to explain on these occasions is how *human life* has come to make better sense to me in the light of my present beliefs. I know so well what I want to say – admirably trenchant and persuasive things! – but on the rare occasions when I try to say them I fumble and stutter like someone quite unaccustomed to the use of words.

———— * ————

Yesterday was a cheerful but *coarse* day. Much enjoyed watching cricket on the telly; gardening; going to the pub; but the very jollity and robustness seemed, at the evening's recollection, to have removed me a long way from any thought of God.

A very unpleasant idea, that I am closer to God when sad; discontented: even depressed. But there is a well-known truth in this – namely that a sad man is likely to be a more reflective man, and probably a humbler one. Yet so far as Christian witness is concerned gloom is the worst possible advertisement. Godly joy is the thing, of course; but this is impossible to simulate.

———— * ————

Pausing at Birchfield, as always on my walks, to look down at that lovely bend and bowl of the valley. The trees are darkened now by the high summer, but all of them looked admirably solid; placed; planted ... And I thought that this really is *our* country now; not with any fatuous sense of jealous

[226]

possession against the stream of visiting cars along the valley, but simply with an intense awareness of our belonging here. We are settlers of course, but settlers who have earned their place by living, working and walking here for eighteen years.

——— * ———

Another stopping place is just after turning the corner of the Copwell drive, where the long field called Starvecrow falls away to the beautiful double curve of the wood along its lower edge, and southward to a view of the blue valley winding away above Tintern. Much further off, the Severn estuary and a vague blur of the Mendips. It must be admitted, too, that the faint orange smoke drifting northward from the Avonmouth chimneys adds to the visual beauty of that scene, though I know only too well from my sailing days that Rio Tinto Zinc are belching poison over the water.

On my way back through the wood I smelled the rich wet mould, steaming in the glades after so many hot days followed by a sudden downpour. Walberswick twenty years ago, when I ran for miles on the marshes and over the sands. One of my rare Wordsworthian ecstasies.

——— * ———

Playing the tapes of their talks sent me by Christopher and Tina I am more sure than ever that these good and thoughtful people – so much more peaceful and serene than I am – are on a different path from mine. When some emphatic statement does emerge from the usual flow of good psychological counselling I find it quite beyond my understanding. This, for example, from Christopher:

'The idea that you have ever done anything – is based on ignorance.
'The idea that you are now doing anything – is based on ignorance.
'The idea that you will ever do anything – is based on ignorance.'

To that I have the reaction of a linguistic philosopher, in

the school of common usage. 'But Christopher, I went for a walk yesterday: just now I am eating; tomorrow it is very probable that I shall be writing a review. A crude response, but this happens to be the way we use our language; and if you are claiming to use the same language as the rest of us then you too must conform to its rules.'

———— * ————

A strange night. My renewed decision to take no more Ativan coincided with an electricity failure. Sleepless, I was reading by oil lamp the vivid description of a young American's spiritual search through several Buddhist monasteries. Very hard rain in the dark night. All my senses heightened; but this was accompanied by a most unusual peace of mind.

And that, of course, is how it should be. Real tranquillity is not sluggish but constantly, acceptingly alert.

———— * ————

Eric Lerner, the pilgrim of last night: 'I was just on the edge, the most distant approach to that space within, standing before an unknown universe of infinite possibility.' What if one substituted 'without' for 'within'. Perhaps we are wrong to think that this would make a great difference. For whether the infinite possibility is located inside or outside the mind is itself a decision made by the mind.

Or could it be said that you look inward with such intensity that the self you are looking at becomes transparent to the outer, divine reality? As if one had to travel through the long tunnel of the mind to emerge, not at some inner shrine, but *at the other side* of self and mind: at the great open space of heaven; the wide reality of God.

And there are some who set out on this journey in what might seem the opposite direction. They stare and stare at the outside world until *that* becomes transparent to God. Devout painters, for example – and no matter what they are painting. Yet they are really journeying through the mind's impression of those outward things; not through the things themselves. So perhaps the journey is always inward; the true goal so far outward that it lies beyond the laws and dimensions of our universe.

———— * ————

'*Rites de passage*.' A beautiful phrase, and an opening into many meanings.

———— * ————

Yet what did it all amount to, the tremendous journey undertaken by this young American pilgrim in the East? He passed stage after stage in the hard process of enlightenment, but came back only to an ugly and painful separation from his wife and a state of renewed bewilderment and loss. The meditation experience, though very intense, seems to have had little or nothing to do with how he would live afterwards.

———— * ————

One evening lately I tried yet again to read a thriller, choosing just the kind I used to enjoy so much; a fictionalized life of Legs Diamond. Found I couldn't manage more than a few pages, though I perfectly recognized that the book was very good of its kind.

This is partly because I no longer find it interesting to read about bad men unless the badness is treated seriously. In an early scene of this book there is a po-faced description of Legs being insulted in a speakeasy, and immediately shooting his insulter dead. This is extraordinary but very boring behaviour: in fact it is much more boring than any of the ordinary reactions would have been.

An act of simple evil, whether witnessed or read about, can cause us a momentary surprise, or shock. But in itself it is empty and without meaning: no more interesting than a stone falling to the ground.

On the other hand saints are the most interesting people of all; each of them amazing but each a very distinct personality. Yet how can this be? Having rid themselves of their differentiating egos you'd think that they would be identical in their blank negation of self.

Perhaps there's a distinction to be made between self and person; and perhaps the person is progressively enriched as the ego-self is withered away. In fact it is *not* the ego which differentiates, for we are drearily alike in our greed, fear, vanity and anger. What is distinct and particular to each of us is our unique, God-given and personal way of serving God.

Still, I regret thrillers: so many happy hours I've spent with them.

31 July

A hard day's work trying to sort out confusions in the last two sections of *Pantaloon*. Whatever happens to it I must make it as good as I possibly can. For the glory of God? I doubt if I have the right to say that yet.

———— * ————

In bed with a heavy cold I brought up one of the speakers and listened to the Berlioz *Requiem*. Transported! As beautiful as any music I know, and overflowing with the glory of God; however vehemently Berlioz rejected him.

———— * ————

But soon afterwards there was a very ugly scene at BH. I'd gone over to start the huge task of clearing up the garden, having begged them to do a little of this themselves. But not only had nothing been done; they were lying and lazing about in the ruined garden; soul music from the open window; one very pregnant girl sitting naked on the edge of the swimming pool in full view of the road ... What's more half the people there were strangers. A crash pad, in fact, just as Mary had predicted.

I delivered a violent harangue, to which nobody spoke a single word in answer. It was Them and Us with a vengeance now; the sweet freaks and children of nature up against the angry proprietor whose only thought was to drive them all away and sell the empty house for a fat sum. A melancholy change.

Or, as some would say, no change at all, but simply the true situation no longer disguised by kindly pretences from both sides.

And Kerry, whom I'd angrily urged to take the initiative in getting the restoration going, wrote us a sad letter and left at once. At first we were furious at this abnegation of all responsibility; but later we realized that he *couldn't* have suddenly turned himself into a boss in that place where no one had ever been boss or bossed.

2 August

We drove up to Manchester – leaving the caravan in an orchard near Worcester – and lunched with Michael Schmidt of the Carcanet Press. I felt like the comic salesman with my leather bag full of samples. But after leaving *Pantaloon* in that charming little office, with the hand-press in one corner, S and I both felt more optimistic than ever before. They seemed the kind of people who would understand the book – and therefore love it, of course, as well as admiring it.

Back down the M6 in cloudburst after cloudburst, stopping for an Indian meal in Bromsgrove. So much good talk between us: on Simon and Kerry, and the many differences between them; on Henry Moore, whose eightieth birthday programme we'd seen last week on the telly; Ivan Illich and our days with him in Mexico; God and free will ... Ah, how well and lovingly we talked over the lobster curry!

And on the next day Tewkesbury and Pershore; but best of all the little church at Elmley Castle, under Bredon, and the beautiful Stuart monument there.

Ross on the way home for drinks and snacks. Intense delight of that first ice-cold pint of draught Guinness in the hotel bar.

In fact the best so far of all our good caravan expeditions; and only slightly marred by a quick sharp row over backing the caravan on to the concrete when we got it home.

5 August

Our *Times* ad of Barn House appeared on Wednesday and Thursday – 'ideal for any form of community or retreat project'. Only one bite, by telephone on Wednesday morning; but when we met the couple – elderly and rich – we knew from their first dismayed glance at the house that they wouldn't dream of buying it. And as we looked at our old dishevelled home through their eyes we saw all too clearly what an unattractive proposition it had become. (How different from the bright, neat and charming house we first set *our* eyes on in November 1959.)

Continued ill-feeling, alas, with the remnants of the community. Surely, we say to each other, they can do *something* to improve the appearance of the place, seeing that the damage has all been done by their long negligence as non-paying guests.

The Rowsons were there, our old original co-founders, and Dave R told us that two of the communards were just going off on yet another meditation course. 'No,' I said, 'they can bloody well stay and do some work, or bugger off for good.' 'OK, *Landlord*!' said Dave; and stabbed me to the heart, as he intended. (But I pulled his stiletto out pretty smartly as I walked back fuming through the woods.)

And all this has led me to being stupidly impatient; often irritable to S. My God, I thought last night in bed, what an endless strain it is to try to live rightly: indeed to live at all, since living wrongly is no reduction of the strain; quite the contrary. 'The third thing,' writes Bennett, 'is universal *baraqa* (spiritual influence) which pervades the world, and to which people become sensitive when their inner enemy has been silenced. This inner enemy stands at the door and prevents the entry of *baraqa*.' 'To hell with *baraqa*!' shouts my own inner enemy, a strong, swarthy, warty old brute who not only holds the door against the Spirit but often swells himself out until he has filled the whole of my inner space.

———— * ————

On Thursday night one of my hypnogogic attacks; the worst

[232]

for years. Almost as soon as I'd put out the light I was in the grip of that fearful seizure. As usual, the sense that I was dying of suffocation, a squeezing paralysis of the chest and throat; yet the conviction that if I went on struggling to escape my heart would literally break under the strain. I cried out to Laura, who I thought was still sleeping in her room next door. She seemed to come in and to be standing silently beside my bed. Then, presumably sinking deeper away from waking reality, I cried out for my mother, who also came in and stood beside me without a word or a sign. My mouth seemed to be wrenched to one side, so that I could hardly speak an intelligible word. 'Like a stroke!' I was trying to say 'Like a stroke!' And then, over and over again, 'Please just say that you're there; say that you're there ...'

At last I despaired of them, and accepted that I must stop struggling and allow the life to be crushed and stifled out of me. And as usual this despairing resignation did whatever had to be done, and I was suddenly fully conscious, but sweating and trembling and with both arms pressed tightly to my sides.

These attacks began during my last, heavy-drinking week at Oxford; and they used to be always associated with drink. They would happen not on the drunk night itself nor on the following hangover night, but, with fearful regularity, on the night after that. Now they come, perhaps about once every three months, for no discernible reason: in the form of no discernible punishment. (It must be nearly two years since I had a fully-fledged hangover; the longest period without one for more than forty years. But it seems there are no prizes.)

——— * ———

Help me, O Heavenly Mother, to exorcize the trivial! Help me to concern myself more with my wife and less with myself.

——— * ———

A splendid programme on Chichester yesterday evening by Alec Clifton-Taylor. All that geological, archaeological and architectural knowledge combining to reveal the town in its fascinating depth. Whereas I'm lucky if I see even the surface,

[233]

so much does seeing depend on understanding. What a lot of time I've wasted which I might have spent acquiring this kind of knowledge! Those thousands of hours devoted to reading newspapers and agitating myself with issues over which I never had the least control. This was seldom due to any heartfelt concern for human suffering: I'm quite sure that I've read the papers, daily and weekly, far more in anger than in pity. (Kept awake at nights for weeks on end in 1956/7 by my bilious rage against Eden, Selwyn Lloyd, etc.)

———— * ————

The Jeremy Thorpe case. As I was gardening yesterday afternoon I had to ward off a sort of slimy fascination.

10 August

A very confused Scotch voice over the telephone. Did I remember a book of poems he'd sent me? Well, they were after him again; they'd got him again; would I phone the Home Secretary at once ... As I questioned him, trying to find out at least his name and address, he broke in with a heartrending cry – 'Oh can't you *help* me, Philip!'

After he'd rung off something stirred in my mind – one of the many poor deranged correspondents I've written to over the last thirty years. Then S reminded me that this was the one who had tried to break into Chequers and had given my name when he was arrested. The Buckinghamshire police had telephoned me at Barn House but I hadn't been able to say anything that was any use to him at all. A little later S even remembered the name.

He had given me a Larbert telephone number, and in the evening I began trying to reach him there. Soon I found myself involved in one of those infuriating telephone mix-ups; constantly getting the wrong number; trying the exchange again; trying enquiries ... My real pity and longing to help soon became muddled by anger and frustration. At last I got through to the right number, but was answered by quite a different voice.

[234]

When I gave my caller's name this other, very rational, very gentle voice, said that G was in Ward 5, and wouldn't be able to answer the telephone. 'Are you a nurse, then?' I asked. 'No, I'm a fellow-patient. But you sound very worried, and I can assure you that your friend is in good hands here.'

What respect, and even perhaps love, I felt for that quiet, kind, unfortunate stranger! But what relief, as well, that there was nothing else I could do for G.

————— * —————

As I was starting the fearsome task of cleaning out the big front flower bed at BH Phil came up and offered me a whetstone for my hook. Then he stood watching me work, with the full intensity of his shaggy earnestness. I gestured, as if whimsically, at a particularly tall clump of dock and thistle; and Phil thought this over for some time before saying, 'If you mean you want me to do some *work*, Philip, I'm afraid I can't because I'm just going up to meditate with Rose.'

Later, refreshed, I suppose, by his meditation, he appeared again and delivered a little homily to me as I sweated away with hook and stick: 'I've noticed that you've become much more anxious and impatient lately. You really shouldn't, you know. Let things happen; don't try to make them happen. You'll sell the house all right, and it only does you harm to fret about it.'

Hilarious, looked at in one way. But luckily, or by the grace of God, I saw beyond the brazen absurdity of Phil's attitude and recognized that the advice he was giving me was entirely well-meant and entirely good. I also realized that Phil will *never* do any work here, however much pressure we put on him; so the angry laughter was easily stifled, and I thanked him quietly for his advice.

Now Rose lies ill in bed while Phil takes Rian for very slow walks down the lanes. Simon is working hard to get enough money for his eight-month Sufi course at Beshara: yet he finds the time to bring us logs, and even to start painting the house. As the one-time community rots and crumbles away this kind-

[235]

ness and conscientiousness remind us of the good years when everything seemed to hum with energy, zest, humour, affection ...

———— * ————

A letter from Sister Benedicta about *Evensong in Peterborough.* 'I liked it very much. In fact your major point about the nature of God is one that has engaged, if not obsessed me for a long time, and I've been trying to find a way of saying it for years...' I am amazed and delighted that she and the Reverend Mother like it so much.

———— * ————

The usual three days at Clovelly with Bun (Lawrence) and Jean and several of my charming nieces. I drank too much, of course, but was never much the worse for wear. Indeed on one evening I suddenly took off on one of my now rare but inspiriting flights of high clowning, raising into a great fantasy of nonsense the whole topic of depression, its causes and its cure. I need just the right amount to drink for this, and a willing as well as a stimulating audience. It is a condition of genuine inspiration; whirling like a dervish; freely levitating; speaking in tongues ... A glorious sensation, and perhaps the nearest I ever come to true possession by the Spirit. (For why should he not inspire us to *comic* joys?)

Lunch with Connie in her Exmoor cottage both coming and going. We were delighted, as always, by her absolute natural goodness, dignity, wit, bright and inventive intelligence. Her comments on *E at Peterborough* were the most useful I've had.

Those six months with her in 1926 must have given me some vision of real love and stability to take with me, somewhere in my agitated mind, through all the distracted years that followed.

———— * ————

Jason and Chrissie came over on Friday to look over BH and work out a rough work-plan. For we've decided to undo all the reconstruction I did with Jeff Sands in 1973/4; which means taking down a floor, rebuilding an interior wall and replacing a staircase, among other minor restorations.

Laura left us for Gloucester on her moped at 3 o'clock on Saturday afternoon: at 6 Paul telephoned to ask why she hadn't arrived. The journey takes about an hour, so S and I were immediately thrown into fearful imaginations. Jason rang up the police in every town on her route; on her three possible routes; while in the kitchen I clasped S tightly and we trembled against each other.

There was about half an hour of this anguish before Paul rang again to say that she'd now arrived safely: she'd felt faint on the way; had laid herself down on the side of the road and passed out. Weird!

We drove Jason and Chrissie back to their Warwickshire village on Sunday morning; and I could hardly conceal my impatience to get them there, get away from there and settle ourselves in some pleasant hotel in time for a long drink before lunch. For this is my vision of total pleasure – to be sitting in a comfortable bar, reading *The Observer* with a pint of Guinness on the table and the lunch menu just about to be brought for our leisurely perusal. The height of worldly enjoyment.

——— * ———

I felt that a bad night was threatening; prayed as best I could and tried to bury myself in a life of St Francis. And it did seem that I was given help; chiefly in the recognition that God shows me my miserable faults and failings *to just the extent that I can bear to accept them.*

A certain irritation, at times, with these tremendous saints for being so conscious of their 'sins'. What the hell had *they* got to moan about!

——— * ———

Sitting quietly with S next day I was strongly aware of our peace. Not that we have it always – far from it – but there are many times like this when we can be together in complete simplicity of unspoken love.

[237]

Later I told her that I thought I was a sort of monk *manqué*, not meaning by that a man who might almost have been a monk, but one who might have made the absurd mistake of trying to become one. If I had done so I would have been impelled by all my most craven emotions – fear of the world and my disordered life in it; a yearning for the rigidity of that regime: no responsibility: absolute obedience; the strictly ordered day. Any abbot worth his salt would have sniffed me out and sent me packing as soon as I appeared on his doorstep.

———— * ————

S and I worked out a very simple prayer to repeat together every morning and evening: 'Lord, help us to see truly and to act rightly.'

———— * ————

The bitter late years of St Francis. The whole ideal of poverty and simplicity had to be pegged down; formulated; set within a rigid structure ... and thus corrupted. So many of us enact in our own lives the melancholy history of the monastic orders. The first fine rapture of resolve; followed by a more or less slow deterioration; followed by a sudden and energetic return to first principles; deterioration again ... and reformation ... (Damn these little white cylinders of corrosive poison!)

So it seems in our own lives that whenever we feel that we've made a little progress the same old faults surge up again and force us back to where we started from. But *not quite* to the same place. The new return may take us just as far 'back' as ever, but the place is different if only because of that apparent advance which has intervened. So the same situation is never repeated, appallingly familiar though it so often seems, and there is, after all, a new chance every moment.

———— * ————

With the old and obvious error about possession goes a slightly subtler error about accomplishment. 'I want *to have read* this book; and therefore to contain it ...' 'I want *to have made* this garden: I want *to have written* this book ...' In fact it

[238]

is desire for possession in another form; another notch on the stick for another Indian killed. The very opposite of Ram Dass's good old Be Here Now; or de Caussade's sacrament of the present moment. The shop-window, not the workshop.

A greedy grabbing at the future.

And thinking again about Eric Lerner's Buddhist pilgrimage, of all the enlightening experiences he acquired, yet the sense of futility at the end, I see that spiritual experience is the last trap of all. Another *thing to have had*: another acquisition. (Of course the Zen masters, and many others, have been perfectly aware of this; but *I* haven't -- and therefore I write it here.)

Even love is useless as a goal. Being an abstraction it also looks like a possible acquisition. Verbs are much better than nouns: to love: to be in a state of loving God and man.

Adjectives are dangerous as well: I want to be a good man, but find it quite impossible to do what good men do.

In the light of this rather elementary discovery, I've now stopped counting breaths in my meditation; for the counting had also become a way of registering achievement and acquisition. Now I deliberately lose count – not so easy! – and concentrate simply on the breath entering and leaving the nostrils. So each breath is now of equal value; indistinguishable because un-numbered.

———— * ————

How splendid that St Francis came from the class which is perennially the most despised of all – the parvenu, money-grubbing, vulgar, rich bourgeoisie.

———— * ————

I went into St Mary's on Thursday morning for a quick prayer after shopping, and found Father Philip sitting in a pew ahead of me teaching two very small children to recite the Lord's Prayer. The scene was deeply touching; and the more so because it was also a little comic. But how hard it would be to describe this in a novel without sentimentality.

[239]

From *Observer* review of *Franz Kafka: Letter to Friends, Family and Editors*. Translated by Richard and Clara Winston (John Calder, London):

But if (this story) is typical of his shrewd, grotesquely defiant attitude to that authority which one can only call The Way Things Are, it is also true that there is an important element in Kafka to which these particular letters do far too little justice. This element is most clearly expressed in a letter of 1903, when Kafka was only 20: 'We are forlorn as children lost in the woods. When you stand in front of me and look at me, what do you know of the griefs that are in me and what do I know of yours? And if I were to cast myself down before you and weep and tell you, what more would you know about me than you know about hell when someone tells you it is hot and dreadful? For that reason alone we human beings ought to stand before one another as reverently, as reflectively, as lovingly, as we would before the entrance to hell.'

Of all the books I have read about him the most revealing is Gustav Janouch's *Conversations with Kafka* which was published in England ten years ago. In 1920, when Janouch was a very young man, his father introduced him to Kafka, who was Janouch père's colleague in the Workmen's Accident Insurance Institution. For the next four years Kafka arranged many meetings with Janouch and often took him for long walks through the streets of Prague. Janouch almost worshipped his older friend, and was left in a state of desolation at his death. And the man who emerges from the wonderful pages of that book is quite recognizable as the boy who had written that we must love one another as if we were standing together at the mouth of hell.

There have been attempts at times to make Kafka into

an agonized protester against the social and political evils of his time. But it is significant that these letters slip by with no mention either of the beginning of the First War, or of its end; and there are not more than three or four casual references to that cataclysm even while it was running its frightful course. Nor do his friends ever succeed in arousing his interest in the Jewish Question; nor is there any way of knowing from these pages that at a certain point he ceased to be a subject of the Austro-Hungarian Empire and became a citizen of the Czechoslovak Republic.

The truth is that Kafka's attention was as much turned inward on himself as if he had been a religious mystic. What he found there was not God, or the Absolute, or Brahma, or Nirvana: what he continued to find was that hell of terror and isolation which he had already been writing about at the age of twenty. And to suggest that this was due to his father-dominated childhood would be as naively Freudian as it would be naively Marxist to see him as the victim of capitalist oppression.

The reason why Kafka remains such a central figure for our age is that he was one of the first and bravest explorers of our inner wilderness. And because he not only explored it but also reported on it with singular brilliance and accuracy; not only reported on it but offered his love to those who suffered there as he did – because of this unique conjunction of virtues and perceptions Kafka was a true saint of our times. More truly a saint than many of those who have used religious faith only as a means of escaping, or denying, the wilderness within.

17 August

A letter from Michael Schmidt: '[My colleagues] Robert Wells and Peter Jones have dipped into *Pantaloon*, and they inform me that this is no work to be lightly dismissed, and that

I have a hard decision ahead of me. Their interest is encouraging of course.'

Yes, it is; and I dare to hope that these young men will see what so many of my own generation have failed to see. My thoughts being turned in that direction it occurs to me again, as a slight balm after so much self-laceration, that I have been fairly wise and patient about this life-work of mine. I have accepted rebuff after rebuff without much fuss or sense of grievance. Is this because I am *sure* of *Pantaloon* in a way that I'm not sure of anything else that I've done, or that I possess? Or is it because I'm no longer very interested in that monumental labour?

——— * ———

Max, the desperate Pole, continues to hover and droop about our roads, raising a sad (reproachful?) arm as we drive past him. But it would be false to write that this miserable *alter ego* causes me much guilt. I know so very well that the kind of help he needs is the kind I could never give him. (Never? Well, it would need a true resurrection indeed to turn me into a man who would welcome him into my house and listen with loving attention to his long complaints.)

'God grant me the serenity to accept the things I cannot change, the courage to change the things I can, and the wisdom to know the difference.'

——— * ———

Reading Michael Schmidt's excellent PN review makes me realize, with a slight start, how *utterly* I am out of touch with the current literary scene. And have been so for many years.

26 August

A wonderful letter from Ronald Higgins about my review of Kafka's letters. '. . . I wanted you to know that I found the second half of your Sunday piece on the Kafka letters profoundly moving and enriching. Indeed I wept reading it – and at 7 a.m.!' I seldom get quite such a warm response as this; but about half a dozen kind letters a year do much to keep up my spirits as a reviewer.

In fact I enjoy my professional work more and more every year. The other day I came across an old *New Statesman* novel review of mine, written when I was 26, and I was amazed at its crudity, clumsiness and conceit. Amazed and pleased, for at least I know that my present reviews are better than that.

———— * ————

'Doubt has to be distinguished from discrimination. Discrimination is necessary. Freedom from doubt does not mean freedom from discrimination, or the ability to recognize what is acceptable and what is not. Doubt is something else. It is based upon a wrong and egoistic demand – that one has the right to have evidence; that one has the right to have things proved to one' (Bennett).

Interesting and strange, for I've always assumed that doubt is a token of humility: 'How can *I* be sure of anything; let alone of the deepest mysteries!'

———— * ————

Thursday evening recollection of the day. The strong sense of a very precarious day, narrowly survived without any gross error. At least three times I *just* withheld a remark to S which might have caused distress or offence or both. Phew!

———— * ————

'No human being escapes the necessity of conceiving some good outside himself towards which his thoughts turn in a movement of desire, supplication and hope. Consequently the only choice is between worshipping the true God or an idol. Every atheist is an idolater – unless he is worshipping the true God in his impersonal aspect. The majority of the pious are idolaters' (Simone Weil).

———— * ————

We've hired scaffolding for two weeks and I've been painting and making good the woodwork of the upper BH windows.

I was feeling quite proud of my work, and might even have begun to enjoy it but for my nagging irritation that neither Phil nor Clifford (a hefty newcomer) was offering to help. At last I climbed down from the scaffold, went indoors and suggested that they might do a bit of work outside. There was an immediate outburst against the 'pressure' I was putting on them. Didn't I realize that Rose was ill, and that they not only had to look after her and Rian but also do all the washing for them both. At which point Rose wailed angrily down at me from her sickroom upstairs, and I, having slunk back to my scaffold, felt that I had indeed become a monstrous land-lord, harrying a poor sick woman and her child.

But doubts about this attitude began to tease me, so I drove back to Woodroyd and asked S whether I was crazy to feel resentful. She was even more taken aback than I was, and we both returned to confront our accusers again. To avoid disturb-ing Rose the four of us went down to the barn to have it out; and S was very scathing indeed about two able-bodied young men thinking it a full-time, indeed an almost unbearably arduous job to look after one woman and one child. They were not put out, though Phil pressed his hands to his ears and moaned that he couldn't stand all this terrible *conflict*. What I should have replied to that piece of holier-than-thou, more-sensitive-than-ye, is that conflict arises whenever people live together, and the sooner Phil realized this the better. The way to deal with it is not to run away and pretend it isn't there but to face it and work through it with as much honesty and love as one can manage.

Yet I do see – with an effort – that it must be very difficult for them to work on a house which is not theirs and which they'll very soon have to leave. (An absurd element in all this is that they did succeed, with the help of a sudden host of visitors, in planting quite a lot of vegetables up in the field. If only that burst of energy had been devoted to cleaning up the house and garden!)

——— * ———

But on Sunday I realized for the first time that this shaggy, scruffy, ever-serious Phil can be seen as a major comic character – though not, of course, as that alone. Simon and I were painting the kitchen-end of the house, high up on the scaffolding which Simon had very skilfully erected there. Suddenly we heard frightful screams from down the hill. I thought it might be one of the Williamses' peacocks; but Simon was so certain it was human that we climbed quickly down from the scaffold, ran across the end of Starvecrow and into the wood. There we found Phil, looking indeed like a woodland creature, but also a little abashed by our arrival. 'It's nothing at all,' he mumbled. 'Only a tree.' 'A *tree!*' said I; but Simon pulled at my sleeve and suggested we get back to our work.

Once out of Phil's earshot I asked Simon what on earth was happening. 'It's only Phil's primal scream therapy,' he said; and when I broke into howls of primal laughter he laughed as well – but a little reluctantly. (How loyal and kind he is!)

And who am I to say that it won't do Phil a great deal of good to let off steam in this way. But it is a miracle that none of the neighbours heard him – for the primal screams were quickly resumed when we'd got back to work again. I suspect that primal screamers are too preoccupied with themselves to be much concerned with their neighbours.

But this is getting bitchy indeed. I've known Phil long enough and well enough to recognize his real gentleness and goodwill.

———— * ————

We took the caravan to the Chilterns on Monday and parked in the prettiest site we've yet found; very small and secluded, tucked away under a fine slope of grass and beechwood. Then to visit Ann Horne in her strange Quaker hostel near Beaconsfield. I was a bit nervous about this, having corresponded so long and earnestly with her; much afraid that I couldn't possibly come up to her high expectations of me as guide and comforter. Nor did I, I'm sure; and a good thing too. S and I made friends with her at once, and the conversation was at least as funny as it was serious. She is not Decca's cousin and best childhood friend for nothing. By the end of the afternoon, when we had to go, I felt that S and I had both come very close to her, and she to us. She suffers a great deal, both physically and mentally, but bears this with the best kind of fortitude – i.e. a fortitude which never tries to deny the reality of the pain, and which includes, when necessary, a total, anguished surrender. I recognize a fellow-traveller through hell, but God, how much worse than mine are the areas she's forced to explore!

It is extraordinary to be able to say that we both love her.

———— * ————

At Uffington, under the best of the white horses, a very old, soft-spoken gentleman offered himself as guide just as we were about to go into the church. I felt my usual instantaneous irritation, but knew that he couldn't be refused. And he proved to be a kind, knowledgeable and amusing guide.

When we came out he 'ventured' to show us a poem which he had written 'under that beech tree many years ago', and which had been published in *The Church Times*; his only published work. It was a poem of great simplicity and beauty. After we'd driven away I wondered whether this apparition had been an angel; for such is the form an angel might surely take; and the message he might convey. The message to me was that I should never close my heart against strangers.

(Not so much 'wondered' as 'played with the idea'.)

———— * ————

Amazing, the unspoiled beauty of the Chilterns and the Berkshire downs, so close to London. Horror of getting on to the M4 and back to the noisy deadness of our world.

———— * ————

One current idea which seems to me false and dangerous – that the more liberal-minded a faith becomes the more attenuated and ineffable must be its conception of God.

———— * ————

BH party, at which Simon presided with great zest and charm. He made a speech of thanks to S and me for 'all they

[246]

have done for us'; and I, thinking of recent tensions, replied with clumsy embarrassment. But many of the old-timers had come back for this occasion – Bec, Dave Rowson, Richard, the Snowdons – and there was an atmosphere of genuine warmth and happiness. S and I led the revels, prancing around together to Dave Snowdon's guitar; catching hold of other hands and drawing them in until the whole roomful of communards, old and new, were gambolling and capering there.

A wonderful last celebration: a healing feast.

1 September

S and I were working together at BH as the last of the stragglers were straggling away. Having the house to ourselves again after nearly five years made it seem weirdly empty: *pleasantly* empty. (But we were both very glad that all the old-timers had left without the least ill will: in fact with apparent affection. Even the late arrivals, creators of the crash pad, had been friendly enough at the end.)

How calmly and thoroughly S works at her windows, scraping off every bit of old paint and crumbling putty! How I rush at my walls, wielding the brush like a weapon!

———— * ————

Oblates meeting at Tymawr, at the end of their annual retreat. Sitting in the library with a priest, half a dozen nuns and a dozen middle-aged or elderly ladies, taking tea and discussing the inspiration of the New Testament. I had been invited to represent the male associates; felt very flattered by this, and greatly enjoyed the whole proceeding. A strong sense of peace and comfort at being with these intelligent and lively people, all of whom share, if not my detailed beliefs, my deepest priorities; values; hopes ...

Even five years ago I would have thought my presence there a ludicrous improbability.

———— * ————

Driving back from BH with S we saw Mrs M by the road ahead of us. 'Don't stop!' I hissed, impatient, as always, to be home – to be anywhere – and impelled, as always, by my hatred of all casual contacts and chatty conversations. But of course S stopped; for Mrs M had been our good neighbour for many years. I was ashamed once again at my boorish unsociability, and the shame was heightened when I heard that Mrs M's husband is ill in hospital.

———— * ————

Barn House Community. Many good memories, and very few bad ones. Even S, for all her reservations over the years, feels that a great deal of good came from the experiment.

Best memory of all. Steve and I working and chatting together on the patch below the yard, while my horrors were gradually overwhelming me. 'You know, Steve,' I suddenly broke out, 'this is all an act I'm putting on. The truth is I'm feeling bloody awful.' The alert concern on the face of that tall, sleepy-eyed young man as he *ran* across the dug soil to me, put his arm round my shoulders and pressed me to sit down on the verge beside him. 'Let's go to India!' he said.

The words were dotty, I suppose, for I couldn't even leave my bedroom, at that time, without fear and trembling. But the kindness and enthusiasm – above all the assumption of our close companionship – immediately made me feel much better. And as I walked back to Woodroyd that evening I knew that this blessing is always *somewhere*, however unblessed my condition might seem to be.

(But the strange thing is that S, who usually welcomed the milkers each day while I stayed up in my room, probably made closer friends with some of them than I ever did.)

8 September

Back from a week with Anne in her Irish cottage; our third visit there; but the last was two years ago, and before that we hadn't been out of England since the American camping trip

[248]

in 1973. What a craven stay-at-home I have become!

A good and very refreshing time with the extended family – Anne, Josephine, Pip and Milly. Two special memories. One afternoon at Dunmanus I swam a long way out, and as I lay kicking on my back I praised the fantastic beauty of the world I saw; praised God for showing it to me. 'Oh God of Peace!' – a long gliding stroke. 'Oh God of Hope!' – a sharp, lively stroke. 'Oh God of Light!' – feeling the bright sky collecting itself above me and falling down like a single ray of light into my open body. 'Oh God of Joy!' – and there was joy. 'Oh God of Love!' – and even love would come.

Not even 'I am happy'; but 'Here is happiness'.

Anne, Josephine and the grandchildren had walked on round the bay to look for shells and samphire, and after our bathe S and I walked along the little coast road to meet them. The second episode was simply that meeting; my sudden awareness that all of us were smiling with love and happiness; that these smiles were quite unlike the usual conventional smiles; that God was with us and within us.

The blues attacked from time to time, and once achieved an occupation which lasted a whole morning. But they were incomparably weaker than they'd been on our last visit here, in 1976.

Then a small triumph at the very end. On that early morning I thought it quite likely that the last-minute chores of Anne and Josephine would make us miss the boat in Cork – as they very nearly did. But I held my peace, in both senses; and continued to do so even when Phine and I were turned back at the dock entrance to change a ticket while the last cars were rolling on to the boat.

Ah, what a joy, the recognition of at least *some* change for the better.

On the voyage to Swansea a studious-looking man was sitting hunched up in rugs reading *The Old Curiosity Shop* aloud to a teenage daughter stretched on the seat beside him. How remote! How splendid! I love these sudden illuminations from lives so different from our own.

Home at ten in the evening, all six of us, and I was glad to be back, as I always am however much I've enjoyed the holiday. Even the pile of letters looked enticing, and the weedy garden more of an invitation than a threat. My own bed again; – the terracotta angel in relief – which Anne gave me for my 60th birthday; Martyn's little watercolour seascape, also a 60th birthday present, and Simon's very pure and simple pot. All these on the shelf in front of me as I lie in bed. The books in their shelves beside me; and the desk waiting quietly for me to start my typing again there ...

Not much regular prayer or meditation in Ireland; but I've found that this interval has made me all the more ready to begin again.

9 September

'One could argue in this way: How could there proceed from me more good than there is in me? If I make progress in the good it must be through the influence of some external good' (Simone Weil).

As an *argument* this could easily be disputed. As an account of experience I find it entirely convincing.

———— * ————

'*Nasut* really means the human world – this world of our human affairs. It isn't really a world – it is a way of perceiving – it is our human environment where we live in this state of separation from one another, each enclosed in our own life and not aware of how we are connected with one another' (Bennett).

———— * ————

Charming dream last night about my father. He, my mother, Tony and I were sitting at some great table set in the middle of a half-ruined city and presided over by one of the family matriarchs; perhaps my Aunt Cecilia. My father was wailing and stretching out his arms like the figure in Goya's *The Shootings of May 3rd.* So I took a huge tealeaf out of my cup and touched him under the chin with it, saying, 'You're playing the role of the mad professor, aren't you.' His face slowly dissolved into a sly, schoolboy grin, and everyone began to laugh.

------ * ------

In St Briavels I met Mrs N, and thoughtlessly, cheerfully, asked her how she was. 'Bearing up,' she said, and I realized at once that this wasn't the usual meaningless answer but an accurate description of her state. Her husband died two years ago; at Christmas her only son crashed on his motor bike and will have to be in a mental hospital for the rest of his life.

She is a quiet, heroic woman, and being a practising Catholic she must believe, I suppose, that these appalling afflictions were sent her by 'God'. Or perhaps they have so deeply embittered her that she has lost her faith.

I think it would be better if she had lost it. For to maintain a humble and grateful faith in the God who inflicted these horrors on her is surely, in our time, a wrong, distorting, *mutilating* operation of the will.

So I risked the impertinence of sending her a copy of *Evensong at Peterborough*. After all, the worst it can do is annoy or offend her; and it's just possible that it might allow her to believe in a God who is not the cause of her misery but a fellow-sufferer in it.

20 September

The General Election postponed. Probably a mistake by the Prime Minister; and I suppose I ought to be more worried about this than I am. After all, I'm still entirely convinced that if the Conservatives are returned they will increase the sum of human misery in this country; and perhaps in other countries too. Yet as soon as I turn my mind back to politics I feel a great weariness of the spirit: a fearful sense of the sluggish, intractable reality of our poor, ill-governed, misdirected country. Maltreated and misguided world.

What can save it now except a new Pentecost; the dove descending over the whole surface of the earth.

———— * ————

In Ireland Anne lent me Paul Scott's enormous novel about the end of the Raj in India. Delighted to find that I am becoming involved in it; that it has rescued me, for the time being, from that imprisoning regime of endless religious reading. It is a terrible thing to shut God up in religion.

———— * ————

Now Jason is at Barn House with Chrissie and his two friends/mates, Lewis and Maurice. They are working away with a will; and on most days S and I go over to join them.

I'm sure Jase and I are both remembering those bad days in that house when I used to harry him so hard about working for his A levels. But now all seems to be well: more than well. The charming nostalgia of sitting for a tea-break in that kitchen where Jason, Lucy and their friends used to congregate all through their teens. Sad irony, though, of the herbal tea on the shelves; the corn-grinder; the butter-churn – all those relics of the community mystique. Which has been replaced, as I said to them, by the teabags-and-chips mystique of their determinedly working-class manner and attitude. (Not that the communards could possibly be described as bourgeois: still less as ladylike or gentlemanly. In fact every one of them would have been firmly pushed by my mother on to a much lower shelf than Jason's. As for Maurice, whose parents are intellectual Jews, another element would have entered her estimate of where *he* belongs. And as for Lewis, J's oldest friend, his parents are copperbottomed proletariat, but he has long ago glided into that indeterminate area where origins no longer have much meaning.)

In fact it was in this area that the communards had also placed themselves, though in a very different part of it from Jason's. Whereas I, in spite of great efforts as a young man, renewed (and bearded) efforts when the community began,

[252]

have never escaped from the class in which I began. (And this no longer seems of the very least importance.)

———— * ————

At one point I did begin to worry about their work: how much it would cost us; whether they'd get it done in time, and do it well enough. But I prayed effectively against this foolish and damaging anxiety. It was quickly relieved and has never quite returned. I see – when I see clearly – that the work will be done, and done far more enjoyably like this than if we had employed strangers to do it.

In fact I now treat the whole operation as a work-in-its-own-right: a creative co-operation; the reconstruction of a fine and handsome house. (And the price we'll get for it? Keeps on crawling back into the mind, of course and alas.)

———— * ————

Painfully fierce row with Dave Snowdon. And Michele is unavoidably involved as well. So we were not to get off so lightly from the ending of the community!

23 September

But Michele came round here yesterday evening, and we were able to talk with real understanding, as always in the past. She brings light and warmth; the Holy Spirit is in her, as well as much common sense. And I know that we shall make it up with Dave as well before very long.

———— * ————

'All I can do is to desire the good. But whereas all other desires are sometimes effective and sometimes not, according to circumstances, this one desire is always effective. The reason is that, whereas the desire for gold is not the same thing as gold, the desire for good is itself a good' (Simone Weil).

Yes, the desire is *a* good; but it is usually a much lesser one

[253]

than the good that we desire. I suppose the proper condition of a human being is to be constantly stretched in longing for what he can't reach; but this state of perpetual strain is surely at variance with the peace of God.

———— * ————

Watched that famous film *Jules et Jim* on the telly. Apart from irritation at Truffaut's mannerisms I was again reminded of how little I have ever been interested in passionate love. (Though I rejoiced in it and suffered from it to the full when I was a young man.)

This is partly, I suppose, because it has been the theme of so much bad or mediocre art in our time. (But from my present position it also looks like one of those noble means which have been turned into inadequate ends: Beatrice was a way to God; transparent to the light of Heaven: Odette is made of some glutinous substance in which men get stuck and blinded.)

———— * ————

Ruby, who used to work for us in Suffolk, paid us one of her periodic visits. A deeper depressive than I've ever been; and with far more obvious cause. But we talk eagerly about our experiences across all the usual barriers of education.

Her visit coincided with our entertaining the DA working party for the day on Sunday. I found the chairing of this meeting very exhausting. To think what a ubiquitous and confident chairman I used to be at Oxford; but now I'm almost desperately aware of the need to prevent anyone being offended by anyone else.

But I like the work, on the whole, and firmly believe that self-help of this kind is one of the few forms of public action which is appropriate in our desperate state of cold dependence.

We drove Ruby back to Kersey, getting up early on Wednesday morning, and she was heavy with misery all the way. I could find very little to say to help her.

Some nostalgia for Suffolk – Hadleigh, Monk's Eleigh, Lavenham, Clare, Cavendish ... The friendly, gentle country-side. But those first ten years of our marriage were not really good years for either of us. I was still a ruthless drinker; and S was the suffering victim.

But nostalgia selects the happy times: taking Jason and Lucy for those huge walks along the valley of the Brett, and all that mythology of the village giants: wading and bathing at Chelsworth; the White Lion at Hadleigh every Wednesday after shopping ... Best, perhaps, that weird weekend with Ben and Jocelyn and the marathon argument about Freddie's first book, and the meaning of meaning. We had arranged the weekend for that purpose; and pursued the argument, without a moment's unpleasantness, from Saturday morning till Sunday evening. Such zest and energy; yet Ben and I must have been nearing forty at the time.

Stevenage, etc: the dormitory towns. Painful reminders of that majority-England which we so easily forget in our beautiful, protected valley. Also the great prairies of the Barley Barons, hedges all torn out and the fields horribly striped with burnt straw.

And when we got back we found the BH neighbourhood seething with frustrated rage. Some Mrs J has let her (rented) field for a rally of Suzuki motor bikes. And there was much shuddering at the prospect of the Modern World, in its most aggressive form, roaring down our lanes and over that beautiful meadow between the oak woods.

I did my best not to share these feelings; but when I examined one of those 1000 c.c. machines I felt real horror and disgust at the hateful perversity of such an object. Having loved motor bikes in my time I respect them still for their neat, light, tidy and compact construction. These monsters not only deny all that with their huge, obscene cylinders and bulging exhaust pipes: their only point seems to be the proclamation of the MALE in all his willed violence and exhibitionism.

Perhaps: yet we heard reluctant admissions afterwards that the rally had been very well conducted; the disco discreet; the young men courteous on those narrow roads ...

Now that we are working three to four hours at BH nearly every afternoon I find I have 'no time' for prayer or meditation. Back here for a quick bath, then out to the pub to reward ourselves for our hard work.

I tell myself that while this period lasts my prayer must be in my work; that this is better, if I can do it, than artificially isolating a daily slot for God. But in fact I still work with all my old ferocity, determined to get a particular job completed each afternoon and blinded to everything except this Stakhanovite ambition. Occasionally I pull myself up, like a man coming out of a state of shock, and paint a few strokes with slow and reverent deliberation. But soon I'm possessed again by the devil of achievement – not 'Now you are *painting – painting – painting* ...' but 'Get it *done!* Get it *done!* Get it *done!*'

And then I reacted strongly against all this; retired to my bed on Sunday afternoon and played Rachmaninov's strange and lovely Vespers – a gift from Ann H when we visited her at Old Jordans. But even there my attention kept restlessly wandering to the book on Von Hügel beside my bed; and it was all I could do not to start reading it before the music ended.

But at least S and I keep to our morning and evening prayer together. This is its present form: 'Lord, help us to receive your loving wisdom, and so to live by the holy light within us. Through Jesus Christ. Amen.' Then: 'And may we love each other, trust each other and honour each other, now and always. Amen.' Then a silent period, which is sometimes a prayer for some particular person.

('And do you really believe,' asks our Composite Infidel Friend, 'that this will do him or her any good?' To which I answer that I don't know whether it does any direct good, but at least it takes our minds away from ourselves and may, perhaps, help us to help that other when we can.)

A good test of a society is how it looks after its old and its mad. By this test we fail abysmally.

———— * ————

'Happy the land that is so ordered that they understand more than they know' (Lao Tzu).

———— * ————

Evensong at Peterborough has now appeared in *Encounter*, and although I try to expect nothing at all from this, a ludicrous vision of mass intellectual conversion tempts my imagination.

———— * ————

A dream almost too typical to be true. Both my wives were standing very close together and telling me that I was about to be submitted to a final test. Would I or would I not get drunk at the party which was just about to begin? If I did they would despair of me and abandon me forever. The next thing I knew I was staggering helplessly through a crowd of laughing faces, but trying with all my might to walk with dignity. Fell down: woke up in horror.

The reason why guilt is worse than useless is that it keeps our heads buried, and suffocating, in our own past.

———— * ————

A very loving letter from Lucy. I was as much surprised by this as I was delighted, for though I assumed she was fond of her father I also believed that she thought me an absurd and perhaps an embarrassing figure. But her letter showed respect as well as love.

It also showed that she didn't believe that *I* respected *her*. How needlessly we suffer from such unexamined assumptions, projecting our own insecurity even into the minds of our closest and dearest.

I told her, truthfully, that I think her job as a psychiatric nurse far more important than mine; her excellence at it far more worthy of respect than my skill at reviewing books.

———— * ————

I would like to write a book, or a long article, in which I would compare the insights of Freud and Fénelon. Reading Fénelon's letters aloud S and I are constantly, and naively, amazed that this seventeenth-century prelate should 'speak' so immediately and intimately to our own condition.

———— * ————

Terry tells me on the telephone that Maurice Richardson has died in his sleep. Old companion of my gamey days: a clever, caustic, disreputable man, and one of the best comedians I've ever known. We once wrote a book together; a sort of modern symposium. But he was a fiercely funny enemy of 'mumbo', and would have detested the pious speculations of this journal.

———— * ————

Sudden brilliance of the chestnut tree across the road. Bright yellow leaves in the sun. How enlivening, inspiriting they are – these unexpected shafts which strike into the heart from the outside world.

———— * ————

S, who endured but hated the violent reconstruction of BH five years ago, is delighted to see it taking its old shape again – particularly the hall, with its elegant staircase and gallery. And I felt, as I worked there, like an admonished child: 'Now, Master Philip, you put all that back just exactly the way you found it!'

I don't share her intense love of that house; or of our Suffolk cottage before it. But I am more and more aware of building as one of the most satisfying and elemental occupations. How well I understand why Jason has chosen it. How little I would have understood this when I used to be driven frantic by my fears for his academic future.

———— * ————

Redemption, yes: Atonement, no.

———— * ————

[258]

Lu's charming account of how the older nurses in her hospital warned her that the patients are always extra-difficult on the night of the full moon.

——— * ———

'The peculiar nature of questions is that they don't have the same limiting character as answers and statements. If one can avoid saying anything, if one can ask a question and not expect an answer, if one can look at a mystery and not expect it to be revealed, if we can look at the veil of consciousness and not expect it to be lifted ... From time immemorial the asking of questions has been regarded as a more penetrating thing than the giving of answers. And the asking of questions is really within the power of us all' (Bennett).

Keats's negative capability; which I made the superscription for my little book called *Towards the Holy Spirit*. Very occasionally, now, I can rest in an ignorance which is a happy openness to belief. This doesn't seem like a foolish credulity: still less like the terrible ignorance of the closed mind. And I hope the time will come when any minor illumination which reaches the mind can be left unspoken: that is, it won't be immediately translated into a possible answer to one of those questions which ache to be answered: it will be thankfully received: and left alone.

——— * ———

I've now given up Paul Scott's Indian tetralogy half-way through. I cannot be interested *for long enough* in what these invented characters are made to do and say. It seems most unlikely that I shall ever try to write another novel; or fiction of any kind. A dying medium? Or has it simply died for me: and to my loss?

——— * ———

Yet I spent much of Wednesday night reading a brilliant little fictionalized biography of a nun who was guillotined in the French Revolution. In a sense she 'failed', so great and obvious was her terror; yet God was with her in that humiliating

[259]

terror even more than he was with those other sisters who behaved with a cold and unblemished courage.

Late that night I felt that my faith had become impregnable.

———— * ————

Dream. By some great effort of mine my mother had been resurrected. Sadness; faint sourness; sense of shame and loss. I woke to the recognition of all that I might have done for her, and failed to do. (*Vice versa* too, of course; but that I *never* fail to recognize.)

———— * ————

Bernanos. His *Diary of a Country Priest* is one of those thirties/ forties books which I somehow failed to read. I found it in the Monmouth library, and as I read it I began to feel that it had been kept for me until it would have the maximum effect. The good bits seem to me as good as any Christian fiction I've ever read. (But what else is there? I can't take Mauriac; and Graham Greene's Christianity is too remote from my own. *Resurrection*, of course, and all the major novels of Dostoevsky.)

Here are some quotations from Bernanos:

'It's a fine thing to rise above pride, but you must have pride in order to do so ... We're all of us liable to lie down in the mud; it seems a cool, soft couch when hearts are jaded. And shame, you know, is a sleep like any other, a heavy sleep, a dreamless intoxication. If a last shred of pride can stiffen the back of some wretched creature, why quibble about it?'

Or this:

'I cannot die without tears. Nothing is further removed from me than a stoic indifference, so how can I hope for the death of a stoic? Plutarch's heroes both terrify and bore me. If I were to go to heaven wearing such a mask, I think even my guardian angel would laugh at me.'

But against all this splendid good sense and loving humility there is a repulsive repulsion at all forms of 'lust', and fearful melodramatics about sins and sinners: 'In their hatred of one another, their contempt, sinners unite, embrace, intermingle, become as one: one day in the Eyes of Eternal God they will be no more than a mass of perpetual slime over which the vast tide of divine love, that sea of living, roaring flame which gave birth to all things, passes vainly.'

Dreadful, blasphemous stuff.

But though I certainly don't share the simple goodness of Bernanos's curé I happily share his strong sense of clumsy failure before God. (The danger of this attitude, though, is a crafty new form of spiritual pride: 'O Lord I thank thee,' prays the publican, 'that I am not as that Pharisee, thanking thee for not being as I am.')

———— * ————

Prayer. Not 'Forgive me for having done X' but 'Help me to know why I did X, so that I may try, with your further help, not to do it again'.

———— * ————

An interview with Jonathan Miller in *The Guardian*. After he has said a lot of interesting things about the higher functioning of the brain Miller is asked whether he believes 'that those higher functions are finally susceptible to chemical analysis? Is there really no ghost in the machine?' He answers: 'It seems very unlikely that we should be so dependent on the brain up to one point, and that suddenly some totally new dispensation takes over in the higher mental functions. I can't believe we get to some level of human activity and it evaporates into the metaphysical.'

This is a bright and disturbing way of stating the materialist position; and a possible argument against a Creator-God. But I see the entry of God into the mind not as a sudden event, either in the individual or in the evolution of the race, but as a slow seepage; an advancing tide. There is no climactic point, either in our racial or in our individual development, of which one can say, before this, No God; after this, God.

As for 'evaporates into metaphysics' that is the stale and emotive language of logical positivism. Miller's materialism is

[261]

as much a metaphysical attitude as any other: and, to the convinced believer, the material world is far more vaporous than the *Milieu Divin*. So what I might say in answer to Miller is that there is a blind and senseless process of evolution into which God is gradually able to enter, bringing light and meaning to the emerging human soul.

————— * —————

Yesterday was a 'good' day, in that I worked hard, enjoyed my work, enjoyed my relaxation after it, gave thought to God on several occasions ... But as I recollected the day I realized that I had failed to do S justice from start to finish. For the only justice I can do her is by *manifest and unceasing* love. (This doesn't, of course, mean frequent kisses and spoken assurances, but the perpetual and loving awareness of her presence.)

16 October

From *Observer* review of *The Other Revolution* by Ariana Stassinopoulos (Michael Joseph, London):

> There is, of course, a pretence of genuine conflict – represented in England by Mr Benn's Tweedledum and Sir Keith Joseph's Tweedledee. Tweedledum claims that further nationalization of the means of production will give people more new things at a faster rate than any other political or economic measure. Tweedledee, on the other hand, believes that this uniquely desirable objective will be much better achieved by returning as far as possible to what he calls Free Enterprise.
> True, both Dum and Dee like to prettify their policies with little chirrups of moral enthusiasm: 'Equality!' chirrups Dum, while Dee sings elegant ditties about freedom. But on examination Dum's equality turns out to mean equal submission to the paternalist State, and Dee's freedom means the freedom of rich men to become even richer. In fact these apparent moral ends turn out to be only means, after all, in the great common enterprise called *La*

Grande Bouffe. 'State control,' shouts Dum, 'will feed you even fuller!' 'No!' screams Dee. 'When the rich get fatter everyone else will get fatter too.'

. . . it is usual for sophisticated religious believers to insist that the Kingdom of Heaven is not of this earth: that spiritual changes within the individual soul are in no way related to such crudities as political and economic ideas. I prefer a statement made by Bernanos more than 40 years ago: 'Willy-nilly the social order must henceforth share the natural burden of humanity, embark on the same divine adventure.' It may be absurd to draw up a blueprint for the organization of the Communion of Saints, but it is surely a religious duty to make at least tentative guesses about the right direction for society to take.

Miss Stassinopoulos briskly dismisses that 'counter-culture' of which so much used to be heard ten years ago. But it seems to me quite possible that if the Spirit is allowed to lead it will lead people directly away both from Big Business and from the Big State; that it will lead them into small co-operative groups and enterprises in which, under God, they can assume a new responsibility both for themselves and for one another. For me Dr Schumacher's message becomes more urgently persuasive with every new lurch we make towards the impossible ideal of universal surfeit.

Perhaps not *impeccably* honest, since I still, after all, prefer Dum to Dee.

25 October

This journal is thinning out fast. So many thoughts, ideas, experiences return again and again and if I wrote them down here at each return no reader would be able to stand it.

In fact, as I've also said before, the repetitions are never exact; but the differences are so slight that I haven't the words to do them justice.

——— * ———

I spent part of the afternoon at BH burning tattered old copies of Gide, Cocteau, Valéry, etc., on the bonfire in the yard. And I've sold, to a man from George's in Bristol, hundreds of novels and biographies for which there is no room here at Woodroyd. A *mild* melancholy at the disappearance of books which have been on my shelves for as long as forty years. But also a powerful sense of relief; the casting off of a very cumbersome burden.

———— * ————

On another afternoon I hammered out all the stones with which I'd blocked up the fireplace here; shovelling away the rubble from behind them, and removed the whole apparatus of the 'coffin' Jotul stove. This had stretched itself out between S and me for the last $3\frac{1}{2}$ years, so that we've had to crane above it to see each other across the hearth. Now the fine great fireplace is revealed again; and we plan to buy a tidy new wood stove which will sit well back under the chimney piece.

So we continue the long process of trying to see each other better.

———— * ————

St Luke's Summer. Trees have the power to startle me more and more.

———— * ————

Penderecki's *St Luke's Passion* – curious chance! It is not a particularly difficult work, but it grates on me by its extreme self-consciousness. This is the almost inevitable fault of so much 'modernismus'. 'Make it New,' cried Pound; and he was right that art dies unless it changes. But perhaps it also dies as soon as it knows that it must change. Haydn was a great innovator; what would now be called a revolutionary. But he moved forward so naturally from the natural innovations of Handel that he saw himself simply as writing the best music he could. The same is true even of Beethoven. The rot began with Wagner: in art with the Impressionists: in literature a little later – with Rilke, Valéry, Eliot and Joyce. But this first generation

[264]

of great conscious innovators were so uplifted by the new joy of making it new that they triumphed over their own ingenuity. Since then most of the epigones have been so conscious of the 'new' in Pound's injunction that the 'it' has become of little or no importance.

There is a book called *Future Shock*; and I know very well what the title means: in fact I feel it mildly every time I go to London. But here we live – except for the telly and a few less important gadgets – almost exactly as an elderly middle-class couple might have lived in the English countryside at any time between about 1920 and 1950.

Escapism? A rubbishy old word, which is rightly disappearing from the current vocabulary; for it's a charge which can be flung in every conceivable direction. (Somebody replied to Marx's quip by saying that *revolution* is the opium of the people.)

———— * ————

S says that I am a puritan; as she is herself, of course. Laughable in view of my public record, but true as well, perhaps. (Here too, though, one must beware of the ease with which words can be twisted and turned in our time: 'Don Juan, *of course*, was an inverted puritan.')

———— * ————

The seven trees on the road to St Briavels. First, the cherry in our own hedge; then the chestnut hanging over the road just before Sitting Green; the two oaks in the field opposite High Vale, and the low cedar in the garden there; the two willows just after turning on to the Hewelsfield road. My resolution to pay tribute to *all* of these on *every* journey. (Resolutions! Resolutions!)

29 October

Dreams heavier than ever now. A general descent/retreat. I feel like a crab jerking itself back and back into its dark cleft in the rock. All the ancient faults jerking me back and back.

———— * ————

An Evening Out. No wonder we've become so anti-social. The weary futility of making small talk to strangers, knowing that they are as bored as I am – not by what we are but by what we are obliged to talk about. S and I have more than enough to deal with here: ourselves for a start ...

———— * ————

'Money! Money! Money! ...' as Mischa Auer, playing his usual foreign scoundrel, moaned in some long-ago film, getting up from a great, rich dinner table and covering his face with his hands.

I saw that the only way to allay this insane anxiety was to sit down and do a sum – assuming the worst possible price for BH; the highest conceivable capital gains tax; the maximum future overdraft ... And that appeased my little demon of Mammon for the time being.

———— * ————

'A slow cure, as the maxim says, is always surest. Diseases of the soul as well as those of the body come posting on horseback but leave slowly and on foot' (Francis de Sales).

———— * ————

'I am not sitting on God's chair; I can't tell whether this is true or not, but it is said that everyone, at one moment in their lives, sees the door (which opens into the Other Kingdom). To know this for certain one would have to be God ... An early Sufi of Baghdad is supposed to have said, "Yes, I found this door. It was the door of self-abasement, and strangely enough nobody was actually crowding into it"' (Bennett).

———— * ————

'Heaven does nothing to win the day.
'Says nothing –
'Is echoed.

'Orders nothing –
'Is obeyed.
'Advises nothing –
'Is right.'
(Lao Tzu)

———— * ————

Second Papal election. It matters more, I suppose, than any other, anywhere. But perhaps this is only Christian parochialism.

———— * ————

We took the caravan to Cambridge again for a DA meeting, at first there was some strain and tension. It is a hard task for us depressives to get this great machine into the air, but I'm sure we *shall* do so in the end:

———— * ————

Evensong at St Neots was the clownish counterpart to Peterborough. We arrived at 6.30 to look at the church, and found that the service was just beginning. We sat down as close to the door as possible, so that we could escape unobtrusively as soon as the pubs opened at 7 o'clock.

———— * ————

Then a more or less disastrous visit to my old Oxford friend, Patrick Anderson, and his friend Orlando in their strange, dark house on a lake near Halstead. Patrick had invited several neighbours in for the pleasure of meeting me, so I drank heavily to prepare myself for this ordeal; more heavily still to survive it. If I could have gone to bed as soon as the last of these strangers had left all would have been well. But there was still dinner to come, and much talk expected of me about modern literature. I cannot have contributed much to that discussion; was more interested by Orlando's sudden appearance from upstairs with two semi-tame foxes; have no memory at all of leaving the house or of S driving me back to where we'd parked the caravan.

She was very good to me next morning, as she always is,

[267]

and always used to be when such events were much more frequent.

A good, sprightly day followed, visiting churches and pubs around Thaxted and Finchingfield; the best bit of Essex, and one we'd never seen before.

4 November

A strange argument with Wilson on Thursday. He is a tough old atheist, but claimed that the susceptibilities of Christians should not be wounded by public blasphemy: this must have started with James Kirkup's poem about Jesus, which I had publicly defended. But why, I asked, should Christians be treated with kid gloves? We should *all* be civil to each other, and respect each other's beliefs. But when some Christian prophet harshly denounces modern disbelievers nobody complains that the victims' feelings have been so deeply wounded that the prophet ought to be prosecuted. The Christians' claim to be thinner-skinned than anybody else seems to me to be both arrogant and cowardly.

———— * ————

On Thursday I also went into the Roman Catholic church to say a prayer, as I often do. Instinctive revulsion, as usual, at the insipid Virgin and Child; but as I hurried past it and out into the sunlight I tried to think harder about this, and with more charity. After all, I too worship God as Mother: and all the familiar Christian icons – the Wise Men; the Shepherds; the Annunciation; the Crucifixion ... have proved their worth as means of prayer. Therefore as occasions of transparency in the world's substance through which the light of heaven has shone.

———— * ————

'Sin' is a bad word because it dramatizes, and thus alleviates, the shame of our daily vanities and fears.

———— * ————

On Monday I fought a strong impulse to work at BH in spite of my exhaustion after our short burst of social life. Common sense won, and I spent a fruitful and calming afternoon in bed.

———— * ————

How much can God work through those who don't believe in him?

This is a hard question indeed. For if, in conscious humility, we say, As easily as he can work through us, then what on earth is the point of all our efforts to make ourselves penetrable; receptive; willing containers for the Spirit? But if we say that God can work only through those who believe in him then how do we explain the extraordinary goodness of so many non-believers? A goodness which goes far beyond what their own rational standards of virtue demand of them.

Things become clearer when we think of the saints; for there have been no rationalist saints; indeed the phrase is self-contradictory, since the saint is a holy man even more essentially than he is a good man. It is even possible to imagine a very good rationalist who is demonstrably more virtuous than a very holy saint. The saint, though consumed by love of God and man, might have sudden lapses – e.g. fits of violent ill-temper – which he would bitterly repent. The good rationalist might be serenely, even ardently benevolent, and never fall from his own high standard. Or if he did fall he would not repent: he would make a sensible resolution not to fall again. There is a great gulf fixed between the two; and how well I understand those who prefer the good, sensible, unpretentious rationalist to the extravagant, often wild, often sickly, often 'impossible' figure of the holy man.

Yet it is St Francis who constantly excites my imagination, not John Stuart Mill; and I would rather read a life of General Booth than one of Voltaire.

For what has happened to me *above all* in these last few years is that my tightly constricted mental and emotional world has been broken through, broken out of. I was not only blocked but imprisoned; couldn't get out or get on. Now faith has thrown back the walls and opened the road again: every frontier has retreated out of sight: every person, object, thought, emotion has become permeable; elastic; mysterious; expandable ...

This is why hope is inseparable from faith. No experience need be the recognition of absolute failure or limitation; retreat or boredom. Even the moment which seems utterly dreary, familiar and arid can shine some light in the mind; and not in spite of its dreariness but because of it.

6 November

From *Observer* review of *The Inklings* by Humphrey Carpenter (Allen & Unwin, London):

(C.S.) Lewis loved his friends as they were not capable of loving him in return; yet if he was aware of this failure in them he never showed any sign of it. He bore even the cold removal of Tolkien from his company without either reproaching his 'friend' or withdrawing any of his inordinate admiration for Tolkien's work. I feel sure that if Screwtape himself had come to Lewis in a state of affliction Lewis would have taken that unconvincing old demon to his heart and given him beer and comfort.

In one of his few polemical passages Mr Carpenter tries to refute the notion that there was something childish about Lewis. Yet I still feel that the devotion of these three men (Tolkien, Lewis and Charles Williams) to make-believe was a limiting rather than a liberating factor. They armed themselves, of course, with all sorts of sophisticated theories about the function of myth; but their love of fantasy worlds does seem to have made them curiously unaware of the real world.

In Lewis's case he not only adored the fantasies of Tolkien; not only created fantasies of his own; he also acted the part of an Old Fogy who belonged to the past more than to the present. In his inaugural lecture as Professor of Medieval and Renaissance Literature at Cambridge he told his audience that the great divide 'was not between those two supposed periods of history but somewhere between the early nineteenth century and the present day, between the greater part of civilized history and what he regarded as the "post-Christian" mechanized society of the present day ... He also alleged that there were still some specimens of the "Old Western Culture" that had existed before this change, and that he himself was one such specimen. "I read as a native texts that you must read as foreigners," he told his audience. "Where I fail as a critic, I may yet be useful as a specimen."'

This attitude is not only dangerously arrogant; it is also childishly evasive. Pretending to be a dinosaur is as foolish as claiming to be the very latest model. The time we live in is the only time we get, and Lewis lived, whether he liked it or not, between 1898 and 1963. His blanket rejection of that almost meaningless concept 'the modern world' meant that he cut himself off from the ever-life-giving present moment. Or at least he tried to do this, and the trying was inevitably a performance.

It was only when Lewis's performance broke down – for example in that deeply moving book about his worst bereavement called *A Grief Observed* – that a man of true and remarkable feeling was revealed. Make-believe is a dangerous game for grown-ups to play; and the wonder is that Lewis was so much of a man in spite of his childish pretences.

11 November

The Kees asked us to visit them and their friends the Goslings, who have just bought a house near Newent. Bob Gosling is a very distinguished psychoanalyst; and they bring up their children on strictly Freudian principles. I can't deny that the whole atmosphere of that house was splendid and delightful;

a rare sense of freedom and order; the kind of freedom which produces a good and fruitful order.

Not that I had much time to study this attractive scenario, for I'd drunk a lot before our arrival, and was soon incapable. Vague memory of S and Cynthia helping me to the car, and Robert dancing and howling with glee in our wake.

Some shame in the morning that these nice people should have seen me in my silliest condition. And how that shame echoes me back through years and years of recurring shame!

But perhaps I've grown tougher with those years: it's even possible, I suppose, that I now care less about how I seem and more about what I try to be. In any case, and with all respect to the Goslings – they are, after all, professional understanders – I soon recovered from my distress. (Rather a quick sequel, though, to the Fiasco at Halstead.)

———— * ————

Tymawr again – after their October holiday from all guests. Immense relief and happiness; refreshment, as if the long month had been a desert.

This, and Laura's present happiness and strength, have greatly revived our spirits. Her new-found independence is an extraordinary achievement. Gift? No, no! He must leave us *some* credit for our own efforts.

———— * ————

I am buying all the books on Gloucester Cathedral that I can find. My aim – my *resolution* – is to know it so well that I could be a professional guide there if I wished.

———— * ————

Working at BH is becoming a way of life for S and me. We spend nearly every afternoon there, and the house is slowly becoming presentable again. Shared enjoyment; shared jokes . . . the special love of two builders and decorators for each other.

———— * ————

'We should carry out our human obligations within the social context in which we are set, unless God specifically

[272]

orders us to withdraw from it' (Simone Weil).

There's much comfort in this, from so austere a source. And here she is, in a different context, at her superb best:

'The proper method of philosophy consists in clearly conceiving the insoluble problems in all their insolubility and then in simply contemplating them, fixedly and tirelessly, year after year, without any hope, patiently waiting.

'By this standard there are few philosophers. And one can hardly even say a few.

'There is no entry into the Transcendent until the human faculties – intelligence, will, human love – have come up against a limit, and the human being waits at this threshold, which he can make no move to cross, without turning away and without knowing what he wants, in fixed, unwavering attention.

'It is a state of extreme humiliation, and it is impossible for anyone who cannot accept humiliation.

'Genius is the supernatural virtue of humility in the domain of thought.'

Passages like this make me wonder again how I dare to think of publishing this ragbag of confused thinking, naive speculation, repetitive personal history. Let me try to reassure myself again – in the manner of Simone W: it is precisely *because of* its clumsiness, naiveté, confusion and confessional brashness that this journal may be of value to others. The spectacle of such an incompetent, yet undiscouraged, traveller may persuade a few hesitant readers to begin the journey themselves.

———— * ————

Christian Experience; Christian Counsel; Christian Living – all these add up to Christian Witness.

But Christian Thinking is a much more dubious affair.

———— * ————

Talking to Father C at Tymawr. He said that he thought God would intervene at the last moment to prevent us

[273]

destroying ourselves by nuclear war. Why did his confidence seem so strange and alien to me? For I also believe that God can intervene directly in the world.

Yes; but not so simply and directly as that; or why is history what it is?

———— * ————

A small sign of grace. On the way to Monmouth last Thursday I was trying to correct my review proofs in the car. Sunlight on the autumn trees of the valley forced my attention away to where it should always have been. I thanked God for this brightening of my eyes.

———— * ————

Dream. The usual type, in which I am hopelessly lost in some foreign town: it is my own fault that I am lost, and everyone is exasperated with me. But this time I felt strangely free and untroubled, accepting my utter futility and uselessness without distress. This was not in any sense a religious feeling, but a sort of sly, underdog's grin.

But why make such hard and fast distinctions? The grinning underdog may also be padding towards the light of the Great Underdog Above.

27 November

Thorpe. I feel so little pity; so much 'righteous' indignation. This is absurd as well as unpleasant, for if he were poor and unknown I would have very different feelings.

———— * ————

Iran. A political situation in which I can't see the faintest glimmer of light. A vile regime will be overthrown by one of two equally vile regimes – fanatically religious and intolerant or fanatically Marxist and intolerant.

When a social-political situation is looked at *only in its own terms* there is no reason whatever to expect a hopeful outcome. In fact it may well be that there is no hope anywhere in social

[274]

or political terms. Yet hope is an indestructible reality within the human soul.

—— * ——

St Francis de Sales. A great and lovable man; but I find his spiritual direction much too florid and literary. An example of self-conscious art becoming a real obstacle to the free movement of the Spirit.

—— * ——

'How many times I've said to myself, "I am being born again; now I am rising from the dead." And what did I see? The same man rose again. He never really died. You see how many ways we can deceive ourselves' (Bennett).

Curious. I have never for one moment deceived myself on that score. It is a grim thought that a series of deceptive rebirths may be the necessary prelude to a true one.

—— * ——

I am working hard on the lecture I promised to give to the Unitarians in April. They need a copy – to be printed – by the New Year; but I have seldom found anything so hard to write. Provisional title – *Christians Then and Now*.

2 December

'To ask therefore by what strange or extraordinary effects the work of the new birth is to be known and felt to be done in the soul is a very improper and useless question. Because regeneration is not to be considered as a thing done, but as a state that is progressive or a thing that is continually doing ...' (William Law).

—— * ——

Persistent difficulty with the Essex Hall lecture. I pray for help; and sometimes feel that I've received it.

—— * ——

We drove to Cardiff docks to buy me a fisherman's sweater.

[275]

The fan belt broke at a most inconvenient time and place; and this brought out all my old raging, intolerant, childish impatience. A great disappointment, for I'd hoped it was now at least partially subdued. (Always such a contrast to S's calm good sense, which she *never* uses as a reproach against me: on the contrary she actively sympathizes with my condition and does all she can to help me out of it.)

———— * ————

A dreadful visit to Em in her new ward. I suppose there is some very persuasive administrative reason for moving these poor old people, and cramming them together here. But what a cost in fear and misery! Em could hardly speak to us; hardly knew who we were.

———— * ————

Essex Hall Lecture. I seem to have acquired surer and wider beliefs every time I have to make some public declaration of them. Yet I can't think of any personal experience which would justify this. Where does it come from, then? By the grace of God, working imperceptibly within me? Or simply by the mind having its own way: constructing new patterns of belief according to its own chosen rules; a preposterous intellectual advance into a vacuum?

15 December

I wrote a reply to Dr Edward Norman's Reith lectures in last Sunday's *Observer*, but I shan't put it down here. All the points I made in it will be made in the Essex Hall lecture, which I *shall* include here if ever I get it into presentable shape.

But how easily and fluently I wrote that reply; and how strangely that contrasts with all this agonizing over my own lecture. I see quite clearly why this is so. The *Observer* article was commissioned at short notice, and had to be written within two days. I also had Norman's lectures in front of me to work on. So it was a professional job of a very familiar kind; a book review with more than a touch of the sermon. Whereas this wretched lecture of mine is not only far outside my usual length, with a dateline nine months ahead, but it had to be written in a vacuum, with nothing to peg it on.

18 December

We had each been in our own kind of private distress – which means that we could suffer only against each other and no help could pass between us. In this condition we had to meet Laura, who was waiting for us outside The George in tears from a row with Paul. How hard it was to comfort her, out of our own separation and debility!

Now snow has enclosed the house, shutting us in with our miseries. If only we had the freedom of spirit to go out, all three of us, and dance together in the snow, under the full moon. To the glory of God. (The glory of God! How such over-used phrases can suddenly light up for me; even in this present darkness!)

21 December

Was there ever a man with a lower pain threshold than mine? Well, of course there was; but God knows my resistance is very feeble.

In this condition I read Mary Craig's wonderful book *Blessings*: and her appalling afflictions made my own seem outrageously trivial; and even frivolous. And therefore even less easy to bear!

Fear of Christmas: imaginations of disaster.

22 December

A rich, sick old man lying in bed as Christmas approaches,

praying for help to sustain him as a loving, merry, life-giving father and husband throughout the 'festivities'.

Sometimes I wish I could have all my memories excised from the brain so that there would no longer be this heavy weight of the past to drag at my feet. Yet I know that all those harsh and repulsive memories are the very material which we have to use in our work of self-erosion.

23 December

We've started reading Basil Hume's talks to the Ampleforth monks (*Searching for God*) and this has blown a clean and cleansing air through my mind. The simple, authoritative voice of a true Christian. (I love the word 'frugality', which seems to imply fruitfulness springing from simplicity.)

Philosophy, whether secular or Christian, seems like a trivial *game* in the face of this quiet and masterly wisdom.

27 December

But Christmas was delightful, after all. My old friend Tom from Cardiff spent the day with us. I knew him as 'Tony' in our bad old London years, and he seemed at that time to have put his Welsh working-class background quite behind him. Since then he has been through many desperate hells of drink and drugs, which drove him not only back to his origins, but also in search of God. We talked of the Gargoyle Club with a shuddering nostalgia.

S, Tom and I went to mass at Tymawr while the children slept; and when we came out he and I imagined ourselves sitting in the Gargoyle with all our cronies of 1940, and somebody telling us that we would be attending a convent mass together in 1978. (But perhaps we wouldn't have laughed. Perhaps the news would have been a great relief to us, like news brought to prisoners that they will eventually be released.)

Jason came over with us to see Em; and the whole atmosphere

of the new ward had mercifully changed for the better. But he, who had been so cheerful and talkative on the way to Gloucester, was struck dumb with distress at what he had seen there; and in particular with pity for Em. (He has known her almost as a close relation since he was seven.) But what I had noticed more than anything was that the sweet light of her smile had come back again. Surely this is the clear light of God which can shine even out of a mind which is utterly confused.

29 December

Suddenly yesterday morning I observed that there was bright blood in my pee. Cancer of the bladder, naturally! But I was amazed to find that this assumption hardly seemed to bother me – though I've suffered so cravenly from Timor Mortis all my born days.

But when S consulted one of her medical books it became quite obvious that the culprit was the beetroot we'd had for supper the night before. So my heroic composure was wasted, in a sense, but it's nice to know that I achieved it, however briefly.

——— * ———

THE ESSEX HALL LECTURE FOR 1979

An address to the Annual Meeting of the General Assembly of Unitarian and Free Christian Churches

'The Modern World' is a phrase which arouses violently different emotions in different members of it, but it might be generally agreed that an apt historical title for it would be *The Age of Analysis*. Indeed scientists have so accustomed us to deciding what a thing is by asking what it is made of that this has come to seem the only reasonable procedure. Think, after all, what brilliant results have been achieved by breaking down the objects of scientific examination into their smallest possible constituent parts.

By what may now seem a highly dubious analogy Freud and his followers set out to treat the human mind in the same way. In the manner of an anatomist Freud divided the mind up into different parts, labelled them according to their functions and set about curing their malfunctions in the same kind of way that an ordinary diagnostician treats the human body. Psychiatrists are now a part of our popular folklore: with a strange mixture of fear, awe and disdain we call them shrinks; or trick-cyclists. And though very few practising psychiatrists are now dogmatic Freudians what has survived is a general tendency to probe the mind with a view to healing it. And this in turn has led us to make amateur analyses of our own minds. 'Trouble with me is I've got a mother-fixation' is a perfectly probable thing to overhear in a pub or on a bus. *The Age of Analysis* has also become *The Age of Self-Consciousness*.

Meanwhile a quite distinct intellectual movement of our time has also sprung from the habit of analysis and has helped to lead us into the condition of extreme self-consciousness. This was the Viennese philosophical school of Logical Positivism which produced as one of its heirs the Anglo-American school of Linguistic Analysis. Very roughly speaking the central faith of these two movements was that most, if not all, philosophical problems could be reduced to problems of language. Professor Joad's famous 'It depends what you mean by ...' on the wartime *Brains Trust* was the popularization of this attitude; and nowadays most of us are at least vaguely aware that whenever we have to think hard about a subject we have to think hard about the ambiguities of our language. We live in *The Age of Semantics*.

———— * ————

So I, a product of *The Age of Analysis*, *The Age of Semantics*, *The Age of Self-Consciousness*, feel obliged to begin this talk by discussing what I mean by its title. But since the first term is the difficult one I don't intend to spend very much time on the other two.

[280]

Time implies place: the words 'then' and 'now' imply somewhere. My somewhere will be what are now generally called the Advanced Industrial Countries – with special reference to England, which is the one I know far the best. In fact this geographical term corresponds well enough with what used to be called 'Christendom' (the obvious exceptions are Japan in one direction; Latin America in the other).

As for my 'Then' I take it to mean any time within Christendom between the first and nineteenth centuries; and my 'Now' shall be our own century with particular emphasis on the years 1978 and 1979. (I am writing this in 1978: I hope to be speaking it in 1979.)

And now comes the hard part. But since a definition has just come my way I shall leap on it with the gratitude of one amateur semanticist to another. Father von Balthasar, who has written a fine and famous book about prayer, has also written a little paperback called *Who is a Christian?* Here, after an uneasy preamble fifty times longer than mine, he finally arrives at his definition: 'A primary and inescapable assertion for everyone who truly believes in Christ's life work is that Christ is the only Son of the Father, the sole intermediary between God and men, the only Saviour, who on the cross has given satisfaction for all: the first-born (first-fruit) of those raised from the dead, who, according to St Paul, is the first principle of all things.'

In other words Father von Balthasar denies the title of Christian to anyone who does not fully accept the doctrines of the Trinity, the (unique) Incarnation, the Atonement, the Resurrection and the Pre-existent Logos.

If he were asked by what authority he delivers this definition he would probably answer, by the authority of the Roman Catholic Church. But he might answer, with a more generally accepted cogency, by the authority of traditional usage: the holding of these beliefs has been very widely associated, and for a very long time, with the claim

[281]

to be a Christian. In fact, of course – as von Balthasar knows well and you know even better – men and women have been calling themselves Christians ever since the first century without conforming to this doctrinal test. And in our *Age of Analysis*, our *Age of Semantics*, our *Age of Self-Consciousness* the term has been scrutinized, disputed and worried over as never before, though mercifully with a great deal less ferocity now than then.

As for me, I must reject von Balthasar's right to tell me whether or not I may call myself a Christian: yet, by the very fact of this rejection, I must try to say what I *do* mean when I give myself that very ambiguous title. Here, then, is an attempt to describe what seems to me to be the essential and enduring core of the Christian faith:

I call myself a Christian because I discern in the New Testament a man whose life, death and central teaching penetrates more deeply into the mysterious reality of our condition than anyone or anything else has ever done. In the Gospels, the Acts and the Epistles I find a total view of what man is, of what he could and ought to be, which evokes a response in me such as no other writings have ever evoked. For me the heart of the New Testament is the assurance that there is a God whose power lies in his total love; that this God not only transcends the natural world but also enters that world through the minds and hearts of men. I accept, with grateful love, the supreme commandment given to his disciples by the Jesus of St Luke's gospel: 'Thou shalt love the Lord thy God with all thy heart, and with all thy soul, and with all thy strength, and with all thy mind; and thy neighbour as thyself.'

I believe that man's highest destiny on earth is to be born again into the Kingdom of Heaven. I believe that God is spirit, and that those who would come to him must come in spirit and in truth. I believe that perfect love casteth out fear, and that the truth shall make us free. I know that for me Jesus is the Way, the Truth and the

Life, and that this way is my only hope of learning to love God as I am already loved by him. I believe that this way can lead us to love our enemies and do good to those who hate us; bless those who curse us and pray for those who ill treat us. I believe that those are blessed whom Jesus named as blessed in the Sermon on the Mount, and that through being blessed in those ways we can receive a heavenly peace which is deeper than any that the world can give us.

When I pray in formal words the words I use are these: 'Lord, help us to receive your loving wisdom, and so to live by the holy light within us. Through Jesus Christ our brother and bringer of light.' I believe that Jesus died for us in the sense that he accepted an agonizing death rather than abjure his message of a heavenly love which far transcends even the most venerable of holy laws and sacred traditions.

I think it likely that Jesus was revealed to his disciples after his physical death, but it is not this belief which leads me to call myself a Christian.

———— * ————

Thus, by painful analysis, awkward self-consciousness, much searching for new words and much reliance on old ones, a man who calls himself a Christian has tried to explain what he means by the word. But although this is self-evidently a personal statement I am by no means resigned to calling it a subjective one.

In the confused and often torrid spiritual climate of our time there has been a strong tendency to say that all ways are equally valid; that the individual traveller must simply choose the path which suits him best. A popular image has been that of a mountain wreathed in mist, and of climbers trying to ascend it by many different routes. It is said that the invisible mountain top is the same, almost impossible goal of every climber, and that although some climbers reach higher than others this is not dependent on choosing any single route which is 'the best'. It is dependent solely on the spiritual gifts and spiritual labours of the individual mountaineer.

Now this is a very persuasive image, and its popularity has surely signified a healthy reaction against that earlier – and peculiarly Christian – conviction that, whereas ones' own route does indeed lead upward towards the mountain top of Heaven, all the others lead steeply downwards into hell. Yet a moment's thought will surely show that though a purely subjectivist attitude to one's own faith may be both humble and broad-minded it is also quite impossible to sustain. Do I believe that the way of St Francis was no better than the way of Torquemada? Or that the attitude of the crusaders towards Moslems was just as right and proper as the attitude of Thomas Merton towards Zen Buddhists?

The answer must surely be, not just that we happen to prefer the attitude of Francis and Merton, but that we believe them to be more in accordance with the will of God and the deepest message of the gospels. Really so. Verily. In truth. And thus I believe that my description of true Christian faith, however inadequate the words I found for it, is not a new-fangled interpretation of my own but the deepest and inmost faith which has inspired all the greatest Christians of all the Christian ages. For I do not believe that the faith I have outlined is in any sense a reductionist one: I am not saying that Jesus was merely a very good man who said some very wise things: I am saying that Jesus was filled with God, and that in most of what he said and did and suffered he was speaking and acting directly under that inspiration.

You will have caught the slightly jarring note of that 'most of'. I do not know how closely the Jesus of the New Testament resembles the man who died at least forty years before the first gospel was written. But I do know that the man who is presented to us in the gospels is the only Jesus we have; and I do know that this man is a humanly contradictory figure who sometimes failed to live up to his own highest teaching. The man who warned us against judging others continually judged the scribes and pharisees with virulent anger: the man who told us to love our enemies sometimes condemned those who refused to accept him to burn everlastingly in hell.

It is an irony of the New Testament that not even Jesus himself could always keep the new and high law which he had given to mankind. And if Jesus was guilty of all-too-human anger how much harder has it been for his followers to love as their master taught them to love. The history of Christianity has been largely a history of their failures.

——— * ———

The History of Christianity! Beset by our modern habit of stopping short at a familiar phrase and looking at it again I begin to think of the works I have read lately with these words for their title. They usually start with the Apostolic Age, attempting to give us some picture of how the earliest Christians organized themselves for worship and mutual support. This is followed by a review of the early Fathers, from Justin to Origen, explaining their various contributions to Christian thought and belief. And so it continues: the conversion of Constantine; councils, creeds, schisms and heresies; St Augustine against Pelagius; Caesaropapism in Byzantium; the papacy in its long struggles for power with kings and emperors; the 'Christian Renaissance' of the twelfth and thirteenth centuries; the Crusades; the Reformation; Nonconformity in England and America; Christian missions East and West ... the Present Age with its ecumenical movement, Second Vatican Council and World Council of Churches ...

Of course this summary does less than justice to much excellent historical work: but the point that must surely strike a Christian is that whatever his faith may be it has not been captured and revealed in the learned pages of these books. What they have told us about is the organization and development of Christian Churches; the public actions of individual prelates; disputes about doctrine between learned and angry men; wars waged in the name of Christianity either against non-Christians or between Christians of different doctrinal allegiances; the attempts to persuade members of other faiths to accept the sole and saving faith of Jesus Christ; and finally the attempts of divided Churches to understand each other better.

Now a traditional Roman Catholic would indeed believe that a history of his Church and its doctrine is a true history of much that is contained in the word 'Christianity'. To a believer of this kind the Church is a holy institution; founded by Jesus himself when he appointed Peter to be its first leader; inspired by God throughout the ages, at least whenever the popes have spoken *ex cathedra*. For such a believer his Church is the Bride of Christ; a continuing incarnation of the Spirit: its doctrine and its discipline lie near the heart of any truly Christian life. To this man the proclamation of the dogma of the Immaculate Conception by Pius IX in 1854 is a historical event of profound Christian significance.

Yet I believe that even a devout Roman Catholic would not feel that a history of his Church and its doctrine is *precisely the same thing* as a true history of Christianity. However strong his reliance on Mother Church; however deep his belief in the divine inspiration of her teaching, he knows that his faith is in more than a Church and in much more than an assemblage of intellectual propositions.

———— * ————

The figure who almost always escapes the dragnet of the historian is the individual private man. To the political historian he is simply a voter; to the military historian an unknown soldier in any army; to the social historian the member of a social class. Yet to a Christian this man is neither less nor more important than the greatest of popes or the most learned of theologians. For the central and enduring mystery of the Christian faith is the individual believer as he stands before his God.

It may be that he reaches this ultimate situation by means of a priest and a Church and a body of doctrine. It may be that he seeks an intermediary in the form of a saint or the Virgin Mary. It may be that he finds help in a particular liturgy or in attendance at a meeting of like-minded worshippers. It may be that he dispenses with all these well-tried aids and relies exclusively on private prayer and the direct inspiration of divine love. 'Thou shalt love the Lord thy God with all thy heart, and with all thy soul, and with all thy strength and with all thy mind.' In St Matthew's gospel this commandment to love God is separated from what follows it by a slight pause. 'And the second is like unto it. Thou shalt love thy neighbour as thyself.'

In either case Jesus makes it plain that the second commandment, or the second part of the single Great Commandment, is intimately dependent on the first. The man who prays well is a man who loves well and who necessarily shows his love by his actions. And this law of the necessary inference is no less applicable to a solitary hermit than it is to a Christian working in a leper colony. For if the hermit is concerned only with saving his own soul, or with the union of his own spirit with the Spirit of God, then, by that fact alone, he will fail in both his endeavours. The true hermit or mystic knows himself to be a channel for the entry of God into the world; an utterly mysterious channel which nevertheless diffuses the descended Spirit into the hearts and minds of others.

———— * ————

If all this, as I strongly believe, is a truism of true Christian faith then it's clear that a history of Christianity becomes a very problematical enterprise indeed. In fact the whole idea of a full and accurate history is an absurdity;

for what can a historian know about the hearts, the souls and the minds of individual Christians over the last two thousand years? Even if he had detailed records of church attendance for every age and area of Christendom; even if he had account-books listing the giving of alms in every congregation since the apostles; even if he could number all the benevolent acts performed by Christians throughout the centuries of our era – all this would profit him nothing. The descent of the Spirit; the illumination of the soul; the manifestation of love – all these are immeasurable by any human standard of measurement.

I had thought, until I thought a little harder, that *A History of Christians* might be a more hopeful undertaking than any so-called *History of Christianity* could ever be. But here the semanticist puts in his oar at once; and I hear the gritty voice of Professor Joad pronouncing from so long ago, 'It depends what you mean by a Christian.' Better, perhaps, to ask what *is meant* by a Christian, and when I ask myself that question I arrive at a working minimum of five distinct meanings. The word is used to mean anyone who would accept the title when offered such alternatives as 'an atheist'; 'a Buddhist'; 'an agnostic', but who goes through none of the outward or inward observances. The word is also used to mean someone who follows the outer observances – says his prayers and goes to church – but whose inner and outer life is otherwise indistinguishable from those of his atheist and agnostic associates. Or the word can mean someone who devotes all his life and energy to what he takes to be the Christian faith, but from this faith the central heart of love seems to be not only missing but flatly contradicted. Or the word can be used of a man who tries as hard as he can to follow the Great Command-ment, who sometimes succeeds but often fails; yet whose failure is always the occasion of a renewed devotion to the light. Finally the word may mean someone who has achieved a large and observable measure of success in following the way of love. I shall speak of Nominal Christians for the first category; Observing Christians for the second; Distorted Christians for the third; Working Christians for the fourth and Saints for the fifth.

———— * ————

Equipped, by the analytical and self-conscious age in which we live, with these five overlapping, these very rough-and-ready categories, the time has come to take another look at the history of Christians, in the hope that something more direct may at last be said about the title of my talk. What I am confronting now is the widely accepted dictum that we – we of the Advanced Industrial Nations; we of what was once called Christendom – are now living in a 'Post-Christian Age'. This phrase has been more on the lips of Conservative than of Radical Christians, but the feeling that it expresses is widely shared by most kinds of Christians and by virtually all non-believers. Yet the harder I have looked at it, in the light of my five categories, the more uncertain I have become about its meaning.

Perhaps I can explore my uncertainty best by beating another enormous retreat and examining, first of all, a period of Christian history very remote indeed from our own.

In the year AD 303 the Christian minority in the pagan Roman Empire had enjoyed almost complete toleration for nearly fifty years. This period was harshly brought to an end when Diocletian unleashed a savage persecution throughout the Empire; a persecution which continued for almost exactly ten years. During that period Christian worship was forbidden and all citizens of the Empire were ordered to take part in official pagan sacrifices. Thousands of Christians suffered martyrdom.

By 350 Christianity had been the official religion of the Empire for a quarter of a century, and the number of both Nominal and Observing Christians had immeasurably increased. We must suspect however, that many, if not

[289]

most of these new converts were time-servers: we know that the Christian emperors, Nominal and Observing, were cruel and barbarous fratricides: we know that the Church was now savagely split by rival factions, each calling the others heretics and each appealing to the current emperor for official support in persecuting the others.

So the Christian historian might conclude that the age of the martyrs was an age of better Christians than the age of the second-generation Christian emperors. It might be claimed that a persecuted Church is more likely to contain good Christians than a ruling and reigning Church. But alas, there is a further irony in store for us. The martyrs may have been heroes of the faith, but many of their kind who survived without apostatizing proved to be intolerant and unforgiving bigots towards those other survivors who had lacked the courage to disobey the imperial edicts. The ex-heroes treated their weaker brethren as irredeemable backsliders who must never be allowed into the Church again, however penitent they might be.

So it seems that although we may be tempted to prefer the martyrs of 303 to the court sycophants of 350 it is too simple to say that martyrdom is itself a proof of true Christian witness; a noble test of faith's endurance.

Yet at this point another historian might remind us that by 350 the Desert Fathers had already established themselves in the Thebaid. These were the earliest Christian monks, many of them mystics of a high order, most of them devoted servants not only of God but of man as well. And perhaps St Anthony and his followers generated enough spiritual force to atone both for the harsh self-righteousness of the surviving heroes and the squalid self-seeking of the courtiers.

But where are the scales to weigh the saints against the rest? They are certainly not to be found on this earth.

———— * ————

Perhaps, then, we shall find a simpler and more encouraging balance sheet if we turn again to that famous Age of Faith which used to be praised so highly by the romantic medievalists of fifty years ago. Surely those great cathedrals of the twelfth and thirteenth centuries could have arisen all over Western Europe only out of communities which yearned for the God of Love in some such way as their towers and arches seem to be yearning from earth to heaven. Surely the marvellous life and ministry of St Francis led to a flowering of the purest Christian love since Pentecost itself. Surely the Cistercian revival renewed all that had ever been holiest in Christian monasticism.

Yes, but not only were the peasants condemned to live in a state of brutish and abject poverty: hardly anyone in the Church considered this affliction a proper subject for their concern. And what are we to say of those monstrous expeditions which were given the lofty name of Christian crusades? What are we to say about the ruthless persecution of the Albigensians, or of the popes' overriding concern that they should prove themselves more powerful princes than any temporal prince?

Would it be more pertinent, then, to this vexed question of our so-called 'Post-Christian Age' if we were to take a period immediately before that great climacteric date of 1859 when *The Origin of Species* shocked so many pious Victorians into incipient disbelief? In 1828, exactly a hundred and fifty years ago, the cloud of evolution was no bigger than a man's hand on the furthest scientific horizon. In England virtually the whole population were Nominal Christians and a majority were in some degree Observant also. Belief in the literal truth of the whole Bible was widespread even among the educated classes. Methodism was consolidating the gains it had made in the previous century. The Evangelical Movement in the Church of England was campaigning not only against the Slave Trade but also against the grossness and laxity still surviving in their own Church from the nadir of the eighteenth century. In that very year the passing of the Catholic Emancipation Bill was an early sign of greater tolerance between Christians of different ecclesiastical allegiances. At Oriel College, Oxford the first seeds of the Oxford Movement were being sown.

Two things emerge with great clarity when we compare the English Christian situation of 1828 with our own: the first is that far more people believed in the full dogmatic apparatus of the Churches; the second is that questions of Christian faith and action were major public issues. Disputes within the Church of England between the Low, the High and the Broad were matters of deep concern to all except the deeply submerged working classes. Today the debate on the ordination of women is good for a jaunty article or two in the newspapers, but is otherwise a matter of purely internal preoccupation to an organization of priests and bishops which has lost the allegience of all but a tiny minority of laymen. Those who are now trying to live Christian lives are faced, in 1978, not with martyrdom, not even with hostility, not even with contempt. They are faced with the deadly indifference of their fellow-countrymen, lightened only by occasional bursts of amused curiosity.

But if we believe, as I do, that Christians have always had to live largely against the dominant society around them is it worse for them to be much or little in the news? Is it a good or a bad thing that the present differences between Christians pass almost unnoticed by the general public? Was it better for Christians when the elevation of a particular bishop could be a cause of scandal not only in the newspapers but also in parliament? If we are agreed that Christianity can never be a matter of counting Nominal and Observing heads, what is – and what might be – the particular quality of Christian life in *our* time?

———— * ————

The Age of Analysis. The Age of Self-Consciousness. The Age of Semantics. And in his Reith lectures Dr Edward Norman has just added, and deeply deplored, *The Age of Liberalism*. What is certainly true is that many Working Christians in the ex-Christendom of 1978 have had to become Thinking Christians as well: they have had to examine themselves and their beliefs in ways which no Christians have ever had to do in the past. We know, of course, that self-examination has always been part of a Working Christian's proper discipline; but what he used to be in search of was sin, as defined for him by his ecclesiastical authority. Our current examination includes a questioning of the very nature of sin, and sometimes a violent shift away from one emphasis and towards another. Away, for example, from failure in precise observance, failure in belief, failure in personal discipline, and towards all kinds of failure in love, failure in honesty with oneself, failure in attention.

Dr Norman is surely right in believing that modern Christians are more tolerant than any generation of their predecessors. But I think he is quite wrong in thinking that genuine tolerance, tolerance as active respect for our neighbour's rights, has been imported into Christianity from some alien humanist tradition. It springs, I believe, from this whole new process of Christian self-examination. Discovering so much wrong in our own history, in our own present thinking and feeling, in our own loveless actions, we have become less piously self-assured about Christian superiority. Analysing many faiths, including the many forms of modern disbelief, we have found much that is good where our predecessors found only evil.

A small minority, then, full of self-doubt, and doubting even some of the most treasured elements in their own faith, surrounded by grey oceans of indifference and much intellectual despair! It sounds a grim enough state of affairs. And indeed there have been many signs over the last thirty years of Christians losing their nerve and reacting with panic to the pressures which this particular age exerts on them. I do not share Dr Norman's belief that Liberalism is the villain of the story: but I do believe that many vocal Christians, confronted by an almost entirely man-centred world, have fallen into the trap of putting the second part of the Great Commandment in front of the first. Avid to show love of their neighbour they have half-forgotten that they can love him truly only through love of God.

This loss of nerve showed itself in a peculiarly abject form about fifteen years ago when several Christian clerics were proclaiming that God had died; when certain theologians were reducing him to such phrases as 'our ultimate concern' or 'the deepest level of our being'; when the phrase 'religionless Christianity' was much in vogue; when even the modern industrial city was elevated to an almost paradisal glory.

Since then that initially healthy wish to understand other systems of belief has induced at least one English monk to write about Buddhism as if it were somehow higher up the social-spiritual scale than Christianity. The perception that peripheral elements of the great Eastern religions can usefully be harmonized with Christian devotional practice has degenerated into respect for forms of meditation which are purely secular and utilitarian. That image of the mountain top, of which I have already spoken, has led some Christians to overlook the fact that at the top of the Hindu mountain broods an impersonal Brahma, while the top of the Buddhist mountain is a holy vacuum, free from any taint of Godhood.

At the same time the magic word 'dialogue' has been treated as a talisman which is capable even of uniting opposites. Many serious Christians seem to have forgotten that Marxism, Freudianism and Sartrian Existentialism are strongly and overtly anti-Christian systems of belief. All of them deride the Christian vision of man as a vessel for the light of God through the medium of the ministry and sacred death of Jesus Christ. All of them deprive man of what we hold to be his deepest humanity – the loving presence of God above him, around him and within him. A Christian Marxist is as queer a creature as a furred fish.

Again, during the most recent period, sections of the younger generation have been swept by various waves of spiritual excitement, charismatic in mood, often fundamentalist in creed. And this movement, so hopeful in its enthusiasm, leads all too easily into yet another form of man-centred blindness. Instead of setting the newly-converted forward on the long and difficult journey of self-erosion it fills him with that conviction of instant and total justification which seems inseparable from a monstrous self-inflation.

———— * ————

Other Christians, of course, have stuck resolutely to their guns, regardless of whether those guns have been spiked or not. A minority of Roman Catholics bitterly regret the pontificate of John XXIII and regard the Second Vatican Council as the opening of terrifying floodgates. Traditionalists in all Churches often seem possessed by the same panic and loss of nerve which has led their radical opponents into a quite contrary form of self-defence. They seem to forget that every 'modern world' in turn has been either stolidly or virulently recalcitrant to true Christian faith and action. They also seem to forget that every modern world in turn has offered its own unique opportunities for Christian endeavour. Instead of recognizing the perennial stubbornness of human greed, cruelty and stupidity – their own included – they treat their human environment as if it were uniquely atrocious and corrupting. Instead of perceiving in the perennial resilience of human hope, human energy and human curiosity a gift of God which should be joyfully accepted and turned to happy account, they turn sourly away from every movement of the mind which seems to threaten any aspect of their great barnacled systems of belief. They forget that every genuine increase in human knowledge must, by that alone, be better than the previous ignorance; that the more we know of earthly reality the more ways we have of approaching the Supreme Reality.

———— * ————

Let's consider the situation once again. A world largely dominated by greed and cruel oppression, in which a small Christian minority confronts either massive indifference or active persecution. The dominant intelligentsia lapped in a benevolent but rather weary humanism – sceptical, critical and deeply suspicious of enthusiasm. Against the oppressive deadweight of formal state religions passionate, non-Christian eruptions of spiritual yearning, often taking bizarre and idiosyncratic forms, and often strongly influenced by wise men from the East. The Christians themselves are divided into those who want to cling to old forms and traditional law and those who want to rush forward too eagerly into alien ways. Surely this is a description of the world of St Paul's epistles.

Of course the differences are enormous; but perhaps there is enough in common between the Christian situation in the first century and in our own to make us feel that our age, too, can be an age of renewal and resurrection. It is time to take stock of our advantages.

First, I would say that in this *Age of Analysis* we are better able than any Christians before us to separate the harmful accretions of the Christian religion from the true heart of New Testament faith. St Paul never spoke an official creed in his life: he never thought that there was anything sacred either in the haphazard organization of the early Christian communities, or in the widely differing rituals which Christians chose to use when they worshipped together. He never supposed that there was anything magical about the role or the function of those who were chosen to preside at acts of corporate worship.

There is a sad law which states that all religions tend towards idolatry: to worship only the highest is too difficult,

[296]

and many of the intended means to that end are elevated into independent ends. Father von Balthasar defines a Christian not by his love of God and neighbour through the medium of Jesus Christ, but by whether he subscribes to a number of theological propositions which were evolved by bitterly disputing men during the first five centuries after the death of Jesus. But it is open to us to recognize, at this time, that formal creeds and dogmas are at best a sort of metaphorical stutter. We may learn something about God through love, through prayer, through loving and prayerful action, through mystical contemplation; but this knowledge can never be formulated in the language of human debate. It is open to us to recognize that we do better to praise God together than to argue about which set of words is the least inadequate to describe him. It is time for us to recognize that there is such a thing as an idolatry of verbal formulation.

When Pope John allowed certain fundamental arguments to begin within the Roman Catholic Church he made it possible for Catholics to doubt the divine authority of the human organization to which they belonged. It began to be seen that Churches were made for man, not man for any Church. It is open to us to recognize, at this time, that there is such a thing as an idolatry of ecclesiastical organization.

In 1889 Edward King, the saintly Bishop of Lincoln, was summoned to appear before a special court presided over by the Archbishop of Canterbury. The points on which the bishop had been attacked were as follows: 'The eastward position during the Prayer of Consecration; lightened candles on the altar; the mixture of water and wine in the Chalice; the Agnus Dei after the Consecration; sign of the cross at the Absolution and the Blessing; the ablution of the sacred vessels.' Not only priests of the Church of England but ordinary newspaper readers and members of parliament were rent with partisan bitterness for and against the bishop and his practices. It is open to us to recognize, at this time,

[297]

that there is such a thing as idolatry of the means of public worship.

None of this implies, of course, that we should dispense with Churches, or with the use of words in our efforts to describe our faith, or with visible signs of invisible grace when we worship together. But it does imply that our present ability to analyse and examine can be used, not to reduce our faith but to purify it of many top-heavy and usurping inessentials.

Indeed I believe that the Churches are now painfully learning the lesson of their demotion from sacred status: the hard reality of their proper function as the servants, and never the masters, of their individual members. I believe that a new humility of the word has led many Christians to search for new, clumsy, untried words with which to express their yearnings and their clouded visions. And I believe that it is now more widely recognized than at any time since the first century that Christians must be free to choose how they shall worship, both together and alone; what forms they shall use and what meanings they shall attach to those forms. (Which doesn't in the least deny that there are those who can and should give spiritual direction, and those many more who should seek it and receive it.) I also believe that although we still have our Distorted Christians, those who believe that everyone outside their own narrow sect will go to eternal perdition, these unfortunates are well outside the mainstream of Christian thought and hope. *Pace* Dr Norman the progression from burning those who differ from us, to damning them to hell, to disdainfully tolerating them, to humbly learning from them, must be a progression in the direction of the Great Commandment.

We may be living in a desert of greed and triviality – ourselves by no means immune to these dreary vices – but there are many and increasing signs of a new thirst for the waters of the Spirit. The waters that Christians offer must be the pure water of the love of God and man, not

the stale and brackish liquid of intolerant orthodoxy, nor
the bottles of cherry pop handed out by parsons dressed
up in the latest gear.

———— * ————

Christians and Humanists are worlds apart – quite
literally so. But there is at least one major Humanist
perception which has been at best peripheral in the
Christian tradition and which Christians should gratefully
accept from their Humanist brothers. This is the perception that every man has the right, in natural morality, to
realize his own potentiality. A man is dehumanized if he
is forced unwillingly into abject poverty; into political and
social subjection; into sickness of mind or body. To heal
a man is to make him as whole as he is congenitally able
to be; to make it possible for him to love and to create
as best he can.

Because Christians have always recognized the enormous spiritual advantages which may be derived from
voluntary poverty, self-chosen obedience, and even wilful
sickness, they have often failed to recognize the crippling
affliction of enforced poverty, sickness and oppression.

In this herculean task of trying to remove the removable
obstacles to men's freest possible self-development
Christians should, and do, work with Humanists as true
brothers. Yet the strange thing about this alliance is that
the visible end of the journey for the Humanist is simply
a stage, for the Christian, on a further and endless journey.
The Humanist ideal is of a man richly self-fulfilled; self-
reliant yet kindly to others; trustworthy, brave and
contented with his lot. The Christian, on the other hand,
relies not on himself but on his God, and is never contented
with his present state. If he has been largely successful in
healing and freeing himself according to the Humanist
pattern he is immediately intent on destroying that very
self which he has been restoring. For the Christian believes
that he must embrace, by his own choice and will, that

[299]

state of deprivation which he rightly rejected when it was inflicted on him either by others or by his own unchosen disabilities.

Here is a passage from the best spiritual director I have yet found, François de Fénelon, Archbishop of Cambrai in the late seventeenth and early eighteenth centuries: 'Almost all who aim at serving God do so more or less for their own sake. They want to win, not to lose; to be comforted, not to suffer; to possess, not to be despoiled; to increase, not to diminish. Yet all the while our whole interior progress consists in losing, sacrificing, decreasing, humbling and stripping self even of God's own gifts, so as to be wholly His.'

To the Humanist, folly: worse than folly – a sick aberration. To many of us would-be Christians, a stumbling block. And how absurd the failing and dejected Christian feels when he reads such a passage, recognizes its deep and necessary truth yet recognizes also that he is far behind many of his Humanist friends in sheer simple decency and goodness.

The best way I know of levering myself out of this self-mocking dejection is to remember that the men and women I most love and admire have all travelled by this path. And I know that there is a further divine paradox – and one which Fénelon fully explores – the heavenly fact that this is not a path of misery but of joy; not of grinding introspection but of flowering in the sun of God's love. I know that the joy of the saints, whether canonized or not, is as far beyond a decent human contentment as the figure of St Francis shines above and beyond the honourable figure of John Stuart Mill. There is another History of Christianity as well as the one we always read – and that is the unwritable history of Christians, known and unknown, who went at least far enough on Fénelon's way to become true vehicles of God's love for man.

We know what terrible crimes have been committed in the name of our religion, but it is quite wrong to say, as some glib Christian apologists have a habit of saying, that Christianity has not failed because it has never been tried. It has succeeded because it *has* been tried – by St Paul and St Anthony and St Columba; by St John of the Cross and St Teresa of Avila; by St Vincent de Paul and Jacob Boehme and Nicholas Ferrar; by George Fox and John Wesley; by Fénelon and Dostoevsky; by William Law and William Blake; by St Seraphim of Sartov and Edward King of Lincoln ...

And as for this so-called 'Post-Christian Age' of ours we have also had our encouragement of saintly Christian witness – from a Péguy and a Schweitzer; a Bonhoeffer and a Simone Weil; an Evelyn Underhill and a Mother Teresa; a John XXIII and a Danielo Dolci; a Huddlestone, a Dom Camara, a Merton and a Steve Biko. They have shown us that *Liberty of the Sons of God* which St Paul looked for, and often found, in the earliest of all Christian communities. And this century has also had its Christian martyrs, quieter, humbler and more forgiving of their enemies than most of the martyrs who died so stridently under Diocletian.

So in the end, though it has served us well, we have to transcend our *Age of Analysis and Self-Consciousness*. God is not to be analysed: Love is beyond dispute: Holiness means wholeness, and cannot be dissected or divided. After so many inadequate words the Christian's last word is simply 'Yes!' Yes to love of God and man; through Jesus; in this place and in this time.

And this must have met their dateline with a day to spar But I suspect that those Unitarians are going to find me sad credulous; even superstitious. For I doubt whether most of the believe even in one God by now.

1 *January 1979*

'The Christian must aim at nothing less than perfectio

[301]

sanctification.' But for many of us this would be a recipe for despair.

———— * ————

Old BH friends to tea. Real friendship, yet the faintest hint of restraint; as if the ending had left a little cloud between us. Time will surely dissolve it.

———— * ————

Geoffrey Hubbard's *Quaker by Convincement*. A good, interesting and sympathetic book. But in it I find an attempt to define God which precisely expresses the inadequacy, for me, of so much modern religious thinking:

> 'By God we mean a spiritual, non-material force or entity *which may or may not have a separate existence away from the material man*, but which dwells indeed in the inmost heart of every man. This spiritual entity is not uniquely personal, but is universal, so that there is a bond between us all which is stronger than any physical bond. In our unity in God we are part of one another.' (My italics.)

This reservation seems to me to reduce God to nothing more than Jung's collective unconscious, or God as a kind of ethereal parasite which can keep alive only by feeding off the inside of the human mind.

———— * ————

A fairly rowdy Beaufort midday, from which we tore ourselves away to the carol service at Tymawr. I felt as if I were dragging myself back from the ancient past of the Gargoyle Club and into a beautiful but not quite convincing present. That past, after all, is undoubtedly *mine*; an ever present reality within; whereas the present which Tymawr represents is still more of an aspiration than a real possession.

———— * ————

Quotations from *The Hound of Heaven* in some book I was reading. The whole image seems very strange: for me God has been more like a scarcely-glimpsed rabbit, whose scut I've very occasionally thought I may have seen disappearing down its hole.

_____*_____

A delightful and interesting talk with our friend Guy Farrer. He had been propelled towards a search for Christian faith by the death of a beloved wife – rather as I had been propelled by my depression.

Guy had lent me Dean Matthews's *The Purpose of God*, on which he is himself basing a much simpler apologetic. But this book, with its painstaking attempt to contrive yet another intellectual proof of God's existence, seemed very remote from the way my own search is leading me.

I have also just reread Isherwood's marvellous *Ramakrishna and His Disciples*; and nothing could be further from Matthews's arguments than this superbly unselfconscious, even 'crazy' Hindu saint. He was one of those who know, and have no need of any argument.

3 January

Some bug, or psychological disturbance, has kept me in and out of bed since Christmas. Yesterday I forced myself to get up and frame off the section of wall immediately facing me as I lie in bed. I hung Breughel's *Fall of Icarus* in the very middle of this wider frame; then fixed up a little spotlight to shine on the picture when I pull a string beside my bed. And having constructed my private gallery I plan to buy many more reproductions over the years, and make a loving and prayerful study of each in turn. The kind of pictures which I have always regarded as representations of heaven: Bellini; Watteau; Monet ... (Buying my way to heaven again? But why not describe it as forcing Mammon into the service of God?)

When I had one of the speakers up here, the wire carefully hooked to the side of the stairs, Josephine said that I was obviously preparing myself more and more for my final retirement to this bed and this room. And I confess that when I'm feeling lethargic the prospect is very tempting. The bliss of being a well-looked-after hermit; visited only according to his own choice of who and when and for how long!

I find it hard to believe that I could have survived the years of my depression without the loving care of S. So perhaps I wouldn't *have allowed myself* to enter that hell unless I'd been sure that her help would be at hand there. Depression as a baleful luxury! (For it certainly seems to be true that those in dire physical need are never depressed: they have no time for depression, being kept so busy by the struggle to keep alive.)

——— * ———

Now we trudge through the snow to Barn House nearly every afternoon to do our work there. And back at twilight, happily tired and very close together.

——— * ———

Thinking of Phine it seems that she is the most special of all my children, being the oldest; the longest known and loved. But then I think of the others in turn, and I realize, with joy, that each one is special, and that the love I feel for them is different in each case but genuinely equal.

4 January

S had sent a Christmas card to Patrick (Anderson) and Orlando; and this is the major part of the strange document which Patrick sent in return – with no covering note:

A VISIT

... the course of my friendship with Philip – an *old* friendship, and few epithets can be more ambiguous in this context, recently and rather laboriously renewed – has always had elements of envy, competitiveness and self-justification. We were intimate only during the year 1938, we met briefly and somewhat emotionally from time to time after the war and wrote to each other now and then during the succeeding years. I think that, while it lasted, ours was a real intimacy. At Oxford we delighted in each other's company but Philip was, of course, a strong heterosexual personality with many friends and interests

[304]

and some considerable knowledge of the world while I was in many ways sentimental and suburban, a muddled immature person despite my quite considerable university status and I can only suppose some degree of forcefulness and charm. We were, in fact, equals as undergraduates whereas in 1947 I was an insecure colonial writer, intoxicated with the modern culture about which I was still learning, while he was a weathered old professional on close terms with many of the leading writers and thinkers of the day. I cannot recall his committing himself about my first publications in this country. When *Snake Wine* appeared to considerable critical acclaim in 1955 he suggested that we should meet and talk about it in a pub, but I don't think much was said. It was perhaps then he told me that he found travel books very hard to get through ... and *Snake Wine* was at least half a travel book. He drank beer, gossiped amusingly and showed a great concern for the cricket scores.

Old friendships, which may mean friendships dead, notably entombed, the shadowy haunters of the perspectives of different lives, are already partly novelistic. They belong, inescapably, to our sense, or our fantasy, of a character swimming through the experience of time. They are distanced by a nostalgia cutting back to innocence; they are lit by a golden, unchanging light. Set early enough, they demand considerable *pietàs*. But they are private as the scar on the knee we cut running and falling on the gravel drive at prepschool or the toughened skin on the back of the neck which is all that remains of an angry adolescent boil. We know all about them and don't want a renewed attention, let alone a reinterpretation, paid to them now. On the other hand, if an 'old' friendship implies grateful continuance, along the lines of 'We've been friends for ages, we've always liked each other', the situation is altered.

When I went to see Philip on the borders of Wales in the autumn of 1976 he was very much the Jesus-Man, long preoccupied with religion, recently beset by melancholia and the founder of an ecology-conscious commune. He wore what looked like a Tolstoyan smock from one of whose pockets he would produce, with a disarming grin, his set of false teeth as though the face were ruefully to acknowledge its skull. For ecological reasons he had wrenched out all the radiators from his house where a single Norwegian stove, the shape of a baby's coffin, did its best to consume the damp branches of that tree-strangled district. Heat was intermittent as was meditation, which took place some-where upstairs. He very quickly declared that God had sent me, for reasons as yet obscure, and grew intolerant (and I thought arrogant) when I started to present him with what I considered to be the least contemptible of my masks, by which I mean that I tried to be entertaining and imaginative and if possible witty in the natural exuberance of my pleasure at seeing him again. He wanted, he reminded me severely on the first evening, nothing false to come between us and I couldn't help thinking that it was he who was making the moral judgements and then demanding that I reveal the spiritual secrets of my life. I agree that, early on, I made one or two foolish remarks but the main area of our disagreement seemed to be that I said I had hero-worshipped him at Oxford while he claimed somewhat similar, if more mature feelings for me. In other words the two novels we had constructed from this part of our lives differed. However my visit, during which we drank a good deal but not really to excess, was long enough for feelings to stabilize, for there to be after-thoughts and new bids for understanding, while it was succeeded by a series of letters in which we seemed to make our positions clear. These letters, some of which dealt with religion (I was then re-reading the New Testament), always led him to welcome the hours of talk when we two old friends should meet again.

Well, what of his recent visit? Everyone agreed it was a great success. Drinks got it going in the first few minutes;

conversation bubbled away in my rarely so crowded study; some pot was smoked later; it ended in kisses and hugs. It was an evening that rose like a rocket to burst in a profusion, a bewilderment of stars. Rocket-like it began with a certain stately slowness as the preliminaries were cleared, the polite fuss with details, the awe and awkwardness of anticipation, but then it soared, busy with its energy and speed, uniting us and our gaze; and, after that *whoosh* of success, how many successive showers of euphoria burned meltingly on the air before the final explosions, the more and more sporadic flashes and liquid trails ushered the darkness back again! Who cared by then? It had been a good effort, a good show. It was, to use the language of the 'quality Sundays', at least a *tour de force*. Since I had masterminded the display, actually drawing up a timetable to convince O that the thing was possible – Arrival and first drinks 5 p.m. – 6; Introduction of five other guests and general partying 6 p.m. – 8; Dinner and intimacy 8 p.m. – 10 – I had every reason to be proud of myself although it was, of course, O who did most of the work and all of the charming. But where, when one began to think about it, were the long hours of talking with the Jesus-Man? Somewhere in mid-flight the rocket proclaimed what I had already masochistically suspected: no, there could be no further meeting tomorrow ... other commitments in Cambridge had cropped up ... Philip and Sally were not only attending a conference on Mental Depression, they were expected at its steering committee. And so, as the rocket burst, it became clear that there was to be no healthily astringent morning walk the next day to pick up its charred stick; no afterthoughts, no affectionate normalcies. (There was not, indeed, to be a single further word.)

And, truth to tell, some three hours after arrival the Jesus-Man was very drunk. He was amusingly roguish and not, as Dylan Thomas might have been, a danger to the furniture. Gloriously articulate he made up little speeches which coiled this way and that before darting at their target: the healthiness, friendliness, entire normality and propriety of another drink. 'Now that is an intriguing question I should very much like to answer . . . if only I had some means of lubricating my thoughts.' The great voice boomed until it tripped on a spluttering laugh. 'Yes, I should say, indeed I should say emphatically, that character is as important to the novel as drink is to a party.' Unfortunately by that time Sally had indicated to both of us that we shouldn't let Philip have anything more, which was pretty embarrassing to us as hosts, and to O in particular in view of his exquisite manners; in fact he continued to dole out tiny gins in beer mugs of water. Once I caught my old friend diving for my tumbler of home-brew. His hand stopped in mid-air and he gave me a look of naughtiness turned comic when found *in flagrante delicto*, a look which parodied greed and shame and disappointment and injured innocence, such as I imagined seeing on the face of some Russian peasant before the Revolution or on an old scoundrel like Zorba the Greek. It was a wonderfully democratic look and all the more earthy for being intelligent. It suggested, as it has done ever since those Oxford days, more of the common touch than I have ever been able to command. It shot at me straight from the youth conferences of the Popular Front and the workers' committees during the Spanish Civil War during which my friend was likely to be accused of lack of party discipline.

As the rocket faded to its last trailing stars I found the remarks I was addressing to Philip being answered by Sally, who acted as his interpreter and, in the role of sweet American wife, stressed the grand simplicities. She is a small woman and rather pretty, with her hair very nicely done and a general air of trimness and compactness as though she were used to keeping a good deal buttoned up. There is nothing showy about her, little obvious Americanism except for a trace of the accent. But her air

[308]

of wisdom and practicality looks as though it was something rather painfully and wearily learned; she has a curious alertness, which troubles me a bit, because I feel she is alert for things I wouldn't myself notice; certainly one's first impression is that she has been locked into the dual roles of wife and even more of mum (not least to Philip himself) and that her acuteness is of the domestic kind – she sees life from the vantage point of a housing-committee or a sick-bed or a shopping basket on a kitchen table. And like most middle-aged women she resents this a little. By contrast Philip is cosmic – by now, indeed, drink has frozen him into a monument whose face I can scarcely see. His great bald head, from which a few wisps of grey hair float out wildly, his powerful fleshy nose, his sensual, extraordinarily *muscular* lips, his deep and authoritative voice, all these features propel him into the empyrean, the cosmopolitan stratosphere of thought; his prime quality is intelligence (his eyes in particular are trained on distance which seems actually to burn them pale or perhaps just to empty them of the nonsense one is talking) but this intelligence is combined with shrewdness, humour, charm and a peasant's body full of lumbering appetite. Intelligence has not made his recent novels a success. Nor has it quite restored his Christian faith or eased his fear of death. But Sally – how she winced at my attempts at self-justification! How genuinely pained and incredulous she was rendered by my self-delusion! And were these home truths of hers so wise after all? We were all lonely, all growing old, all feeling misunderstood or undervalued; writers were incorrigible egoists; all men retained a good deal of the small boy. Was not she, too, in danger of being neglected? How often had she been engaged in the conversation? With the exception of O, who was on his best behaviour, we had all by then drunk a good deal and I'm sure I had begun (but not for very long) to thud my obsessions into the gap between Sally on the settee and Philip upon his chair. Why didn't he discuss my poems with me? Why did we never telephone each other? Why the mystery about their goddam caravan?

And then they left, Philip staggering to the car rather more easily than Sally had feared. It all still seemed euphoric, the final burst of the rocket. In the dark of the drive I did something I have never done before, I flung my arms about my old friend and hugged him. But he was ponderously climbing into the car and very likely did not notice.

Certainly the fact that no thank-you letter has come has been a blow, although this is normally a prime punctilio of O's rather than mine. Should I not, in the spirit of love (a favourite Philip word), persist despite everything? I was, after all, the first to let down the friendship when I did not write from New York. I know, of course, I know, that I back out too easily. On the other hand there are standards which I believe I do honestly prize: standards of civilized, often serious discourse, of sensitivity, of the appreciation of various kinds of beauty. It may have been entirely forgivable to renew a friendship after two years by both getting drunk *and* cutting the visit short – we all enjoyed it at the time while Philip said several times how happy he was – but surely, afterwards, one of them should have written?

First reaction – defensive indignation. Second reaction – irritation that old Patrick should have laboured away at such an elaborate literary vehicle for the delivery of his insult. (How much larger than life that visitor is! How patronizing P is about the little American wife!)

The third reaction was amazed incredulity that he should have accumulated so much anger and envy over the years, for none of us, I suppose, thinks of himself as really enviable. Yes, I am lucky in my wife and children: lucky in my job; lucky to have plenty of money. But a *success*! A figure fit to be shown off to the neighbours!

[310]

After all, how long ago I beat a forced retreat from that world of literary London which Patrick evidently longed to enter – and after how many public humiliations! And what about my life-work still unpublished; perhaps unpublishable?

But the fourth and last reaction to Patrick's strange compilation is guilt – as it was meant to be. I cannot deeply blame myself for getting drunk, considering how early the drinks began to be poured; considering the ordeal of being presented as visiting lion to so many strangers. But I should have recognized how much I must have wounded Patrick by failing to talk about books, and about his own books in particular. I should certainly have sent a letter afterwards, to thank him for the visit and to make what amends I could. 'Insensitivity' is a fair enough charge, I'm afraid.

5 January

Is S a mum to me? In those circumstances, of course. But there are just as many in which I'm a dad to her. And how lucky we are to have such a loving parent each, as well as a loving spouse!

But the real problem about describing my reactions to Patrick's document is the great difficulty of bringing in *spiritual* failure and success without insufferable priggishness. Of course I still mind, and mind a great deal, about the kind of success that bothers Patrick so much. I also know that the state of one's soul can't possibly be measured in the same sort of way as the state of one's literary reputation. But it *is* true – and therefore I must say it – that I now mind more about doing the will of God than about whether or not I can get *Pantaloon* published.

And alas, this will seem to Patrick, if he ever reads it, like the most snooty response I could possibly have made. (And I feel that there should have been a way of writing it which would *not* have offended him – but to find the words for doing that I should need to have a soul in much better condition than mine is.)

———— * ————

[311]

Kierkegaard's *Journals*. His constant originality of mind – of which I haven't a scrap.

———— * ————

Hearing S chattering away to Phine downstairs makes me worry again that I may be oppressing her by my taciturnity and love of privacy.

Irritated – perhaps by guilt – I began to congratulate myself that *I* don't need to gabble in this way. But I realized almost at once, that my constant reading is a sort of desperate gabble with the writers of books; just as far removed as vocal chatter from the peace, patience and fullness of true silence.

What's more, S's chatter is largely due to her genuine interest in other people. How much more she knows about our neighbours than I do – not in the way of gossip but because of a real and benevolent interest in their lives.

———— * ————

But why is Kierkegaard in such a constant nagging fury against almost all his fellow-citizens? This interferes grossly with his own peace, and therefore with his powers of meditative thought.

———— * ————

'Behold, I make all things new.' But the things which he makes new are themselves old, and retain the virtue of their antiquity even when they are transformed.

———— * ————

Kierkegaard insists that God must be feared. I see that there must be *awe* before God; otherwise he is no better than a sweet old gentleman. Or lady. But surely it is the greatness of his love which should inspire our awe; and this is the direct opposite of fear. (Fear is *always* the enemy; the deepest of all the roots of evil.)

———— * ————

Breughel's Icarus has had a lucky fall; missing the sun, he has fallen into heaven itself. He won't drown in that paradisal sea; he'll swim to the shore, join the fisherman, the shepherd and the ploughman, and work with them there to the further glory of God.

———— * ————

Sun on the snow through my window: Mozart: Breughel: Traherne's *Centuries* open on my bed: two bottles of Sam Smith's Strong Brown Ale (the best beer I know). *Happiness.*

———— * ————

The Agnus Dei. So charming, yet so absurd. Neither lamb nor saviour nor saviour-lamb can bear our sins for us. What Jesus did was to lighten our sins, in both senses, by shining his light on them and showing us their true nature. Sometimes he makes us see that they are much less important than we thought; and sometimes he sharpens our awareness of how much they divide us from the God of his revelation.

———— * ————

For me to enter the Breughel, as I long to do, would be exactly the same as for the picture to enter me.

———— * ————

One day I might write an admiring commentary on Kierkegaard's *Journals*; as once I planned a detailed refutation of Rochefoucauld. (So much easier, always, to write with something *there* to hang it on.)

10 January

We went up to London, chiefly to have dinner with Polly and Peter (daughter and son-in-law) and to meet, after a long time, my ex-sister and brother-in-law (Anne's sister and her husband). I spent some of the happiest months of my life in their large and comfortable house near Peebles, fishing; skating; running over the hills; reading the great unreadable English classics in the splendid library. But now they live in Corfu; and although they've asked us to stay, and although I'm devoted

[313]

to them both, to go there still seems to me like going to the moon.

Martyn and Pinkie were there too, and though they live only in London and Yorkshire I don't suppose we see *them* more than twice a year.

A very good time with the granddaughters before dinner; and the whole evening was a sad/happy reminder of how wonderful – how full of love – such occasions can be: that is, meetings with family (Anne and Josephine were there too) and *close* friends.

True I was tipsy by the end; but not enough to spoil my own pleasure or anyone else's – so S assures me.

At least our secluded life surely enhances the rare pleasure of such an evening. (But back to bed for two days, of course, after the utter exhaustion of 24 hours in London!)

11 January

Courbet's apples are now in the place of scrutiny and honour. More real than real. And as the reality of earthly objects is intensified so they move towards the condition of heavenly objects. Such signs are what we should always be looking for.

——— * ———

Real flu and bronchitis now. Ill-health is a great deadener of the spirit – except for saints. Prayer needs a vigour of concentration which the muffled mind finds very hard to achieve.

——— * ———

If only I could read Chekhov's stories again! I can imagine no better way out of this stuffy little shrine of holy books.

——— * ———

Ann H included in one of her letters a glowing tribute to Beethoven. I took this to be addressed to *me* at first; but at least had the grace to write and tell her about my fatuous mistake.

——— * ———

[314]

Instead of the Chekhov stories, which seem to have disappeared in the recent holocaust, I've been trying to read *The
Possessed* again. I'm rather put off by all that deep, crafty and
long drawn out hatred of Sepan Trofimovich. I cannot hate
like that; and I know that this is *not* due to apathy or moral
indifference but simply to my mistrust of any platform on which
I might stand to do my hating *from*. I am in no position to
despise anyone in the way that Dostoevsky despises that poor
old silly Liberal.

(Nor, for that matter, was he; for nothing so ill becomes a
Christian as a sneer.)

———— * ————

O Lord, I cried, in the desert of the early hours, help me
to see which way to go. And the simple fact was presented to
me again – but freshly; as if for the first time – that my proper
way is by manifested love for S. (It is this quality of newness
in what has long been 'known' which makes me believe that
certain messages are indeed from God.)

———— * ————

Far Away and Long Ago. Now those two phrases tear at the
heart! And though I know very well that attention must be
paid to the present time and place; that nostalgia can be
sentimental and evasive; yet the present moment is nothing
without all the earlier moments which it contains. This view
of a snow valley would be nothing unless I had seen many other
and very different views.

———— * ————

Preyre quotes from Proust: 'In myself, no doubt, since I was
a man, one of those amphibious beings who are simultaneously
plunged in the past and in present reality, there was always
a contradiction between ...'

Preyre comments: 'From these remarks it seems that man lives
in several worlds: a so-called real world, a world of dreams,
a world of imagination, a world of memory and the rest.'

Yes; and one might add *Le milieu divin* to this list. In fact it may be that one of our tasks on earth is to unify all those other worlds and so to achieve a depth of vision which allows us at least a glimpse of God's domain.

——— * ———

Also from E-Alexis Preyre's *The Freedom to Doubt*: 'It is noteworthy that the problem of the soul's immortality becomes less important if one believes in God.'

A *profound* truth. The deeper our experience of earthly light – the closer we get *from here* to the beatific vision – the less we need to rely for our illumination on what Robert Graves once described to me as 'a second helping'. (Not that I wouldn't choose a second helping if offered a choice of that or 'unification with the Godhead' – i.e. a personal obliteration. But only if the next helping involves a further work to be done: *in my present state* eternal bliss has no allure for me at all.)

——— * ———

Simon's beautiful little pot on the shelf underneath the Courbet apples. A *frugal* beauty.

And Anne's Byzantine angel on the other side.

This is the perfect shrine for me now.

——— * ———

Twenty days without smoking!

12 January

In Monmouth Father Philip quoted to me the words 'Circumstance is the voice of God'. He takes this to mean that God arranges the circumstance in which we can hear him speak. I take it to mean that God can speak to us, if we have ears to hear, in every circumstance which happens to happen to us.

He also told me that he'd heard from a friend in Oxford that I used to be 'a bit of a lad' when I was young. A way of putting it, certainly; and a useful phrase to remember when falling into too noisy a grovel about past sins.

The real fault of Christian obsequiousness before God is that it demeans *him* so. If he were really so 'superior' to us as to make us feel utterly insignificant, unworthy etc. then he wouldn't really be superior at all. He would be just like one of us lording it over another of us. The purpose of his love is to raise us up to him. As far up as he can get us.

The notion of God as Judge is one of the most persistent and one of the most pernicious. It springs, perhaps, from our strong belief that he does indeed know all about us; that to him 'all hearts are open, all desires known', and from him 'no secrets are hid'. But it is through his love that he knows us; and love transcends all judgement.

———— * ————

I still have to come to terms with my mother; to get beyond all that long, even if long-suppressed, resentment and reach back to the primal and immortal love. She must somehow be included in that Heavenly Mother to whom more and more of my prayers are addressed.

(But an irreverent little memory immediately intrudes itself. When I came back to Ganthorpe from Oxford there would often be a new crucifix hanging on some wall or other. Once I confronted a particularly large and demanding version immediately opposite the front door, and I paused, with my mother beside me, and struck an attitude of quizzing connoisseurship. 'Who's it of?' I asked; to which she answered, surely without due consideration, 'A friend – to some of us.')

———— * ————

Beyond Good and Evil. You might as well say Beyond Truth and Falsehood; which no doubt *has* been said by some of the great mystics of 'the negative way'. But I come back to the fact that 'the Battle of Hastings was fought in 1066' is quite a different kind of statement from 'the Battle of Hastings was fought in 1067'.

Satan as the Father of Lies. 'The truth shall make you free', etc.

———— * ————

[317]

Christianity must always return to certain absolute simplicities, such as the love of God. But there are also certain shallow and very tempting simplifications, such as fundamentalism, which are really a way of giving up the hard struggle for truth; evading the real difficulty of loving God and man in freedom of heart and mind.

———— * ————

'Each of us in the circumstances of his life must ask, "what would the Lord have *me* do?" That question, honestly posed and faithfully responded to, leads to perfection. Tolstoy, in spite of his extreme pronouncements on non-violence, was scripturally accurate when he wrote: "Christian teaching does not lay down laws for everybody, and does not say to people, "All of you, for fear of punishment, must obey such and such rules, and then you will be happy'; but it explains to every individual his position in relation to the world, and allows him to see what results, for him individually, flow inevitably from that relation"' (Peter de Rosa).

———— * ————

If the publican commits the lesser sin and the pharisee the greater sin, then Jesus was guilty of forgiving the lesser sin but failing to forgive the greater one. (Admittedly self-righteousness is the most formidable barrier against receiving any help from either God or man. But I doubt whether that barrier is ever pierced by angry abuse.)

———— * ————

One of my most persistent errors is that I still – if only half-consciously – look for some future event which will change the whole course and texture of my life. This resembles nostalgia, in being another way of evading the present moment.

19 January

Worse industrial troubles on the way. And I shiver with

[318]

nervous agitation for *this* skin; this skin so well protected from even the slightest genuine privation. (And even if genuine privation did come our way we ought to welcome it – as a means both of sharing the common affliction and also of clearing our clogged communications with God; clogged by too many possessions.)

——— * ———

Laura's heroic job-hunting and job-finding in Gloucester. So radical a change in so short a time! A minor miracle of flowering – or rather of tender shoot growing into resilient sapling.

——— * ———

'Humility is above all one of the qualities of attention' (Simone Weil).

——— * ———

Kierkegaard writes that we must *choose* suffering in order to learn God's will from it. This seems very perverse. In fact if our suffering is chosen we can presumably choose it to stop at any moment. And this is the negation of true suffering, whose essence lies in its inescapability; its infliction by some force which is beyond our command, whether within us or outside us. Chosen suffering is literally *voulu* – i.e. contrived and artificial.

——— * ———

The revolting term VIP; as in 'the VIP lounge'. Our odious 'respect for persons' which means the opposite of what it seems to say. It means respecting a few people – for all the wrong reasons – and disrespecting the great majority.

——— * ———

Kierkegaard: 'Suffering directs us to look within.' Yes; that is the real point.

——— * ———

'Heavenly Mother, help me to show the light of your love in the world.' If taken literally this form of prayer is an entirely superfluous petition. She gives all the help she can, whether we pray for it or not. But this is an essential way both of

[319]

approaching God and of exhorting ourselves to have greater faith in her.

———— * ————

Donne magnificently answers Kierkegaard's demand that we should choose the way of pain:

'Foreign crosses, other men's merits are not mine . . . Since I am bound to take up my cross, there must be a cross that is mine to take up, a cross prepared by God, and laid in my way, which is temptations or tribulations in my calling; and I must not go out of my way to seek a cross; for so it is not mine, nor laid for my taking up.'

———— * ————

Always distinguish between choice and preference. I read in the newspaper that 5000 people have been drowned by floods in Bangladesh; but also that a very inconvenient local strike has now been settled. The total effect of reading these two news items is to give me more pleasure than pain. Yet if the *choice* had been mine I would, of course, have chosen that the strike should continue and the people be saved from drowning. We cannot help our preferences; but we are largely responsible for the choices we make.

Yet the preference in this case, and so many others, is *despicable*; and I know that there is only one way of making the preference correspond with the choice; and that is the way of total change; rebirth; enlightenment; salvation . . . Nothing less will do it. 'A good man out of the good treasure of the heart bringeth forth good things: and an evil man out of the evil treasure bringeth forth evil things' (Matthew 12:35).

14 January

Suppose I know that a certain South American village is on the verge of starvation; and suppose the following choice is available to me; a) I can send a body of coldhearted but competent officials to the village who will arrange for centrally-distributed supplies to be made permanently available. This will enable the villagers to lead ordinary lives until they die in the course of nature. b) I can send a great saint to the village, who will arrive with empty hands but a full heart. He will bring so much love to the villagers during their remaining days of slow starvation that many, perhaps all of them will die in a state of holy joy.

My strong impulse, of course, is to send the saint. What might prevent me from doing so is simply my deeply ingrained respect for freedom of choice. I am almost sure that if the choice were put to the villagers they would choose food and life rather than love and death. I cannot feel that I have the right to override what I believe would be their own choice, even though I may be convinced that they would all die in praise and glory under the saint's ministrations.

But when I put this problem to S she had a better reason for choosing a) – namely that you cannot tell what those prolonged lives might have produced in the way of love. You cannot assume 'ordinariness' in a world where, by God's grace, the extraordinary can always happen.

Yes; but there is something else about this which nags at my mind, and which I can't quite reach.

———— * ————

Certain small miracles have been happening lately. For example: I was looking for the little ear-plug of the portable radio, and had *perused at least five times* the open space of the shelf in the big sitting-room cupboard. The sixth time I looked the plug was lying exactly in the middle of the shelf. I was alone in the house.

Or this: yesterday I had dumped on my bed the contents of my brown satchel, which should have comprised two notebooks, my watch, my handkerchief, my spectacles and my pen. But there was no sign of the pen; so I looked for it in nearly every conceivable place before looking on the bed again. Still no pen there, so I looked in all the remaining conceivable places. When I looked on the bed for the third time the pen was lying there, plain to see *and poked through the chain of my watch which I had picked up during my second perusal of the bed.*

I told S about these events, knowing perfectly well that she would ascribe them to my well-known ability to lose almost anything almost anywhere. And so she did. Yet *I know* that in each case a trivial but genuine miracle occurred.

Why? God knows. But though I certainly don't understand them I take a certain pleasure from these events, as I do from anything innocently out of the ordinary. (I even wondered whether dear Ben could be trying to communicate.)

———— * ————

The desert again last night. But now there is always *a sort of* knowledge that there is hope at the heart of darkness. (It seems like a completely dead knowledge: a dry, remembered fact to which, in spite of its apparent lifelessness, I must cling with all my might.)

———— * ————

'There is something mysterious in the universe which is in complicity with those who love nothing but the good.'

Simone W at her best again. What more perfect statement of minimal religious faith!

———— * ————

Magic – which is not at all the same as the miraculous – is directly opposed to belief in a just and loving God. For example the magical Roman Catholic belief that the only *true* host is one which has been properly consecrated by a properly ordained priest means that if a priest happens to have got the words wrong, or to have been wrongly consecrated himself without knowing it, then the host will be without 'efficacy'. And whatever the priest and the people may believe to the contrary they will not have received the objective benefits which the *true* sacrament would have provided. How odd of God!

How even odder of God to send unbaptized babies to Limbo, or to treat differently those souls of the dead who received the last rites from those who did not – e.g. because a snowstorm prevented the priest from arriving in time.

I know that sophisticated Catholics find various ways round these traditional magical beliefs, but in so far as any element of magic remains it is a form of blasphemy, since it implies that God can be compelled to give or to withhold according to the use or non-use of spells.

19 January

> A prayer. Heavenly Mother,
> Light of the World,
> Peace in our hearts.

——— * ———

Looking at S across the hearth as she was watching the telly I felt my whole body and mind *suffused* with love for her.

——— * ———

Father Philip in Monmouth. How much I've come to value our weekly half-hour together in The Swan. This time we arrived, in a fumbling way, at a declaration of our friendship and of its importance to both of us. He is a depressive (as well as an epileptic) so our meetings are sometimes like a minimal DA group, but held in mutual consciousness of God's loving help.

——— * ———

I bought a chess set in Monmouth; and yesterday evening I taught S the rules. I dare say she will soon be beating me, as Anne did within a month of my teaching *her* to play in 1940. How furious I used to get at those defeats: but this time I confidently expect chess to be another token of our companionship. (Companionship and love. Of course people can be companions without loving each other; but they can also love each other without being companions. In our case it seems that we express our love more and more in the things we do together and the way we talk together. She used to complain that we hardly talked at all when we were alone; we certainly do so now, and not by any conscious effort on either part.)

[323]

24 January

Health at last fully regained: earth itself again and heaven almost believable.

We went for a beautiful and happy walk through thick and still tumbling snow, looking down from our white world at the pale green fields along the river.

3 February

Prayer. 'Now may the peace of God fill me with light.'

———— * ————

Noisy and boastful people in the bar of The Wyndham Arms after I'd done my long morning walk there through the snow. I quickly quelled my revulsion by remembering that fear is at the back of nearly all loud and exhibitionist behaviour. Christianity has surely been wrong in supposing that pride is the *fundamental* sin; and it is a modern, non-Christian perception that fear lies deeper than pride: that pride is nearly always a mask for fear.

———— * ————

Forking hay out of the barn here, to make room for logs. I rejoiced in doing hard physical work again after more than a month without it. A mild and quite pleasurable melancholy, thinking of Martin's great enthusiasm during our brief farming years; good days in the hayfield and four or five of us perched on the topheavy pick-up as we swayed along the Upper Meend.

———— * ————

So Aquinas renounced all his intellectual work before he died. Because he saw further than all that. Because he saw that all that was more of a hindrance than a help.

———— * ————

Why is there no representation of Jesus sitting with his legs crossed? Why would that be disrespectful?

———— * ————

Now, as I pray, sitting at the end of my bed in an imitation lotus position, my eyes cross and recross Courbet's apples in a set and repeated pattern. I cannot even begin to pray without order and regularity; – and how those apples glow when I use them in this way!

8 February

From *Observer* review of *Blessings* by Mary Craig (Hodder & Stoughton, London).

The Christian paradox is that though we must *willingly* accept unavoidable suffering for ourselves we must do all in our power to alleviate the afflictions of others.

———— * ————

I tried to read Viktor Frankl again. I still see that he ·is the best, wisest and most humane of all psychologists; but even he feels bound to use that intolerable jargon. (No worse than the jargon of Christian apologetics; but every bit as bad.)

20 February

A mad lady suddenly appeared at the house, having hitched from Devonshire to see me. By the grace of God I was able to receive her warmly; and as we talked to her she became less mad: a kind of wild wisdom shone out of her paranoia, and I felt sure that she too was a messenger if only we ourselves could muster enough wisdom to hear her message.

She left next morning, having entrusted me with a great parcel of her writing.

———— * ————

And on the telephone another constant caller, full of fear and anger. Yesterday S talked to her for half an hour: I could not have stood it for more than five minutes.

———— * ————

Wednesday was a day of exemplary rectitude: – and extreme non-happiness. (I know, of course, that this non-happiness is the usual condition of most people, but I cannot resign myself to it. Better – *almost* – the sharpness of real pain.)

———— * ————

Iran and Pakistan. How appalling if they can rid themselves of our Western corruption only by reverting to a barbarism which is worse than anything we brought them. My father would have been bitterly and ironically distressed.

———— * ————

We were invited to two parties in London where we would have met many old friends whom we hardly ever see. 'We *must* go!' said S and I to each other. 'We must make this effort to join the world again.' But as the dates came closer we both felt a growing dread of the journey; the delightful but over-stimulating company; the sharp disturbance of our present well-ordered life. So we went to neither party. (But how hard and happily we work at BH together: and then the rewarding pub at half past six.)

March 4 to 11

But then a week of hellish and growing separation from each other; like two people drowning separately and trying desperately to touch fingers as the sea engulfs them.

Finally we went off to a Cotswold hotel to see if walking in an unknown area might do us any good. After much walking and praying the knowledge did suddenly come to me – high above Chalford – that now is within eternity as well as in time; that the relationship between soul and Holy Spirit is the eternal tension; the eternal act of creation; eternal love. And for that moment I believed that I was surrounded by heavenly brothers

[326]

and sisters, and that it was they who were giving me this message.

A mystical experience? Scarcely that; but an assurance, after so much pain and shame, that we had not cut ourselves off by our folly from the ceaseless and loving *attention* of God.

15 March

We had to go and have drinks with a couple who live the other side of Monmouth and whom we hardly know. One of those inescapable obligations. The husband was a rough-tough sporting business man; and as we were talking I realized that there were three possible levels of communication between him and me:

a) our present one, making polite, meaningless noises to each other.

b) the angry argument which would certainly follow if we stumbled into any social or political issue.

c) the confession that we are fellow-men, full of fear and anguish, calling for help.

a) and b) are not really communication at all: but how seldom, even with old friends, do we ever communicate on the third level. Yet it is only there, in the sharing of affliction and helplessness, that the fruit of love can grow.

——— * ———

When we got home from the Cotswolds I found a letter from Michael Schmidt cautiously but definitely accepting *Pantaloon* – on condition, of course, that he can get the grant from the Arts Council. But at the same time I also realized that somewhere on that expedition I had lost my treasured fisherman's jersey. And my irritation about the jersey almost completely kept out of my mind the extraordinary news that *Pantaloon* will (presumably) be published at last, after so many years of hope and disappointment.

Even when I woke next morning the jersey loomed much

larger than *Pantaloon*. Perhaps it is simply a case of 'Wolf! Wolf!' – or rather it's opposite – apparent good news so often having come to nothing. Or perhaps, as the years pass, I really care less and less about the fate of that book.

——— * ———

Beer, after all, has hardly ever done me an injury; and now I take my first gulp at the Orepool not only with a sense of just reward for a hard day's work, but often with an almost sacramental joy.

Why not? 'Malt does more than Milton can
To justify God's ways to man'

——— * ———

Thoreau's famous claim that most people live in a state of quiet desperation. Perhaps much of the pain I suffer comes from my unrelaxing refusal to accept that condition for myself.

23 March

Working upstairs at BH I leant over the banisters to talk to S and happened to hear a line from Henry V on the portable radio: 'Think, when we talk of horses, that you see them.' A merely serviceable line; yet at that moment more impressive to me than any of the great passages would have been. What absolute mastery and authority.

And this, which I found in some anthology, has its own perfection too; enhanced, I suppose, by my knowledge of what happened to the men and women who used to sing it:

To conquer them by love, come in now, come in now.
To conquer them by love, come in now.
To conquer them by love, as it does you behove,
For He is King above; no power is like to love.
Glory here, Diggers all.

If English radicals had gone on singing songs like that, and

[328]

meaning them, perhaps they would have conquered long ago. (But such songs are never sung for long.)

———— * ————

A letter from Patrick Anderson's friend Orlando to tell us that Patrick has died of (a mercifully quick) cancer. Orlando believes he was already afflicted, though without knowing it, when he wrote his furious letter to me. The letter I wrote back to him wasn't an angry one; it was apologetic, but also tough in the way that I felt it should be – that is, I refused to patronize my old friend. But if I had known that he would be dead in a few weeks' time would I have written as I did? No, of course I wouldn't; but nor, God forbid, would I have written him a letter of Christian propaganda. Since I am not a saint, and therefore lack not only the right words but also the loving heart to inspire them, any approach of that sort would only have added to his bitterness against me. (There are times when holy words are an insult.)

Orlando's account of their coming very close together as Patrick was dying moved me deeply. I shall miss P very much, and our strange, spiky, intermittent but true affection for each other.

———— * ————

Also the death of my cousin K: doubled up by arthritis, abandoned a few months ago by her husband after a marriage that had lasted – by hook or by crook – for nearly half a century. She had been brought up a Quaker: but lost her faith long ago. Yet her smile when I last saw her, still seemed Quaker in the very best sense; gently and affectionately amused.

———— * ————

Love your neighbour as yourself. But it isn't that we really *love* ourselves: we cherish and cosset ourselves; scrupulously attend to what we take to be our own best interests: nothing is too good for us. To treat another person in this way would do him harm.

———— * ————

[329]

It is no use saying that S and I must love each other *in spite of* the faults which each sees in the other. This involves a critical standing-off; a form of appraisal which is quite incompatible with love. Knowing our own faults, knowing the faults of the other, we have to love the other *in full complicity of failure, folly and weakness.* And it is only through this acknowledged complicity that we can hope to strengthen each other and ourselves.

28 March

Now we've taken to playing chess with our neighbours, the Hammonds – I with Jeffrey and S with Nasi. It seems that a real affection is growing between the four of us, and that the difference of age and background are not so important as people think. A famous English ex-pop-star married to a Persian girl. both aged around thirty: an upper-middle-class English intellectual married to a middle-western American; both around sixty. A strange quartet, it might be said, but our friendship only shows how little such labels matter.

The chess is a minor but rewarding ritual; even a blessing.

11 April

'The day is not distant when humanity will realize that it is faced with a choice between suicide and adoration' (Teilhard de Chardin).

Or this:

'Only through one of the greatest and innermost renovations it has ever gone through will the world be able to save and maintain itself' (Rilke).

———— * ————

Still in search of healing we spent a day's retreat at the convent. I read as little as I could: we attended all the offices, from mass until evensong: we walked slowly together in the

[330]

garden ... I can't say that either of us felt any dramatic transformation, but there was the steady, day-long reminder of a place 'where prayer has been valid'.

Perhaps we were made even more aware than before that we are both addicts of hurry and bustle, in different forms. If she could sit still for even ten minutes a day, not even trying to pray; trying to do nothing at all! If I could read nothing (except books to review) for three months on end!

———— * ————

Gerald Vann's *The Divine Pity*. This wonderful little book shows that when a good and strictly orthodox Christian is writing from the soul the dogmas are not so much unimportant as transcended; used and absorbed by the deep and enduring truths.

———— * ————

Dying We Live. The superhuman, God-given strength and love of these Christian martyrs writing from their Nazi prisons in the months before they were executed. (It occurs to me, of course, that many Communists must have died just as *bravely*, entranced by their vision of an earthly paradise. But I'm bound to say that I think they died in delusion, while the Christians died on the right road to the truth.)

We visited Simon, Mary and Rose at Beshawar (Sherborne House). This eclectic institution in the Cotswolds runs strenuous eight-month courses in meditation and comparative religion. It seems to be Sufi-based; and in the middle of the course they were all transported to Turkey to see, among other things, the great tomb of Rumi.

No doubt that our three friends – and ex-communards – were all looking the better for their intense activity: Simon seemed to have had about five years taken off his thirty odd; his face glowed with health and happiness and he emitted a strong aura of peace instead of the nervous tension which sometimes used to radiate from him like a reversed magnetic field.

———— * ————

Now for us too the really good days are back again; an active

[331]

but unhurried rhythm of life which is the only kind which can give us the peace we need so badly. (Yet I notice, again, that *extreme* cheerfulness sometimes seems to make me not only forgetful of God but also very ready to snap at S. As if that dangerous exuberance could lead as easily to singing happiness or to explosive self-assertion.)

———— * ————

I like good pubs for their own sake; but they are also the best possible meeting places. Neutral ground which either party can leave at will.

The next best is to visit other people in their own homes, where the leaving is at the visitors' choice. Far the most dangerous is to invite guests into one's own house, simply because of the absurd convention by which the host has no right to declare the meeting at an end. (I understand the virtue of hospitality; but how much easier it would be to practise, for people of my temperament, if there were no danger of the visitors staying too long. But again – virtues are seldom easy to practise; so why should this one be an exception?)

———— * ————

Consciousness. It is impossible to see it as something which arrived on the scene at a certain time, and may disappear again when its time is up. For us consciousness is the supreme reality, and we cannot imagine any stage or state of All-That-Is in which there is no consciousness anywhere.

This is one strong reason for believing in God: 'I am always about in the quad.'

———— * ————

'Man's true freedom consists in his receiving himself from elsewhere, that he does not owe it to himself that he is, that he is not his own creator and thus cannot free himself from himself ... For it is the mystery of human personal being that it is summoned from elsewhere, and that it exists in response and as response, and that therefore man is wholly himself when he is not caught up in himself, but

[332]

has the real ground of his life outside himself' (Gerhard
Ebeling).

———— * ————

We went up to Manchester for me to give my talk (*Christians
Then and Now*) to the Unitarians. They are very pleasant people,
but, as I'd expected, many of them were plainly shocked by
my credulity. One fat, elderly, very robust minister from
Massachusetts expressed surprise and dismay at my belief in
God (in spite of the fact that my God is strictly unitarian).
After a few minutes' discussion I asked him how he differed from
Bertrand Russell. 'Not very much. Not at all, in fact. Like him
I believe in the nobility of man.' 'Well, what do you preach
about?' 'Ethics. I tell them to be good.'
   And after my talk a lady doctor came up to say how much
she had appreciated my emphasis on the *spiritual* side of things.
   For all their obvious goodwill and benevolence we found
them more like a friendly society than a religious sect. And
I suppose sternly orthodox trinitarian Christians would say that
this is where you inevitably end up if once you start com-
promising on any aspect of the True Faith. I don't believe it
for a moment. The essential Christian belief about man's nature
is contained in that quotation from Gerhard Ebeling. Within
that conviction of man's dependence on a God who is outside
him as well as within him 'a thousand flowers may bloom'.

16 April

From *Observer* review of *Man of Nazareth* by Anthony Burgess:

   I recognize everybody's right to create a fictitious Jesus
   to suit his own taste (Mr Burgess has invented an intellectual Jesus, with a good knowledge of Latin and Greek).
   But I have never read a modern life of Jesus, whether
   fictional or comparatively 'straight', which did anything
   but grossly diminish the Jesus of the Gospels, and not only
   by reducing his stature but by weakening his credibility

[333]

as a human being. Semi-mythological figure though he may be, the evangelists' Jesus has the pungency, the actuality, the historical credibility of a real man who really lived, taught and died in the Palestine of the early first century.

25 April

Jason and Chrissie were married on Saturday: in the registry office at Gloucester, with a large party afterwards in the shell of Barn House. We had imported trestle tables and a few chairs from the Breckweir village hall; scattered cushions along the walls of the big sitting room; hired one lady to do the catering and another to do the flowers.

It was a cheerful occasion, but since they've been living together for more than four years, not a particularly dramatic one. In so far as we have gained another splendid daughter S and I are very pleased. In so far as J was brought rather reluctantly to the 'altar' I sympathize strongly with him, but can't help rejoicing in this act as a symbol – at least – of stability and enduring love. Their chances of this are certainly far better than mine and Anne's in 1939: better, too, than anyone supposed when I brought my unknown second wife to England for the first time in 1951.

I am certainly an old fogy in this – that I believe, with all my heart and mind, that married love, or its equivalent, is something which must have time to mature; must be able to survive the most lacerating hostilities; is capable of becoming the most precious and illuminating of all human relationships. In other words, that marriage *can be* a sacrament.

———— * ————

Articles in the Colour Supplement about the joyful experience of an afterlife by people who have 'died' – technically – but been brought back to life. Certainly an immediate state of joy *for all* suits my concept of God better than any other

[334]

posthumous condition.

On the other hand the doctrine of purgatory, provided it is accompanied by the notion of active work to be done by the soul on itself, and not just of passive purgation, makes perfectly good sense too.

——— * ———

The General Election. I voted Labour, as usual; and I am as much against the Tories as ever I was. But I wasn't consumed by hatred for them, as I have been too often in the past. (Not that our new prime minister is the neighbour I find easiest to love.)

——— * ———

A few Sundays ago I had been moaning to Sister Paula about my enforced retreats; renewed failures; months of work apparently gone for nothing ... 'Back to square one,' she said briskly. And very comfortingly too, for if even the sisters go through this miserable experience there must be hope for us all.

——— * ———

Here is a question which I would like to set in a Moral Philosophy Paper: 'If A loves X and B hates X is it always the case that A sees X more clearly than B does?' My answer would be an unequivocal yes if the love is true love; that is, clear-sighted love. But then the answer is tautological.

Nor can one deny that hatred has its own sharp perceptions.

Yes, but these perceptions are swamped and distorted in the general falsification which hatred imposes on the hater's mind and heart.

The belief that all men are lovable, which is an *essential* article of Christian faith, is a long way from any personal capacity of the believer to love all men.

——— * ———

'You must have pity for all, and the greatest pity for those who have the greatest need of it. But humbly,

[335]

reverently, not conferring a gift but asking to be given one; otherwise you will not have pity but the terrifying vulgarity of condescension and all the ugliness of pride. (Think for a moment of whether you are ever "shocked" in the colloquial sense of the word: if you are it is a lack of wisdom, for you ought to know more about human nature, including your own; it is a lack of humility, for you are presupposing that the thing that shocks you is something far below your own moral level – and if that is the way you think you will never have the gift of divine pity' (Gerald Vann).

—— * ——

A saint is defined somewhere as a man who is transparent to God: you can see God through him.

—— * ——

Every form of competitiveness is harmful. The worst form of all is to compete in righteousness. The good man always wants others to be better than he is.

—— * ——

She is my dearest *life*.

—— * ——

'Depth without action is inhuman, and action without depth is folly' (?).

—— * ——

A hasty letter to Ann H about one of her prose poems caused her deep misery, and quite justified resentment. If I had made my criticism more carefully it would have been no less honest but far less wounding. So much harm can be done by a moment's carelessness; a moment's inattention.

—— * ——

I found myself criticizing S for reading so little; and here again the annoyance I caused was entirely justified. Her way is not my way; but it is certainly not a worse one.

[336]

This was an amiable argument, though, which ended with a decisive quip from her: 'Poet and Peasant, eh?'

———— * ————

God's forgiveness is not an action, or even an activity, but a permanent condition. To know that my sin is forgiven at the very moment of its being committed is the true state of penitence. For that knowledge is not accessible to me so long as I am still in a state of sin.

I recognize more and more that if I have any godly function on earth – and of course I have; everybody has – then it is to act as both a warning and an example on the very lowest rungs of the ladder. The present account of my hopes and fears; large failures, small successes; humiliations and perceptions (perceptions often from the heart of humiliation) is meant for the spiritually backward – who nevertheless know enough about the Spirit to be in a state of often subdued but never extinguished hope.

———— * ————

I must always distinguish between my two selves: 1) a knotted bundle of worries, vanities, ambitions and fears which blocks the passage of God to Earth; 2) a unique channel for God's light and love.

———— * ————

'Hence faith is by no means a mere act of choice, an option for a special solution to the problem of existence. It is birth to a higher life by obedience to the Source of Life: to believe is thus to consent to hear and to obey a creative command that raises us from the dead. And what can be a deeper motive for belief?' (Merton)

And in spite of that warning phrase, 'the soul wounded by inordinate self-expression', Merton is well aware that certain souls must continue to risk wounding themselves in this way:

'There have been so many words uttered in contempt of truth, in despite of love, honour, justice, and all that is good. Even these concepts themselves (truth, honour, goodness) have become sick and rotten to us, not because

[337]

they are defiled but because we are. Nevertheless, we must risk falsity, we must take courage and speak, we must use noble instruments of which we have become ashamed because we no longer trust ourselves to use them worthily. We must dare to think what we mean, and simply make clear statements of what we intend. This is our only serious protection against repeated spiritual defilement by the slogans and programmes of the unscrupulous.'

———— * ————

Now that Jeffrey and Nasi have offered to share their huge walled vegetable garden with us our own garden is freed for my ambitious plans. I mean to terrace the whole slope, making four successive levels and four dry-stone walls at each descent. This will be at least as big a job as the creation of the water garden at BH ten years ago. And now I'm ten years older.

But this doesn't worry me in the least. Making new gardens has been one of the joys of my life, and I know I can still do the work. The element of dread comes from thinking about the complete garden, in a state as close to perfection as I can bring it, and the obligation to keep it so. A few odd weeks of depressive lethargy – or simple laziness – during the summer months and the whole thing sinks into that state of overgrown untidiness which changes it from a joy into a source of anxiety and guilt.

Still, I shall make the garden, and trust in God for the capacity to maintain it. (Though gardens can no more be kept in a state of immobility than souls can. An ancient analogy, and a very good one.)

———— * ————

When I start thinking of this journey in terms of God's glory instead of my own improvement, *that* will be the 'great leap forward.'

———— * ————

Strange that most of the religiously minded people I know seem to be far more conscious of God-within than of God-outside. With me it is quite the opposite: I often search in vain for the smallest spark in my own soul, but God in heaven reaching towards earth becomes steadily more real to me. (No, *not* steadily: by spasms: by fits and starts.)

20 May

Quoted in *The Common Experience* by J. M. Cohen and J. F. Phipps (Rider & Co., London): and in my *Observer* review of the book on Sunday.

On January 23rd, 1961, I came home after an evening lecture at the house of some friends. It was a freezing night ... I had absolutely no premonition of anything un-usual, but suddenly, I don't know exactly what happened, but it was a bit like a long electric shock. Of course this was quite different, it wasn't mechanical, it was a person; I could have no doubt about this at all. There was a feeling of heat and light rushing through my bloodstream, sweep-ing over me and paralysing me almost, as if some person outside were blowing something in me to white heat, and I was sobbing tears of love and gratitude. I was longing for it to go on, and for some time it kept returning more and more strongly, leaving me weak and shivering in be-tween. There were no visions or voices, but the person com-municated with words, or rather ideas, or certainties, with a sort of close intimacy, much more closely than into my ear or imagination.

As I wrote in my review, I find a passage like this more vivid and moving than even the most eloquent classical account of mystical experience. How I wish ... but I really accepted long ago that this sort of thing is not for me.

——— * ———

A visit from Martyn and Pinkie. What a shock to realize that it is *two years* since they were here last. How graceless and unsociable this made me feel: the more so as their short stay was unalloyed happiness. As Pinkie said, though without the

[339]

least hint of reproach, 'we haven't got so many years left that old friends can afford to go for long without meeting'.

———— * ————

Another great satisfaction came from our meeting with Dave and Michele in The George. We had a very enjoyable, even affectionate talk: and all that unpleasantness between Dave and me seemed as if it had never happened. So the last wound left by the ending of BH has now been healed.

———— * ————

Jeffrey (Hammond) now comes to Tymawr with us on Sundays; and seems to enjoy it as much as we do. It makes him and Nasi seem even closer neighbours than before: and now we've heard that another close neighbour might want to come, and perhaps his wife as well. True, there isn't much room for guests in the chapel; but what pleasure it gives me to contemplate the growth of a regular Tymawr congregation gathered from the few houses at the bottom of our loop-road. A little, loosely knit group of neighbours, strengthened in their neighbourly affection by the threads attaching them to that organized and enduring group of sisters.

And when I contemplate this possibility it seems to be much more than a means of giving me greater personal protection – though that enters into it, of course. My hope is for a free community, growing together in 'the liberty of the Sons and Daughters of God'.

A dream, of course, but what a pleasant one!

1 June

The virtue of hope implies the recognition that you must often *hope against hope*. A hard virtue in a hard world. Its marvellous fulfilment is Dame Julian's All shall be Well; but any premature reaching after that assurance leads only into a fatuous optimism.

———— * ————

At least my worry about Laura is a fairly pure concern for her happiness. (And it is a foolish sophism to say, 'Ah, but you want her happiness only so that she shan't interfere with your own.' Don't look gift horses in the mouth!)

———— * ————

We towed the caravan to Cambridge again for a DA working party. It was addressed by a very intelligent psychiatrist who nevertheless took it wholly for granted that his function towards depressives is simply to get them back into working order. In my vote of thanks I managed to suggest that an out-of-order depressive may be in much better condition than a busily satis-fied competitor on his way up a 'career structure'.

From Cambridge to Lincoln, where I had glanced briefly at the cathedral when I was walking from London to Ganthorpe at the age of eighteen. This time we both thought it one of the most beautiful buildings we'd ever seen.

Then, via Southwell – true 'romanesque'; a dark, Roman triforium – to a camp site just outside Dovedale. Real happiness there for three days, though I nearly ruined my longest walk by morbid fears of frightful news somehow reaching the camp site in my absence – S awaiting me in tears, to tell me that Jason . . . Lucy . . . Laura . . . Phine . . . Poll . . . (Another failure to be Here and Now, for even if a child were dead the anticipa-tion of the news would have been useless. Worse than useless.)

So I suppose the mild, and very familiar bad news when we got home shouldn't have upset me much. In spite of a near promise of funds if I could find a publisher the Arts Council has not only refused a grant for *Pantaloon*, but has done so almost with contempt.

In The George I suddenly felt very ill; rushed out and vomited profusely in the Gents. And I was immediately relieved not only of my stomach pains but of all my grief and irritation about *Pantaloon*.

It seems more and more clear that this work will be published *only when I no longer care whether it is or not*; either because I'm dead or because I no longer need to express myself so inordinately as all that.

But that evening I also began to understand that *Pantaloon* is as much a pilgrimage as this journal is meant to be. (Though I never saw it in that light when I was writing it.)

3 June

In one of Beethoven's quartets the words *Neue Kraft Fühlung* appear in the margin, not just as a statement about himself but as a direction to the musicians. I too, this bright and windy morning, feel an access of new power; extraordinary refreshment; hope as a total assurance of God in his heaven ... *No more cigarettes*.

——— * ———

'This was my world from now on. I myself have chosen it. More than ever before, the life of the world as I knew it seemed empty, devoid of all meaning, and I understand why, once on the Spiritual Path, one can never go back; not because one learns extraordinary secrets ... but simply because there remains nothing to go back to' (Irina Tweedie).

This, from a book called *The Chasm of Fire*, surely speaks for almost everyone who has ever tried to set out on that path. (Irina Tweedie is an Anglo-Russian lady who put herself in the hands of an Indian guru for many years. I don't much like the sound of him – human, all too human in his arrogance and bad temper; even cruelty – but he seems to have given her what she needed. Such strange vehicles for his grace God chooses. Has to choose?)

——— * ———

Why are there so few wise teachers here; or even capable spiritual directors? It is not in our tradition: and how much that says against our adulation of the ostensibly autonomous, self-sufficient individual.

——— * ———

[342]

Pantaloon. God has given me great strength, and even some measure of wisdom, in dealing with all these disappointments.

———— * ————

In one little Derbyshire village we went to the annual ceremony of blessing the wells. Each of the five village wells had been 'dressed' – that is, flowers had been intricately threaded into a frame above it to form a Bible picture. They were hideous pictures, since our summer flowers look much too garish when pushed together like this. But the designs were made with astonishing skill; and how little it mattered that they were ugly; how much it mattered that this traditional and very difficult craft was still practised by the young people of at least a dozen villages in that area. May they never give it up! May wells be dressed in Tissington. Till Kingdom Come! (As Rupert Brooke might have written, I am forced to add by my deplorable literary self-consciousness. It is sad that such simple and expected ideas still embarrass me.)

———— * ————

But why this prejudice against books in some Christian quarters? For me a book is simply another human being talking to me as clearly as he can: and if I had never received such communications I would never even have started on this journey.

———— * ————

Pip (grandson) becomes more delightful and accessible with every visit now. I foresee great happiness with him, as I have already felt it with Milly – four years older.

———— * ————

A dream of love and madness. My mother, my father and Tony were all mad; so I sat them on the chimneypiece (hearth?) and went in search of Lucy (qualified to help them). But I was told that Lu was out in the rain; and I knew that this had some terrible hidden meaning. I woke in the anguished conviction that something frightful had really happened to her, and I couldn't get rid of this until it was time to get up. I

[343]

immediately rang her up at the hospital, and found that all was well. (But these days I worry more about her than about anybody else. She is so vulnerable behind all that courage and reserve.)

———— * ————

'How can love be said to know? Because when a thing is loved it becomes in a special sense, as the old theologians used to say, "Connatural" to the lover: it is immediately experienced. You know a great deal *about* the thing you love, but if you put down on paper all that you thus know you do not really touch on the essential because the essential is something that will not be put down in rational terms ... You are beyond the realm of knowledge about things: you are in the realm of that *connaissance toute cordiale*, that knowledge of the heart, which, because it is a direct experience, is a union not only of mind with its object but of the whole being with the thing loved' (Gerald Vann).

———— * ————

Records and tapes put carefully in order. The great satisfaction, of making these little inroads on confusion.

———— * ————

A Godsend. This invaluable word has been corrupted into meaning any piece of fortuitous good luck,

———— * ————

That jolly Monmouth fishmonger, whom I knew so well in his shop over so many years, has now become a gloomily officious traffic warden. So much can be done by a uniform and a little brief authority.

———— * ————

I dreamt I was thirty years old; and when I woke up I felt a stunning shock at being recalled to my real age.

———— * ————

'Oh, to get back to our blessed routine!' I said to S. Then

[344]

quickly corrected myself: 'I mean, of course, to our *creative order*.'

———— * ————

What a switchback of a life we lead. But each downward swoop, we must again remember, is a new and different one, so we never traverse the same bit of track a second time. (A dubious analogy, though, since on a switchback each descent and rise is lower than all those before it.) The hope is that this alarming rollercoaster (as S calls it) will lead us up and up until we are finally shot off the end into some unimaginable higher realm.

———— * ————

Friday is usually the best day of the week, chiefly because I spend the morning writing my review. This *rappel à l'ordre* – obligatory work; professional work – steadies me down after the too-frequent hecticness (in recent weeks) of our Monmouth symposium.

———— * ————

The importance to me of Jesus as 'brother and bringer of light'; which are the words I use when I pray to him. As a unique hybrid he has no meaning for me at all.

———— * ————

Each new freedom that we take – sexual freedom is the best example – demands a new, more difficult, more subtle discipline.

6 July

A delightful visit from Ann H. Since she can hardly ever face moving from her Quaker hostel it was a great sign of love that she asked her brother to drive her here. Too much to say, and far too little time to say it. I told her that she inhabits a lower corner of hell than any that I've ever visited, and therefore a more distinguished one. For she suffers not only from depression, guilt, etc., but also from almost unremitting physical pain.

And two days later a marvellous yet mystifying letter: 'Oh the joy of seeing you both and the whole visit. It is impossible to thank enough for everything, above all for the glorious welcome. You can't imagine the loving CALM, relaxed, utterly HAPPY atmosphere radiated by both of you. It really is almost impossible to believe that either of you ever has a care in the world ...'

Strange and wonderful. And yet there has been other evidence that people see us in this light. Surely there must be some truth in it, then; some grace received by us of which we are almost totally unaware but which can sometimes be apparent to friends and visitors.

There is nothing better in this world than to be a witness to the love of God. And there's no danger whatever of my resting on these golden laurels: too many painful scenes keep me firmly in mind of the other reality. (Not that those pains disprove the love, or even the calm, which Ann observed here. The weirdness of life – and particularly of lives lived in the hope of God – is that these opposites can somehow coexist, the pain, rightly faced and accepted, feeding the love.)

——— * ———

In Van der Weyden's *Pietá* the donor, kneeling there with his coarse but willing and respectful face, is every bit as prominent as Jesus and Mary. At first I thought this a shocking piece of sycophantic commercialism; but I now see that it is entirely right. For the donor is all of us, crudely and inadequately adoring at a scene which is *both* one of deeply private grief *and also* part of a mystery which is being performed for the whole world.

——— * ———

Sitting in Newland churchyard on Sunday evening (depression of the third, or mildest, order) I expressed my self-disgust to S in words which shamed me even as I was speaking them. For I knew very well what I was up to – extracting repeated assurances from her that I am really a good and respected man in spite of my many and abysmal faults. She supplied what I was asking, of course; and it was as right for her to show me this charity as it was wrong of me to demand it.

———— * ————

The Vietnamese boat people. A hideous symptom of our time. Driven off every shore; dying by the boatful, or on tiny islands.

And would I take one of them into this house if I were asked? No, I would not. No, I *could* not.

'My Lord and God, take all from me that blocks my way
  to thee.
My Lord and God, give all to me that speeds my way
  to thee.
My Lord and God, take this my self from me and give
  it as thine own to thee.'

(Nikolaus von der Flüe)

But the self who would not/could not take a dying child into his house is scarcely one that God would wish to receive as a gift. The strange truth is that you cannot give your self to God until that self is a gift worth giving. (Yet if the child were here, on the doorstep, I wouldn't hesitate to take it in. So what I do – presumably – is to dull my imagination in order to avoid this unbearable immediacy.)

28 June

'*Souffrir passe: avoir souffert ne passe jamais.*'

———— * ————

When we find it impossible to speak or act out of felt love we must act on the memory of love and the certainty of its return. But any *simulation* of love is immediately detected and rightly rejected.

At our very worst moments there is at least the thudding

[347]

reminder that *we are landed with each other*; that he/she is what we have to work with whether we like it or not. (And this can turn from heavy resignation into a strange sort of satisfaction.)

———— * ————

Stripped of every scrap of dignity; the one filled with anger and the other with noisy self-pity; no more contact possible between us than between two rocks; no conceivable communication with any conceivable god ... Is it possible for shame and pain to be greater than this? Yes; it is always possible. In such a state all prayer sounds repulsively false; unctuous; even derisive (because the empty words turn back against the one who is trying to say them).

But when she said, 'I'm sorry, but I have nothing to give you' I felt close to her for the first time that evening. For I was also too weak and empty to give anything at all. So although we were apparently so far apart, we could at least share our indigence; our incapacity. Perhaps we could even share our separation.

At the worst, I can remind myself, whether in my guilt or in my anger, that we have given to each other and received from each other more or less equally. We are not a lopsided couple.

30 June

The worst element in acute suffering is the sense of imminent disintegration. So I try to clutch myself together, holding on tight to all the bits that are threatening to slip away.

But perhaps I shouldn't cling so tight. Perhaps I should allow myself to dissolve, in the pure trust that I shall at last be reconstituted in a more godly shape. (But what a mess that would leave for others in the meantime!)

Merton puts it better of course:

[348]

'We have to be able to relax the psychic and spiritual cramp which knots us in the painful, vulnerable, helpless "I" that is all we know of ourselves. The chronic inability to relax this cramp begets despair. In the end, as we realize more and more that we are knotted upon *nothing*, that the cramp is a meaningless, senseless, pointless affirmation of nonentity ... our frustrations become absolute ... There is only one remedy – the surrender that seeks faith in God as a gift, and that is willing to suffer great indigence and peril while waiting to receive it.'

———— * ————

Sometimes it seems that a loving couple must hammer away at each other's faces in order to break the crust, film, wall of glass between them. They think they are trying to hurt each other, but they are really trying to reach each other; to see each other 'face to face' at last; and so, at last, to love each other truly.

2 July

The absurd but almost ineradicable conviction that only what is done arduously, even painfully, can be of any value. But it is the natural grace and ease of good people which delights us almost more than the goodness itself. Well; that is an essential part of their goodness.

———— * ————

'Stupidity' and 'silliness' are both vices. 'Simplicity' is akin to idiocy. 'Unintelligent' sounds dreary and almost contemptuous. Why is there no word to express the opposite of 'intelligent' without the least hint of disparagement? After all many saints have been – that word.

———— * ————

People become more difficult to meet and books become more difficult to read. As if I were being slowly forced into becoming a solitary and a contemplative. But this fills me with panic and

[349]

rejection; for I know that I'm not ready for this, and I strongly doubt that I ever shall be.

3 July

Kierkegaard shrewdly insists (but over-insists, as so often) that it is our very imperfections which should give us grounds for hope: there is always a task to be done.

———— * ————

There are many people living in 'quiet desperation' who wouldn't presume to describe their suffering as spiritual. But their pain certainly deserves this awkward but uplifting word, since it springs, at its deepest root, from horror at the apparent meaninglessness of life. And at that level they know that the stock humanist answer – we ourselves must give a meaning to our lives – is a hopelessly barren one. For how can we live by constantly putting the same food into a cupboard from which we are constantly taking it out again?

———— * ————

'Begin the life of devotion, the life in which morality is transformed into worship by the alchemy of love' (Gerald Vann).

———— * ————

So often I crave for perfect order within me and all around me: a decent, serene, dignified man, living in a house without blemish; a garden without a single weed; a society smoothly organized to the satisfaction of every member.

How false this longing is, for the condition I suppose myself to be longing for is one of total sterility and inertia.

———— * ————

If good can spring from evil why shouldn't evil spring just as naturally from good: a perpetual and unavoidable alternation?

The answer is that while good may *grow* out of evil the reverse

[350]

process is not one of growth but of collapse; retreat; disintegration ...

———— * ————

'I long for the time when men will turn away from this most barren discussion on God, immortality and their souls' (Hale White).

But here we are, still at it after a hundred years!

'I believe that mind never worships anything but mind' (Hale White).

What could be simpler than that? What could be truer?

'He was on the point of sinking, when he bethought himself that if he was to die, he might just as well die after having put forth all his strength; and on the instant, as if touched by some divine spell, the agitation ceased and he was himself again' (Hale White).

I have never been at such an extremity, but I believe there have been moments of near despair when I've been touched by the same divine spell.

Reading Hale White ('Mark Rutherford') again I'm vividly reminded of how much he meant to me when I first read him thirty years ago. I think we are wrong to suppose that we have somehow left those tormented, God-seeking, God-doubting Victorians behind us. I believe we have more grounds for hope than they had, if only because faith has been freed from some of its shackles. But I feel a strong sense of brotherhood with that honest, awkward, desperate yet indefatigable man.

———— * ————

Gerry's excellent pamphlet called *On Being Incarnate*. The tone is a little too rationalist for my lusher taste, but there are any number of fine perceptions. This, for example: 'When Jesus says "I and my Father are One" and "When you pray say, Our Father ..." he is not referring to two different fathers.'

The great value of Jesus to me is always as a brother, however much wiser, holier and more loving than I am.

———— * ————

I must embark on a slow-reading course.

——— * ———

'It is hard to really love others if love is to be taken
in the full sense of the word. Love demands a complete
inner transformation – for without this we cannot possibly
come to identify ourselves with our brother' (Merton).

——— * ———

We live our normal lives within certain conceptual spheres;
and we would instantly go mad if they collapsed. But it is
possible to include in our limiting sphere of concepts the concept
that there are other and greater spheres than ours. This is the
beginning of wisdom: its continuance is to try to penetrate, or
at least to enlarge this invisible but imprisoning bubble. 'Where
the spirit of the Lord is there is liberty.'
Canon Allchin is saying the same kind of thing in his fine
book, *The World is a Wedding* (Darton, Longman & Todd,
London):

'This is to make large affirmations about the nature of
human life which the greater part of the daily experience
of most of us hardly seems to corroborate. It is to say that
man's life is lived on the verge of an unbelievable fulfilment,
and that even here and now, through all the fragmenta-
tion, the waste, the tragedy of our existence that fulfilment
is made known. Here and now we are being drawn into
it. Even here and now there is something unspeakably
wonderful about human life when it is received as God's
gift and lived in His presence. We share our life "with
angels and archangels and all the company of heaven".
The world of time and the world of eternity are nearer
to each other than we usually think. There is a good deal
of coming and going between them.'

'We can all do good deeds, but very few of us can think
good thoughts' (Pavese).
It is also true to say that we can all think good thoughts

but very few of us can do good deeds. The point, I suppose, is that really good thoughts and deeds are inseparable.

———— * ————

Sometimes it may be useful to regard God simply as the best (by far) of all our means of apprehending ourselves and the world.

———— * ————

The task is not to destroy orthodox theology and replace it with a new one; but to replenish orthodoxy by a deeper perusal of its terms. Thus the Trinity has become, for me – Heaven (the Father); Earth (the Son); and every occasion of their meeting (the Holy Spirit).

———— * ————

'All is imagery. Or rather, all is experience which only images can adequately convey' (Bishop John V. Taylor).

8 July

An article on DA had appeared in *The Yorkshire Post*, and the very pleasant young woman who had telephoned me for information forwarded the letters which resulted from it. Not a flood, but enough to keep me busy for two mornings. Each one has to be written differently according to the letter received; not just saying different things but saying them in different ways. So there is an art in this letter-writing, and I take pride in doing it well.

Most of my depressed correspondents drop off after a time, not, alas, because I've cured them, but because they discover that they can't get enough help from letters to make it worth the effort of writing. (And I know very well that the effort can be overwhelming.)

———— * ————

'The way of tribulation remains equally long and equally dark to the very end – it must be a different way which little by little gets lighter. Neither does one know when the change will come, nor exactly whether nor how much nearer one has come to it (for that cannot be known in the dark). But one believes that the change will come, and then with the happiness of eternity. When the child in the dark room waits for the door to be opened and all the hoped-for glory to show itself, then even at the last second before the door is opened it is just as dark as before. And so long as there has been no agreement between the parents and the child as to how long he has to wait, he still does not know whether there may not be a long time to come. But it is quite certain that in the second the door is opened the glory will show itself. So it perhaps occurs to the child sadly that he has been forgotten. But then the child says to itself: how could I believe that my parents would behave like that. So the child endures in patience; for to make a noise for fear of being forgotten is, he knows quite well, to spoil everything. Oh but it is so hard for a man to hold out thus and set everything upon the last moment! We would so much like it to show itself little by little i.e. we would so much like to spoil it for ourselves by getting something in advance' (Kierkegaard, *The Journals*).

Yes, but it is also possible that at the last moment we too shall be crying, 'My God, my God, why hast thou forsaken me!' And it is possible that even when we cry out like this on the point of death we shall believe that God hears our cry with deep love and a pain which is even greater than our own.

9 July

Laura's new distress. I suggested that we might go and stay with her in Gloucester for a few days, to help her get over the worst of it. Then the thought half-formed in my mind that to do this might interfere with the spiritual work on which I'm so assiduously engaged in this house. I cut that short, with a raucous inward guffaw. (As if to say, 'Keep away from me, everyone! I'm busy learning how to love God and my fellow-men.') And then I careened over towards another ludicrous error: 'Ah, what a splendid opportunity to try out my holy love!'

Yet the simple truth is that I love my daughter dearly, and will do all I can to help her.

She was crying in a train a few days ago, after a row with Paul. A middle-aged man tried quietly to comfort her, and as she was getting off at Gloucester station he gave her his card. On it was an invitation to call on him and his wife in Cheltenham whenever she chose; and the little message ended with the words 'Every blessing'.

Now she has gone to supper with these kind and Christian people, and has got much comfort from them both. It is hard, in such a case, not to see the finger of God, and Professor W a true godsend. (But very rash to see this too often.)

———— * ————

I was reduced in bed one night to crying out for a sign, though well aware that this is not the etiquette at all. So I turned to the books beside me and tried Kierkegaard again: this time a little paperback with the repellent title of *Edifying Discourses*. There, where I opened the book, I found my state described in detail, and almost in the words I had been using myself. And it ended with words of perfect comfort:

> 'Alas, this certainty was denied you. But when the busy thoughts had worked themselves weary, when the fruitless wishes had exhausted your soul, then perhaps your being became more quiet, then perhaps your heart, secretly and unnoticed, had developed in itself the meekness which received the word which was implanted in you, and which was able to save your soul, that every good and perfect gift cometh from above.'

It was not that these concluding words described any previous state of my own mind, but that they induced in me the state which they described.

I have never before felt so certain of an answer to prayer.

Male associates day at Tymawr. All except three of us were priests; all except four I had already met, and liked. We sat round the warden – Father Sylvanus from Mirfield – on the sunny grass, and about half the sisters were sitting with us. What a *fête champêtre*! What delightful, easy talk; we telling the sisters what Tymawr meant to us, and they telling us how much we meant to them. Reciprocal back scratching of the very nicest kind.

After tea had been brought round by Sister Benedicta Mother herded us all down to the hayfield, where the parsons stripped off their robes of office, sometimes revealing very flamboyant shorts underneath. And we spent a delightful hour there, the tractor and trailer, driven by Sister Mary Jean, collecting the bales as we piled them up and loaded them.

That was a *heavenly* afternoon – another word which should be rescued from debasement.

———— * ————

'Let us run with patience the race that is set before us' (Hebrews 12:1).

And not try to run any other, for that destroys all patience and all hope.

———— * ————

I have never seen such elder flowers as these. But that may be because I paid so little attention to trees until that surprising walk in the winter of 1977 when I seemed to be looking at a tree for the first time.

———— * ————

The film of *Oh What a Lovely War* on the telly. How much the satire bored and exasperated me, for all satire springs from hatred and contempt. But I was moved to tears by the soldiers and their songs. Innocence and anguish, braced by heroic irony.

17 July

Yesterday we went to Cheltenham and bought two beautiful bicycles; light, fast and many geared; very expensive.

Guilt? On the contrary. 'My Lord and God, give all to me that *speeds* my way to thee.' Strongly approved of, also, by Illich and all good conservationists (though these are not, perhaps, quite the kind of bicycles they mean). And in September we shall speed on these elegant objects from Cherbourg to Chartres. A pilgrimage of sorts.

Or this might, of course, be simply another example of my naive materialism: that old rune of mine which runs:

> In order to dispossess yourself of what you possess
> You must go by the way of a surfeit of possession.

Time will tell. But the ways of God are *so* mysterious that he might even find a use for two Claud Butler super-tourist models; with dropped handlebars; light alloy frames; centre-pull brakes; Derailleur multi-speed hubs ...

25 July

I'd hoped to cut the journal short at that point, on a note of gaiety; even of defiant frivolity; the literary equivalent of a painted Japanese wave, with the crest turned back on itself.

And so I might have done if I hadn't been sharply directed – by Fate? by Chance? by God? – towards what will surely be a very different ending. We'd taken out our bicycles and spent the first two afternoons riding them very gingerly along the bottom of the loop-road. But on the next two afternoons we'd been emboldened to walk them up the steep hill to The Cherries, and then to ride along the hilltop roads to Bream and Hewelsfield. A real taste of ecstasy in the wind up there, swooping along those gentle switchbacks, and beginning to manipulate the complicated gears with a little more confidence.

But when we'd got back from the second of these cheerful

expeditions, full of hope for France and the journey to Chartres, I stooped to pick up the loaded coal scuttles, as I've done a thousand times before, and felt an ominous sharp pain in the small of my back.

Since then I've been lying propped up in bed, working my way through the present version of this journal, and pruning it as severely as I can. I found a great deal which cried aloud to be blacked out with my felt pen, but suspect that this may be a job which can be done properly only by some kind, understanding but ruthless friend (Robert? [Kee]).

But on the whole this reading gave me more pleasure than I'd expected. At least I can detect a gradual change from mainly literary preoccupations to an attempt at a more direct account of this strange and roundabout journey. (Even with these qualifications the word 'journey' seems too definite; too confident. But surely I am not in *exactly* the same place as I was in two years ago – so there must have been some movement in between.)

————— * —————

And now those elegant bicycles in the shed seem like impatient horses kicking up their hoofs in the stable for lack of exercise. They also seem like symbols of a premature leap towards earthly bliss – perhaps towards heavenly bliss. In much the same way as that impudent 'ending' of 17 July seems premature and over-confident.

So how shall I know when to end?

I've sometimes felt that the only way to cut short a book like this – which can't have any logical or natural ending – would be to break off in the middle of a sentence. But this would be just as self-conscious a device as my attempt at a farewell flourish from the seat of a brand-new bicycle.

1 August

And now I can no longer deny that I'm filled with fear and nervous apprehension. The immediate cause is the forthcoming

[358]

visit – three days from now – of the Kees and the Kilmartins. How can I possibly entertain these old friends as they deserve, my back being what it is? (But at other times I'm deeply thankful for my injured back, knowing that I shall be able to use it as an excuse for escaping to my room whenever the company becomes too much for me.)

What is it *exactly* which fills me with so much dread?

Certainly not drink alone, but the general over-excitement of such a visit. The dangerous stimulation of that lively company, which may lead me into all sorts of foolish antics and over-talking. Or it may strike me utterly dumb and senseless, so that I shall sit like a boorish lump of gloom at the dinner table.

Not least the vast amount of work that falls on S.

And then there are those delightful but almost unknown Goslings who are coming to dinner on Saturday. (We've met them only once before, and then I was very drunk and silly.)

8 August

But in fact – and *of course* – the weekend was thoroughly enjoyable and affectionate. Such kind friends and such enlivening talk. And one of my best self-intoxicated, wine-aided (Spirit-inspired) flights of fancy – a conversation between me and God, in appropriate voices, delivered at dinner on Saturday.

As for S she was not only a wonderful provider, as she always is, but has survived without a trace of that nervous tension which sometimes follows so much gaiety. Whereas I am back in bed, of course; and not only because of my back: the weekend, for all its pleasures, has left me very tired. But also more convinced than ever that this confinement has been imposed on me for some good purpose. Perhaps to find the right way of finishing this book.

Yet the sad thing is that I now know I shall never get enough practice on the bike before September 11th, when our passage is booked for St Malo. (Again like mettlesome horses, these superbicycles are far more difficult to ride than the old cobs that both of us are used to.)

This must be a great disappointment to S, who had grown more and more enthusiastic about the expedition. But she never shows her disappointment, of course.

9 August

A very cheering letter from Cynthia; more than a conventional letter of thanks. It really seems that she, Robert and Sarah had enjoyed themselves here; and she even writes that she hadn't seen R laugh so much for a long time.

10 August

Warm messages, too, from Goslings and Kilmartins.

If only we could see our friends more often: and perhaps it may be possible when I get through this particular forest. Or rather these miles and miles of scrub.

16 August

A letter from Robert this morning. It seemed like a ray of heaven's light shining directly into my darkness.

'Dearest Phil and Sal,

'I'm sorry to have been so long in saying what I have been feeling so strongly ever since our lovely time with you the weekend before last; but what I should have said before and what I have been feeling all the time since is that you are the two people who most of all make me optimistic about life with your effortless radiation of its real reality and fun. Now don't get me wrong or jump to euphoric conclusions: you haven't won me over to you-know-who, and of course I know quite well that like the rest of us you're hysterics, depressives, alcoholics, schizo-phrenics, sexual maniacs, hopeless parents anonymous and all the rest of it. But you are true to something good in it all – which doesn't just mean to all that's funny, though the funniness is good and you are that.

'So thanks for all that as well as everything else. And that ends my sermon for today ...'

I see Robert's sad face light up as he has lit up mine with these magical and almost incredible words. That he writes so much the same as Ann H wrote after her short visit here surely must mean that other people can see something in us of which we ourselves are unaware. And the joy Robert got from being here seems all the more real for that self-mocking addition which is so characteristic of our ordinary talk. He knows all about the disabilities from which S and I suffer; and he even implies that if we didn't have these to share with 'the rest of us' he wouldn't have felt such happiness in our company. (A dangerous line of thought, though: 'Good old, bad old us!')

When S came back from Monmouth I showed her Robert's letter at once; and she was delighted, but not nearly so *surprised* as I was. She has always been very fond of R; at least as fond of him, in her quieter way, as I have been; and the extreme openness of his letter didn't amaze her as it amazed me. Nor would she accept my bubbling insistence that what R had seen here could only have been the work of God. 'I just don't *feel*,' she said, 'that I've been changed in the way you're talking about.'

This cooler reaction disappointed me a little, but didn't suppress my extreme elation. Or my faith that there was indeed some holy mystery at work during that weekend, enacted within Robert every bit as much as within S and me.

(At best I see this difference between her and me not just as a difference of temperament but also as a misunderstanding between two different forms of humility. S cannot accept that we have received an extra dose of the grace of God, and believes that Robert's happiness here was simply due to the close affec-tion there has always been between the Kees and the Toynbees.

In other words, to the ordinary working of God in all human beings. I agree about the affection, of course, but feel sure that Robert wouldn't have written a letter quite like that even two years ago. So I do believe that God must somehow be perceptible through us now as never before – hysterics, alcoholics, sex maniacs though we are.)

As for putting R's letter into this journal I shall have to get his agreement to that, of course. But it would be a silly falsification to keep it out if he has no objection to its appearance here. A mock humility. Even the hiding of our light under a bushel. The light of God, that is.

(Besides, didn't I give poor Patrick a run for his money, in quite the opposite direction!)

17 August

The Kees' letters have also started an immediate improvement in the state of my back. I've suspected for some time that although the original injury was perfectly straightforward, its prolongation has had various ulterior purposes.

——— * ———

I had to postpone last week's review, having tried to type it on Friday and finding that I couldn't get any further than the title of the book. All through the week – until yesterday – the obligation to get this done had been oppressing me as it used to do, week in, week out, during the worst years of my depression.

But now, having written the review this morning, and done it well, I lie here basking in this achievement, but still more in the undimmed light of the Kees' letters. (I've made several tests for complacency and vanity, but can't detect any at all. Only gratitude to God and gratitude to Robert and Cynthia.)

And just now God seems to be present – no, *shown* – in everything that comes to my attention: sky and trees; my father's smiling face on the wardrobe; Ben's death; the gift of mechanical genius; the vision and scholarship of Kenneth Clark; S's voice talking to Laura on the telephone downstairs, and L's unheard voice at the other end.

An omniverous gaiety.

———— * ————

'Fear not, for I have redeemed thee; I have called thee by thy name, and thou art mine' (Isaiah).

23 August

Not that I ever expected that mood to last. Nor could I even detect, in yesterday's greyness, that it had made any difference at all to the texture of our lives. Yet I know that it *has* made a difference; a change that can never be reversed. *La joie passe: avoir connu la joie ne passe jamais.*

———— * ————

One lesson from rereading this journal is that poetical language is the worst sort to use for religious discourse; for it compounds the removal of religious speech from the everyday and the commonsensical. Better to say the simplest things – 'God loves all men' – and to let them echo as far as they can.

———— * ————

I've also become more aware – painfully so – that in this domain of the Spirit there can be no intellectual or emotional revelation, however slight, without some corresponding new demand for a change of life.

These demands are seldom obeyed; but the virtue of hope certainly includes the intention to obey them better in future.

25 August

I got up on Monday, with idiotic determination, and rode my bicycle for half an hour. The result is that I'm back in bed and my back a little worse than before. So I decided to ward off boredom and gloom by trying out my own version of the traditional (Eastern Orthodox) Jesus Prayer. Those words – 'Lord Jesus Christ, Son of God, have mercy on me' – are wonderful and enviable. (They are the words which the anonymous nineteenth-century Russian pilgrim used to repeat to himself every day, and often nearly all day, until he was in a daze of glory.) But since I've never been able to accept the unique Incarnation I couldn't use that particular prayer and had to compose one of my own.

I arrived eventually at something I've been working on for many months; and which at least has the merit of being in the same rhythmical form as the Jesus Prayer. 'Heavenly Mother, Light of the World, Have mercy on us.'

On the first day I limited myself to four well-separated half-hour periods of repetition. On the second day I did three separate hours – after breakfast; after lunch; before supper. I felt, perhaps, a little 'high' at the end of the third hour; but chiefly grateful that this occupation had strengthened me against the gloom which had been threatening before I began the experiment. On the third day I achieved four hours, and at some point during the third I did have a feeling that the words had begun to glow a little at the edges.

But on the fourth day, aiming at five hours, I broke down during the second hour in a state of horrified surfeit and disgust. Now it seemed that I had not only emptied the words of all meaning, but had made them worse than senseless – abusive; sardonic; contemptuous.

I groaned for help – but soundlessly at least.

———— * ————

I have never really reached Thy Will be Done: only Help me to Will that Thy Will be Done. But I know that 'Have mercy on us' is not a plea for a mercy which might be withheld, but a reminder of the abundant and ever-present love of God.

26 August

What seems to have happened is that I did receive a breath of holy joy – partly from Robert's letter and partly from my own prayer – but then I tried not only to hold it in but also to inhale more and more of it, as if to burst my lungs. If I had breathed easily and naturally the joy might have stayed longer and had a peaceful effect instead of a disturbing one.

The folly of excess again. But in a most strange and unfamiliar form.

28 August

The contract for the sale of Barn House has at last been safely signed and sealed. So we now have a great deal of money in the bank, of which some – but how much? – will be given to Oxfam as a conscience saver. The gift won't be very effective in that function, but at least it may keep a few children alive.

Meanwhile, in our unregenerate state, the thought of that solid sum to be transferred to a building society does give a certain cowardly comfort. It is also, of course, a barrier between us and God. Considering the interest which will accrue to us I am again scandalized by a system which so brazenly adds more to them that hath. (But not, apparently, too scandalized to take advantage of it.)

———— * ————

A good test of a faith is whether or not it seems to have given greater freedom of mind, spirit and action. I am certainly conscious, some of the time, that my mind and spirit are far more free than they've ever been before. But I am bewildered, and sometimes worried, by the fact that I also seem to be more physically constricted than ever before. Yet rather than try too hard to break out of this particular constriction I believe I should try to accept it – at least for the time being – and make all possible use of it.

[365]

Perhaps my recognition of a far wider and deeper reality has made me more aware of my constant failure to reach or apprehend it. And the result of this is that I sometimes feel a greater sense of restriction than ever before. There is this contrast between what is believed in, guessed at, *almost* seen, and the familiar, unchanged reality of daily life.

———— * ————

Lucy, who still does a lot of hitchhiking, tells us that some cars slow right down, as if to give her a lift; then the drivers, and sometimes a whole family, make abusive gestures at her and speed away. What sort of people *are* these? I believe they are the kind of people who would volunteer to become concentration camp guards.

———— * ————

Thinking again about our newly-acquired money I note down that 'there is nothing worth wanting except the love of God and man'.

But this is an example of the kind of dramatic and false condensation of faith which Christians should be careful to avoid. I know that what we should *most* want is to love God and our neighbour with all our hearts, minds and souls. But this is very different from saying that no other desire is of any value. What about a passionate desire for scientific truth? Or to create beauty? Or to live, though without faith, both honourably and kindly?

A Christian must believe that God is in all these noble ambitions; yet they are seldom the means of leading a person to the Christian's supreme ambition.

———— * ————

There are two famous Christian ways – the way of Martha (good works) and the way of Mary (prayer and contemplation). I am very incompetent at both; but perhaps there is a third way, which is to share this moral and spiritual incompetence with others, and encourage them not to lose hope by keeping

[366]

one's own hope alight in the murky confusion of repeated doubt and failure.

———— * ————

Still in bed for most of the day, and still working over this journal and trying to remove as many bloodstains as possible from that 'wound of inordinate self-expression'. Moments of nausea, which come from this rubbing my nose in my own sickening person. (But I'd guess that nearly all personalities are sickening under such close scrutiny.)

I also notice that there are such frequent, and sometimes violent changes of mood that the journal reads almost like a case history. This condition may be fruitful; and not only as a warning. But it is hard to endure. I long for a more even keel: calmer waters; a haven of peace at last. (For I know that real peace is more fruitful than any amount of turmoil, however closely examined for hidden patterns of light.)

But the effect of Robert's letter has certainly not been to enlarge, gild or glorify the ego. I believe more than ever that what he saw and felt here was the grace of God, working in all of us whether we knew it or not.

30 August

Heavenly Mother, give me the strength to stay out of bed this afternoon, and to do something useful with this depleted and injured body. (Much of the trouble may well be psychosomatic, but only idiots imagine that this means it isn't 'real'. I have never been a hypochondriac, as S confirms: I love health and happiness and long to possess them all the time. I long to be a cheerful witness to what is, after all, a joyful faith in the power of God's love for men.)

———— * ————

'What then of the Church? A born-again company of believers? Perhaps. A company of travellers ... diverse, open, caring, living in the Way, trying to do God's will

[367]

as Jesus declared it? Certainly' (John Simmonds; Methodist minister).

4 September

A very cheerful visit to Peter and Polly's house near Rye. I wasn't quite a witness to the love of God, but a good time was had by all, which is not to be sneezed at. Bob* and Decca were there: and Decca and I clowned away together, as of yore.

S and I felt a great admiration for Poll, who is the most radiantly *easy* of all my children. She is a wise and loving mother; an unobtrusively good housewife and entertainer of friends and relations. The best kind of Martha – and one who would be much too good-natured to make any complaints against Mary.

Pleasant games with the children; I even swam in the sea with Peter, Polly and Milly and never felt a single twinge from my back.

On the way to Rye we called on Ann H and had lunch with her. As usual this was a happy and very talkative meeting, with much more to say than we had time for. Vigorous discussion on reincarnation. A medium has told Ann's daughter that her mother is now paying, by her many dire afflictions, for having been a brutal general in an earlier life, who massacred thousands of prisoners. This is poisonous rubbish to S and me; but it seems to give Ann a strange kind of comfort. 'After all, it means that there is some *sense* in my suffering, doesn't it?' Her friendly Christian Science healer also believes in this tale, but tells her that it's possible to work out, and escape from, a bad karma *in this life*. Sheer revisionism! I doubt if any genuine guru would approve.

When I talked about this to Decca, with concern, Decca shared the concern but told a very funny story: Wife, in touch with dead husband through medium: 'Well, dear, what do you do over there?' 'Oh, we run about a bit; then we eat a bit; then we have a bit of sex; then we run about a bit again; have a bit more to eat, and a bit more sex ...' Wife: 'Goodness I

* Bob Treuhaft, Jessica Mitford's husband.

never knew heaven was like that.' Husband: 'Oh I'm not in heaven: I'm a rabbit in Australia.'

——— * ———

From the latest number of *New Fire*.

'Whereas science is positive, contenting itself with reporting what it discovers, scientism (the religion of science) is negative. It goes beyond the actual findings of science to deny that other approaches to knowledge are valid and other truths are true. In doing so it deserts science in favour of metaphysics – bad metaphysics, as it happens, for as the contention that there are no truths save those of science is not itself a scientific truth, in affirming it scientism contradicts itself.'

5 September

Reading Father Gerard Hughes's *In Search of a Way*. A splendid book, in which he uses the framework of a walking pilgrimage to Rome to expound a liberal Christianity of the very best sort – i.e. the most generous but the least sloppy. How admirable that a Jesuit should defy his superiors and give communion to all-comers.

The fact that Father Hughes was already in his mid-fifties when he achieved his great pilgrimage makes our plan to walk part of the way to Chartres seem even more insignificant than it did before. (Yes, but perhaps our little amble might be acceptable to God as an equivalent of the widow's mite.)

Walked down the hill for a swim in the Wye: only the second time I've done this since we came to live at Woodroyd. A baptism into new strength? Now physical health has become the first object of my prayer. How much I want to be a smiling friend; a welcoming host; a quiet listener ...

——— * ———

From the *Wisdom of the Desert* – edited by Thomas Merton:
'Yet another elder said: if you see a young monk

[369]

by his own will climbing up into heaven, take him by the foot and throw him to the ground, because what he is doing is not good for him.'

I wish I could have shown that to Barn House John; though I think he'd have ridden over it without a moment's hesitation.

———— * ————

A *Resolution*. That every day I will break my routine somehow, in however small a detail.

———— * ————

Woodroyd Cottage. My –
Nest;
Bolthole;
Retreat;
Fortress;
Womb;
Prison;
Watchtower;
Sickroom;
Chapel;
Woodland bower;
Great War dugout;
Cork-lined study ...

My back is evidently recovered at last; so it hasn't saved me from the dreaded/longed-for journey across the sea. But what with this lumbago, as John E diagnoses it, and attendant disabilities, I've been in bed for most of the day during the past six weeks. Try to see this as a legendary preparation for the journey to Mont St Michel and Chartres. Revival of the wounded Fisher-King; or something of that sort.

———— * ————

Much reading lately of books with titles like *Life after Life*. The usual shame: a dog returning to its vomit. But damn it, the evidence *is* strong; and though I find the notion of eternal bliss almost as appalling as eternal punishment I would dearly love to move into a different realm in which I could pursue the Way further.

———— * ————

Our friend Jim's back, very erect, disappearing into the dim light of Agincourt Square. And in his desolation he remains wonderfully tidy in his clothes; well-shaved; his nails perfectly clean. A brave man, fighting hard for his respect: and how much S has done to help him win it back for himself.

9 September

Tomorrow we leave for Portsmouth. Zero hour; then over the top.

For me this has become an elderly version of the tremendous challenge I had to face in 1950. Wifeless, and longing only to hide my face in the cottage, and protection, which G had offered me, I went to *The Observer* (on Patrick O'Donovan's advice and recommendation) and accepted the job of roving correspondent in the Middle East. I had never been a proper journalist before; knew nothing whatever about the Middle East. But I went out to Cairo, by the grace of God; encountered, and survived, many horrors there and elsewhere; came back to England a year later married to S.

What I most fear now is that I may have to turn back. Reach St Malo, perhaps, only to find that I can't make it, and must drag poor S back home again. A frightful thought.

Yes; but if only I *could* do it!

Yesterday we went to Bristol and bought boots, rucksacks, etc. They seemed absurd when we tried them on: an unconvincing disguise: costumes for a play which will never be acted.

10 September

We had decided to stay tonight in some small hotel near Portsmouth rather than get up at five to be sure of catching the St Malo boat. The sun was shining brightly on Tintern Abbey as we drove past, and this seemed a good omen for our journey. But as soon as we stopped at the first likely hotel we were told that it was full, and that all the hotels for miles around were likely to be full as well. Some sort of naval exhibition was being held in Portsmouth all this week.

We tried three or four more places without success; but without agitation either. Our calmness was due, in S's case to a natural disposition to take things as they come; in my case to the fantasy of a stern pilgrimage in which many trials of patience and courage would have to be met. This was only half-serious, of course, but it was already proving a useful device in the kind of situation which used to cause me – and those with me – a great deal of trouble. But I shan't talk about my extravaganza to S; for this is the kind of thing which tries her patience as much as full hotels try mine.

Eventually it was she who noticed a 'Bed and Breakfast' sign in a beautiful bit of country between Petersfield and Winchester. At the end of a long drive we found a charming Queen Anne farmhouse and a very clean bedroom overlooking a small green valley full of horses. Propitious!

11 September

A calm, sunny and rather boring crossing to St Malo. It was 9.30 when we got off the boat, and already dark; so the first of our tasks in France was to find that little walled town among all the complexities and misleading lights of the docks. The packs seemed badly-fitting rather than heavy during the half-hour we spent stumbling over railway lines and hawsers. But when we found the town gate and the castle beside it they looked welcoming as well as imposing.

But here too the hotels were full, and it was obvious from the gaiety of the little streets that the season was by no means over, as we'd hoped it would be. In the end we had to settle for a fairly squalid dump over a café, where the sheets were damp and grey and looked like breeding-grounds for bugs. I remembered such rooms from Paris in the thirties, and accepted its sour dankness with scarcely a shudder. S needed more courage, and showed both the courage and her need of it.

We sat in a pavement café at the main crossing, and watched young people dancing to the guitar or strolling very slowly up and down, arm in arm. It is eight years since I was last in France; easily my longest absence since childhood. For about sixteen years – from 1935 to the early fifties – I regarded this as my second country, and knew almost as much about its politics and modern literature as I knew about England's. In those years, speaking quite good French and having several French friends, I was at least able to play the part of an honorary Parisian. Even during the next fifteen years, when S and I often went to France with Ben, he and I had enough professional connections to make us feel that we were something very superior to tourists. But since then I have lost touch with French writing, lost almost all my interest in French politics and seen nothing of my closest French friend for more than ten years.

But as we sat in that café I calculated that I must have spent, in all, at least a year of my life in France, and many hundreds of hours doing exactly what we were doing now. The only new element in the café life was our pocket chess set, either on the table between us or held up like an open book by each of us in turn. A desultory game, much interrupted by our comments on the people around us.

And this time I was in no doubt at all that we were tourists among tourists (though none of the others, I would guess, supposed themselves to be pilgrims as well).

12 September

In spite of those grim beds we slept well, woke unbitten and ate a good breakfast in the café downstairs. We spent the morning walking very slowly and happily on the walls, visiting the church, drinking (expensive) beer and (cheaper) Pernod. It was a bright, windy, exhilarating day.

After a modest lunch we took the Cancale bus from outside the walls, but got out of it at the little inland town of St Meloir. This left us only four miles walking in the afternoon, which we did very slowly – to my Old Adam's occasional impatience, quickly cut short by the pilgrim – under a hot sun and through endless cabbage fields. S's orange pack and my scarlet one must have contrasted oddly with grey hair and balding head; and one kind driver stopped to offer us a lift. We refused it, of course, but almost regretted this by the time we were walking down the long cliff road into this famous little oyster town.

By the time we'd climbed the six flights to our hotel bedroom I was far the more exhausted of the two; felt sick with tiredness and even wondered, for a very uneasy half-hour, whether the pain in my back was starting up again.

But by dinner-time we were fresh again, and very hungry. We ate well in the hotel dining room and then strolled along the dim pier to find the tide just reaching the end of it, and fishermen working by lamplight in the holds of their boats. There were two or three other elderly English couples taking the air on the pier, and we wondered whether any of them were also on their first holiday without the children. Whether they, too, felt the slight strangeness and melancholy of being alone together on holiday again after so many years.

Then the thought of God came into my mind, after a long absence, and added, perhaps, a certain depth to these shadowy and superficial emotions. At least they were no longer fortuitous and isolated, but attached to every other loss and new beginning. (In God everything is related to everything else: enter his truth by any occasion and there is at least a faint glow or murmur of the whole Kingdom.)

13 September

But a bad night followed, turning and turning on that unfamiliar bed, and longing for the beloved bed I'd left so rashly behind me. I reproached myself for my impatience of the afternoon, and thought again how good it was of S to come on an expedition so little suited to her usual tastes. I thought of walking alone through Austria and Yugoslavia in the summer of 1936, usually sleeping in haycocks under the moon, too poor to eat anything but bread and cheese or drink anything but water; sleeping, at last, in that great dormitory of an Allogio Popolare in Trieste ... And now the very thought of doing even a journey like this one without S makes me shudder with fear and misery. 'Old men should be explorers ...' Eliot was right, of course, but he wasn't advising us to trek through Amazonian jungles; he was thinking of the jungles within; and in those I have certainly done some hacking, sweating and peering during the last few years.

But as for the outer world this particular old man is now so housebound; so clenched into his own little corner of England, that even this pleasant Breton town on the English Channel seemed, at night, to be darkly alien and hostile all around me. I heard the tide wash loudly against the seafront, and then recede to leave a black and hollow silence through the window.

Then the word 'Vigil!' suddenly presented itself, and my mind was immediately relieved of almost all anxiety. This was partly because the idea was absurd, in a homely and familiar way; but partly because the notion of an old and ailing knight on a pilgrimage of healing had begun to be almost real to me.

This morning we left the packs in our bedroom and walked four miles along a cliff-top path from Cancale to Port Mer – a name so pure and simple that it fitted very easily into the proliferating legend. Yet that bad night had left me in a rather dim and dismal state; and I found the walk quite hard going even without a pack. But my spirits lifted a little when we suddenly saw the first of our two shrines – Mont St Michel, a dark blue cone about fifteen miles across the hazy air of the bay. After a swim from the pleasant sands of Port Mer, and lunch in a pleasant small hotel there, I felt better still. We walked back by road; hot and dusty but happy and frivolous.

At dinner in Cancale that night there was a vast seafood dish on the menu which cost about £19; and most of our fellow-diners were eating it. Enormous pink bibs were tied round their necks by the waitresses, which made them look both privileged and ridiculous. They grinned self-consciously at each other; but how they tucked into those great mounds of lobster and *écrevisses*; of crabs and *langoustes*; prawns, oysters and mussels! What a cracking of shells and gouging of claws; but not a word spoken. It made us feel almost austere with our escalopes and salad.

(But the truth – and perhaps a sad one – is that I can't take the rapturous delight from food that I used to take. I don't think this is due to any newly acquired disrespect for fleshly pleasures but simply to a general decline of all the appetites as age advances.)

14 September

We stood on the outskirts of Cancale hailing cars and lorries for forty minutes without success; and I noted the coldly dismissive glances of the drivers with sadness but without anger. We nearly always give lifts in England; and this little experience made us resolve to stop, in future, even when we feel least inclined for company.

In any case the amiability of the man who finally stopped for us more than made up for the almost violent indifference of the others. One just man can save a city.

He put us down at a cross-roads where we were able, after another short wait, to take a bus to Pontorson, the dull little town which 'serves' Mont St Michel from six miles inland. Here the first hotel we tried claimed to be full but we knew this was only because of our rucksacks (and later we saw several full cars unload themselves there). This gave me a pleasant but fatuous sense of having rejoined, after many years, the enviable ranks of the undesirables. The knight, disguised as a beggar, had

[376]

joyfully suffered another of the pilgrim's predestined humiliations.

To this was added a groaning stomach and the dreaded trots
for much of this fifth night away from home.

15 September

But both of us were fresh and cheerful this morning, waiting
in the sharp morning air for the bus to take us on that longed-
for last stage to Mont St Michel. Pontorson, by far the dreariest
place so far, seemed like the necessary purgatory before we could
come to this shining paradise, climbing so steeply out of the
miles and miles of sand. (The sea has receded so far since the
Middle Ages that by now it washes the base of the holy citadel
only at the highest tides.)

I am no good at describing great works of art and won't
attempt to do what Henry Adams and many others have done
so much better than I could. But certainly I'd never realized
how *extraordinary* this place is; how astonishing the feat of building a great abbey on top of a wild island rock; the fantastic
late Gothic spikes of the chancel; the sheer height of the
buttressed walls on the north and south ...

The hotels and junk shops are kept severely down to the first
sixty or seventy feet; so as we were walking up that cobbled
lane we emerged quite suddenly from all the babble of our own
time on to the battlemented wall, with a wide view of sands
and the pinnacle still far above us in a sky which seemed almost
silver as we looked up at it against the sun.

Sitting on the very pleasant terrace of our hotel (beer about
80p a small glass) I read a short history of the Mount, and
found that it wasn't a very inspiring one. During most of its
medieval existence the abbey was at best a breeding ground
for rich prelacies all over France; at worst a harsh oppressor
and exploiter of the mainland peasants. Then the Revolution
turned it into a prison, which it remained for much of the nineteenth century. What greater descent could one imagine, from

[377]

a temple built in the sky for silent and holy aspiration into an island dungeon where man's inhumanity to man was blankly at work again?

But now there are three monks in residence, and from what I know of modern religious orders they will at least restore the spirit of the original foundation. Perhaps they will improve on it. This is a holy place, in spite of its gloomy past, and we both felt happy and refreshed as we walked through the garden on the seaward side; then up as far as the abbey door; then over the sands to look back at the whole island from the north. (We are leaving the abbey itself until tomorrow.)

One of the strangest tasks which this pilgrimage imposes on me is to spend money freely, and without a murmur. This sounds ridiculous, fatuously paradoxical: but although extravagance is certainly among my vices, meanness has always managed to insinuate itself as well. My tendency is to spend a lot and complain about the prices. But if I make a fuss on this journey – or rather if I continue to make a fuss – I shall be spoiling S's pleasure as well as my own. And although there have been some trials since we left home, and there will surely be more, the expedition will have failed miserably unless we both enjoy it. To travel happily together is at least as important as what we see or feel in the places we visit.

16 September

I slept well last night, and went to sleep remarkably early. So I must be getting accustomed to the stern hardships of this crusade!

Mass in the abbey at midday. The officiating monk looked too like Donald Pleasance* for immediate comfort; but we soon got used to this and enjoyed that friendly celebration very much: swallows swooping and squeaking high up in the chancel; the extraordinary clarity and purity of the air, and a real sense of being raised towards heaven, perched up there in the sky.

*A well-known actor.

There was a congregation of about a hundred; and three women in white robes serving the three white-robed monks. One of these women brought us a warm *handshake* of peace – not the formal kiss of Tymawr – which we passed back to the row behind us.

I took communion, and S did not. I made this decision without any heavy deliberation, for this has never been the supreme Christian occasion for me – how could any liturgical act be raised above the simplest act of charity? What it meant for me here was what it means for me, more strongly, at Tymawr; that we are partakers of the one bread; that we are united in our will to love God and to love each other through our faith in the love of God.

S stayed in her place because she thought it wrong to presume. But I judged that they would not have withheld the wafer if they'd known what we are. (Also I'd just read Father Hughes's account of how he gave the communion freely to all-comers when he was chaplain at Glasgow University.)

After mass we perambulated the abbey in a guided party. The amazing extent – extension – of these halls (Salle de l'Aquilon; Salle des Chevaliers ...) and chapels; refectory and promenade; cellar and almonry. Most marvellous of all were the cloisters, suspended in air above the rambling gardens to the north. But everything was astonishing: miraculous: if not an outpost of heaven on earth, at least a place where the peace of heaven has been invited to descend.

In the afternoon we walked to the end of the causeway and back, watching the thousands of Sunday cars pouring into the giant car park. Why do they come? There is no beach to play on here: and only a few of these visitors seem to climb above the level of the shops and cafés. In fact by the time we got back that lowest level had become as crowded as an Arab bazaar, milling with good-humoured family parties. God knows I'm the last person to sneer at them for neglecting the abbey: I'm only a recent convert to diligent sightseeing and the joys of architectural splendour.

But they can hardly have come here simply to buy the

appalling trash in the shops, or even to sit in the pleasant cafés and hotel bars. So I suspect that they too are pilgrims, drawn by the potent magic which this place diffuses far and wide around it.

As we were coming back from our short but very hot little walk we suddenly saw a bright straggle of colours – mostly reds and blues – stretched out on the sand about half-way across the southern bay. I asked the car-park attendant what this meant, and he told me that these were young people who went on guided walks across the bay and back – about ten miles of almost desert conditions. Another group of pilgrims.

As we were looking up at the ramparts I had the pleasant fancy of a party of fifteenth-century English knights galloping fiercely through the shallow seas to attack the walls, only to look up and see what we were seeing now – the bright, sleeve-less shirts, the dark glasses, the cameras and the candy floss.

S, after our evening prayer – 'And thank you for the happi-ness of this holiday.' P, a little taken aback, 'Well, and thank you too.' For a minute she kept a straight face, before admitting that it wasn't me she'd been talking to.

17 September

Two final thoughts as the bus was driving us away and we were looking back at that shining pile behind us. The myth of St Michael and his host is among the silliest of Christian legends, in spite of all that Milton made of it: how, for example, did he protect those great unarmoured wings from the slicing swords of Lucifer's wicked angels? But in that other dimension, how appropriate that a pilgrim-knight should make this the first shrine of his pilgrimage, to receive up there the blessing of the holiest soldier ever imagined.

It was an early rising, and for me a painful wrenching out of a bed which I'd just begun to make my own. How can I explain to those who've never been confined as I have just how painful these constant uprootings can be?

But they can be very exhilarating, once the worst is over. Particularly in that dazzling sunrise over the sand, with the magic mountain glowing behind us and throwing its giant shadow across the western bay. (There were also huge Japanese rubbish-gobbling machines under the walls, hard at work getting rid of yesterday's massive detritus.)

S's rheumatic shoulder has begun to bother her: and I'm sorry that she hasn't the advantage of sharing in my fantasy.

A rheumatic shoulder was to her, a rheumatic shoulder and nothing more – not a welcome test of her patience and endurance. But she seems to be bearing it well enough, without the help of that mental caper.

My 57th day without a cigarette; though I do take an occasional puff from one of S's. And alas, I draw the smoke into my lungs with undiminished satisfaction. Will the day ever come when I shall feel *only* revulsion?

Three trains took us from Pontorson to Alençon; and I realized as I got into the first that I hadn't travelled by train for five years or more.

The first change left us far out in the country for more than an hour, so we walked from the station to a tiny hamlet called Le Repas and drank some beer there. A name of the deepest significance, not surprisingly.

Looking through the windows of those excellent trains I experienced for the first time since we left England that wonderful skinning of the eyes which used to be the chief reward for going abroad. Because everything is a little unfamiliar everything becomes noticeable: and so we see twice as much as we usually see in our usual place.

Walking from the station at Alençon to find a hotel, I realized that our resemblance to genuine long-distance walkers is seriously impaired by S's dangling handbag. This quite destroys the effect of my noisy and brawny walking stick.

At the hotel by three o'clock – how good it is to take off our heavy boots, even after such very modest walking. The manager told us that we could get a meal at any time of day in the brasserie across the street. But when I asked for the menu the young waiter behaved with astonishing and almost violent rudeness: '*Vous voulez manger! À cette heure du jour! Qui vous a dit que vous pouvez manger ici?*' This was accompanied by slamming our beer glasses so hard on the table that they spilled on to my paper, and then making off for a door at the back of the café. As I chased after him my rusty French *flew* to my rescue and I complained vigorously and eloquently before he had time to get away.

My pleasure at this linguistic feat easily overrode any doubts I might have had about the appropriateness of such a reaction to my shadow role. (But though we know that many tests are set, we can never be sure whether we've passed them or not. Perhaps that forthright indignation was just what was demanded of me on this occasion.)

After being fed at last, and apologized to by another waiter, we walked a little way up the street to the house where St Thérèse de Lisieux ('The Little Flower') had been born and bred. A fearsome shrine! The wall of the birthroom, carefully reconstructed so as to contain the actual bed, etc., had been opened up, and a little chapel built alongside the house so that this bedroom formed a sub-chapel on the south side. In the house itself photographs, authentic baby clothes, hairbrush, christening robe ... In the chapel hundreds of plaques, covering the whole of the north and west walls, with such inscriptions as '*Reconnaissance profonde, Petite Fleur, pour toute voltre bonté envers moi.* 1925.' Unspeakable stuffiness; mustiness; mouldiness; – even a sense of evil, as if this shrine had been corrupted by a soft and insinuating superstition. Dulled trumpets of the Church Triumphalist; that frightful epoch of Catholic arrogance and right-wing frenzy. (How many priests and prelates were Dreyfusards?)

And yet, of course, there's much more to it than that. Sensible people say that she was the greatest saint of the last hundred years. I've read the *Histoire d'une Âme* with admiration as well as with some revulsion. It seems too, that new discoveries are now being made which show her in a much more robust light than any that's been allowed to shine from her before ...

If this is another test, as of course it must be, then I shall be very prudent in my response. However repulsive I may find this cult it remains obvious enough that Thérèse Martin was ten times closer to God than most of us will ever be.

Through the restaurant window this evening – a foul meal – we saw a sign to Chartres. And every evening in bed I read a bit more of George Henderson's great detective work on the cathedral and its builders. (S read it before we started.)

18 September

We had determined that this, at least, should be a full day's walking; and as a token of our resolve S even allowed me to pack her handbag in my rucksack. We set out from our hotel at 10.15.

Walking through the dull and noisy outskirts of the city was just as good *for the pilgrim* as walking through the most beautiful country in France: perhaps better. But for the two holiday-makers it was a dreary time.

However it turned out that this was the day when the allegorist had his wildest fling. About seventeen miles ahead of us lay the town of Mamers (*Ma Mère*), and though we doubted our capacity to reach it on foot we assumed that we could take a local bus at the end of the afternoon. The last sombre outposts of Alençon, a wide road lined with roaring and hissing factories, was called St Paterne: a few miles beyond it lay the Forêt de Perseigne which ended at the village of Neufchâtel. And the map showed that Le Val d'Enfer de-scended on to Neufchâtel from the north, through the depths of the forest.

So first of all the pilgrim had to pass through the harsh reality of the sainted Father; dreaded source of his overbearing super-ego; perhaps the necessary victim of his still murderous and unconquered oedipal compulsions. Then came the forest of the Persian (Pagan) knight, who would have to be fought and vanquished before Sir P could reach the great walls of the New

[383]

Castle. These would be manned by a host of demons who had descended from Hell's Valley; and the knight would have to lay siege to those terrible fortifications. All this was a necessary preparation for coming at evening to the Holy Mother of Heaven: or, in the alternative terminology, for re-entering his mother's womb.

I kept this to myself as we trudged along, but the allegory had been so perfectly provided for that it was taking a stronger and stronger hold on me. It loosed its grip, though, when we suddenly came, at exactly half past twelve, on an elegant-looking bar-restaurant just two miles from where the forest began. Here the excellent food and drink quickly turned me back from a poor but brave pilgrim into an amateur walker, with a car in Portsmouth and plenty of traveller's cheques in his rucksack.

But the forest road rose steeply after that, and we plodded along in silence, stopping often for short rests and often having to step on to the verge when two great lorries came thundering down on us from both directions at once. But just over a mile from Neufchâtel we found a special Forestry Department track leading straight on towards the village, while the main road curved away to the right. This track was marked *Zone de Silence*, and all cars and transistors were forbidden. It was an avenue of very tall and straight beeches, with the sun streaming through them from the right. It is no fancy to say that this track looked like the immensely long nave of a cathedral, with silver columns and a roof of bright, almost emerald green leaves. Many different kinds of birds were singing loudly as we walked along it: and the whole of that sacred and beautiful approach seemed like a heavenly encouragement to attack the bastion of hell which we would find at the far end of it.

But after all this Neufchâtel was a dull and disappointing little place; and it was a sobering shock to realize that it was already half past five: this meant that we'd done our walking at an average of just over two miles an hour.

Luckily the last bus of the day was soon to leave for Mamers, so we sat in a tiny café to wait for it, pleasantly tired, and refreshing ourselves with ice-cold Pernod. It was only when the bus had left Neufchâtel that I realized that I'd left my stick behind in the café. This caused me real dismay, for I always use a stick when walking; and it was only when I returned to the half-abandoned allegory that I found an immediate consolation. That stick had certainly been as trusty as any sword or lance, for I'd used it on many walks at home over the last few years, and always taken it with us in the caravan. But clearly the knight must surrender his weapon before he can enter the shrine of the Heavenly Mother. And Herr T of the case history must – at least temporarily – undergo castration; sacrifice his organ of virility – before he can make the healing return to his mother's womb.

Mamers was a gentle and charming town, as it had to be, and we found one of those old hotels which still lie – grey, slate-roofed and heavily shuttered – gently decaying at the far ends of quiet courtyards in provincial towns. It was called 'L'Hôtel de l'Espagne et du Cygne' – Spain, where all chivalry began at Roncesvalles but where the swan sings the song of his very last journey.

An enormous bedroom, with two great beds which were fit for a king and a queen, but a beautifully modern bathroom attached. This was by far the most expensive room so far; but also by far the best earned.

19 September

In that splendid bed I had a dream which was worthy of it: S and I and a few of the best BH communards were composing a musical play together; and when it was performed it was going to change and glorify the whole world. We'd slept nearly eleven hours, but were stiff enough this morning to prefer hitching to walking. As I knelt with my back to S so that she could fit the little blue haversack over the poles of my rucksack I became Sir P again, kneeling so that his squire could attach the plate to his back. And on our short walk to the eastern

[385]

edge of Mamers a new notion suddenly intruded itself and this both sharpened the whole fancy and also brought it down many pegs from the high and holy romance of yesterday. It was a vision of myself and S as Don Quixote and Sancho Panza, making our way through this new don's imagined landscape. Each of us was the right build for the allotted role; and of the right nature, at least on the occasion of this journey, but in our case it was the short, broad and realistic figure of Sancho who led the way, setting the pace; the tall, fairly lean Quixote who dropped along behind. (And who'd learned, from the bitter experience of four hundred years, to keep his fancies to himself.)

The process of demoting the allegory was completed by the fact that we were now making for a town called Nogent; our last stage before Chartres. For of course the Knight who had lost his organ of virility at Neufchâtel was No Gent any more; and the ludicrous facetiousness of this downfall made me start laughing as we trudged past the last houses of Mamers.

So then I told S the whole tale; and at first I don't think she was too pleased with the role I'd finally given her. I pleaded that Quixote is mad and Sancho magnificently sane: that she knows very well, in any case, that she is neither my servant nor my squire. But she was fully mollified only when I said that I also know very well how shrewdly sane I can be in defence of my own interests, while she is quite capable, at times, of nobly erratic derangements. (And I can see that even the most proudly stolid and down-to-earth of men wouldn't be quite pleased to be told he was wholly Sancho with nothing quixotic about him.)

Again, as we stood beside our dumped rucksacks looking old and decrepit as we could (I took out my teeth to make the impression even more vivid) we were disdained by the same succession of dismal faces. But it wasn't more than forty minutes before a young man in a battered van offered to take us as far as Bellême. He was very pleasant, of course; a native of this unassuming but quietly beautiful country and enthusiastic about its charms.

At Bellême we stood for an hour and a half without any luck

but our mood was kept sweet by several drivers who stopped and spoke kindly to us, but who weren't going our way. (This name presents so few problems for the allegorist – or liturgist, as David L has since suggested – that I now decided to give up the whole scheme.) But as we stood by the road, almost absently raising our thumbs, I had plenty of time to think back about yesterday's walk and all its fancies. I knew that I'd gone a long way towards accepting them as at least in some sense relevant and real. Perhaps this playing with names and roles seems whimsical at best: at worst pretentious. But I did feel that I'd almost moved into a dimension – or framework – or means of perception – in which the journey really did take on a strange and holy aspect. And I thought that if I'd followed Blake's advice and persisted in this folly I might, after all, have become wise; have been led, by this road of excess, to the Palace of Wisdom. For Don Quixote wasn't *only* mad.

But even if I'd wanted to take that risk, the risk of real insanity, I knew that I could never have gone much further than I did. I played a game with myself (as I might have played it best, among all my friends, with Paddy) but played it with a certain seriousness. And what still lingers this evening (in Nogent) is the fading vision of a real illumination.

Our bus, which left Bellême at 4.30, was the essential country bus, constantly veering violently to left or right whenever a sign pointed straight ahead to Nogent. We weaved back and forth across the main road; and although this caused a faint stirring of my old impatience I soon realized that by taking this zigzag route we were seeing a remote and enchanting countryside which few motorists would ever see. A marshy country of little streams and ponds, with villages called St Jean de la Forêt, St Pierre la Bruyère, and, best of all, La Fontaine aux Lièvres. (I thought that Hare Fountain would be impossible in England; – but we have, after all, our Old Sodbury and our Nether Wallop.)

It seemed a long, hard, uphill slog from the railway station, where the bus put us down, to the old centre of the town. But here we found a delightful grey square, a good and cheap hotel, and a café half-way up a flight of seventeenth-century steps where we are now drinking cold brown beer before dinner. (Pelforth Brune is the nearest approximation to Sam Smith's Strong Brown Ale: not very near.) For me, as I sit here playing chess with S, writing up these notes and watching the evening light of Nogent in a warm dusk, this is the highest point of the holiday so far.

The only disappointment is that there is no bus to Chartres tomorrow. We'd hoped to take one to within four or five miles of the city; then walk the rest of the way with that famous view of the cathedral across the flat land of the Beauce continually before our eyes.

But since we're to meet Bob and Decca the day after tomorrow, and want to see something of the cathedral before our meeting, we shall have to take a train all the way from here tomorrow morning.

A quiet excitement as we contemplate the goal of our journey. Warm pleasure and love as we sit together here in perfect agreement of mood and inclination.

20 September

I put on clean trousers, clean socks and shirt; shaved very carefully and carefully cleaned my nails. (But S lost a front tooth in her breakfast croissant, as if to remind us of our dissolution and mortality.)

A prayer in the beautiful late Gothic church of St Hilaire by the station; but when we'd bought our tickets it was announced that the train would be twenty minutes late. No impatience, though: the cathedral had already been waiting for 800 years.

We bowled pleasantly along between small woods and valleys before coming out on to the plain at Courville, fifteen miles from Chartres. After that last stop S and I took our packs to the end of the carriage and pressed our noses to the windows on each side, peering forward to catch our first glimpse of the most famous twin towers in Christendom. (I'd been to Chartres once, and many years, before, but must have done no more than my usual ten-minute tour of the cathedral between drinks.)

It was S on the north side who saw them first, and beckoned me over. They were perhaps five miles away, and curiously blue in the misty air, just as Mont St Michel had looked, across the bay from Cancale. And because of our long expectation, our studious — for us — preparation, the reality was deeply satisfying: the fulfilment of a promise which had in it a faint element of surprise: — so there it was, after all, just as they'd said!

We walked there straight from the station, aware at once that we'd moved back into the tide of tourists which we'd left at Mont St Michel. And there was a curious pleasure in joining them again, seeing the ancient American faces and hearing the indomitable American voices. Was there, though, some disappointment as we came out into the square and saw the west front no more than a hundred yards away? Of course there was: but this was a disappointment which we'd thoroughly anticipated. Strangely disturbing to an English eye is the fact that the stone is cut into such small, neat and smooth blocks that it looks at first as if the whole front and both the towers are made of pale grey bricks. Also the north tower had scaffolding all round its middle ...

But still! But still!

Postponing the final act of penetrating the Portail Royal we found a good hotel and settled down to a good lunch. Over food, wine and chess we agreed that the cathedral had become almost menacing, so much had we read, spoken and thought about it: so long, it now seemed, had we been travelling towards it. STUDY ME! it was saying, across the rooftops. But also GET WHAT YOU CAN FROM ME, AND WHATEVER YOU GET WILL BE ALL YOU DESERVE.

By the time that we were actually approaching the great triple doorway our entrance seemed more like an ordeal to me than a long-awaited pleasure: the first real test after so many fanciful ones on the way.

[389]

Coming up to the door, ten days almost to the hour since we left home, a colonel-like figure with bald head and white moustache turned and smiled at us. He went ahead and held the door for us: '*Merci,*' I said, but his answer was, 'It's all right: I'm English.' So I can say that the first words I heard on entering Chartres Cathedral were the very words that I always crave to hear. '*It's all right* – God is Love ... *It's all right* – you are on the way ... *It's all right* – you'll see heaven's light ...' And these words should come, if possible, from divine or at least from angelic lips.

Still, one can't have everything. 'It's all right – I'm English' was also good.

As at Mont St Michel words fail me here, looking down the middle of the nave as the east windows gradually settle into their proper colours. This is not because no words could ever do justice to the beauty and holiness of what I saw, but simply because they are not the sort of words I could ever find.

Yes. Yes. Yes. Acceptance at least as strong as amazement.

When we came to the shrine of La Vierge Noire du Pilier, that warmly beautiful little sixteenth-century figure, lit by great banks of candles, we were both glad to sit down among the handful of other worshippers. Here I felt much more at home than in the sublimity of nave and aisles: at home as I'd felt during mass at Mont St Michel. For me this was the real heart of the whole cathedral; the mystery in honour of which every statue and window had been made; the great walls built and the towers raised; our own small journey undertaken.

> 'Heavenly Mother
> Light of the World,
> Have mercy on us.'

But when we walked on again, round the ambulatory and back into the nave again, the rest of the cathedral seemed even lonelier than before; and further away. We heard rain on the windows – the first since we'd left home – and this reminder of rain on my bedroom window made me suddenly long to be back there. The great object, the great *thing*, seemed very alien;

far away in time as well as in space; too pure for me; too perfect for love. Perhaps there seemed to be too much of heaven there and too little of the earth I know.

We sat for about ten minutes under the crossing, and soon this rather bleak mood was partly dissipated by an episode which S saw but I missed. A schoolboy, about eight years old, satchel strapped to his back, had come through the North Porch, walked – 'very neatly and properly' – across the whole width of the cathedral and out through the south door, never once glancing to either side. This was clearly his daily short cut home from school; and the quiet intrusion of ordinary life was comforting as well as comic.

This evening, as were having dinner in a small restaurant near the grandest hotel who should come in but Bob and Decca. A happy, and partly accidental reunion, for we'd arranged to meet at the west front tomorrow morning. They immediately continued the good work done by the schoolboy with his satchel: the world again and all its pleasures: much cheerful talk, and brandies afterwards in the splendid Hôtel du Grand Monarque. (Where they are staying, needless to say: just as we – needless to say – are in the second best hotel across the square.)

Or one might cast B and D – a last fling of that now forbidden fantasy – as the appointed Mockers: not hostile, in my mythology, to the Vierge du Pilier, but charged by her to lighten the solemnity of her adorers.

When we described our journey Decca promptly calculated that we'd carried our packs for an average of only 1.4 miles a day. 'Ah,' I said, 'but you must remember all those hard slogs from the station to the station hotel.' But I must admit that her teasing calculation did rather put the 'pilgrimage' in its place.

21 September

Yes, but I won't quite relinquish the notion of a pilgrimage, for this has at least been a proper journey; and for me an

[391]

unexpected achievement. It would have been very different if we'd taken the car to St Malo and driven to Chartres in a couple of hours.

The exchange rate has been falling steadily and sharply throughout our journey. We got 9.50 francs for the pound in England, but when we cashed some traveller's cheques yesterday it was down to 8.95. As if our poor country has been crumbling away behind us.

This morning the nave of the cathedral seemed almost welcoming; it no longer vaguely alarmed and distressed me as it had done yesterday afternoon. But as I stood there, with the brilliant windows on every side of me, I still found that my eyes were straying towards the softer light from the candles round the shrine of the Vierge du Pilier.

Asking for the key to the crypt in a print shop we were told that a mass was just about to begin there. A lean, handsome Jesuit was officiating – introduced to the celebrants before the mass began. It was strange being down there, the mass celebrated immediately under the crossing, so that we were sitting sideways on to the altar, under the north transept, but most of the congregation were unseen by us round the corner of the crypt and under the nave.

Again the handshaking. And now even stronger than at Mont St Michel the sense of fellowship down there: almost as if we were again a forbidden sect celebrating our rites in the catacombs. (What greater contrast could there be in the setting of these two masses – high up in the sky and deep under the pile of a great cathedral. To amend the psalm slightly: 'And if I ascend into heaven, thou art there: if I make my bed in the bowels of the earth, behold, thou art there also.')

For me a pleasure of hearing mass in French is that I miss a good many of the words, but hear the important ones all the more clearly: '*Dieu*'; '*Sauveur*'; '*Saint-Esprit*'; '*Partagez*' ... So the whole celebration seems less specific than in English, and I can feel the more included because of that. (Though not so warmly included, of course, as I do at Tymawr, where I hear every word perfectly. I thought of Tymawr down there as I

[392]

recognized the separate section of the mass, and it didn't seem far away at all.)

In the afternoon we looked much more thoroughly at the Grand Portail and the North and South Porches. The statues, like any great work of art, come more and more alive the more one looks at them. And the more *humbly* one looks at them. Humility is needed here because these statues are very alien to an English eye; almost a different civilization from the little South Porch at Gloucester.

Then we walked right round the east end and tried to disentangle the apparent confusion of the buttresses.

There is a fine statue of Marceau in the middle of our square. He was a real soldier of the Revolution – pre-Napoleonic; beginning his short career by taking part in the attack on the Bastille. He came near to being guillotined during the Terror, but survived to become a general; to fight bravely for a revolution which he must have known had been betrayed; and to be killed in battle at the age of 28. This brave but melancholy figure aroused atavistic emotions when I stood looking up at his statue against the sky. He was born in Chartres, but it would be hard, and foolishly perverse, to try to set him in the aura of Notre Dame.

Dinner with, and on, Bob and Decca in what we'd hoped, from a three-year-old Michelin, would be the best restaurant in Chartres. From that point of view the evening was a failure; very slow and sour service; undistinguished food, and wine that even my palate condemned. But we surmounted these disabilities easily enough, and had an old-fashioned evening of lively talk. How glad S and I were that we'd arranged to meet them here: a splendid counterbalance to the high demands of the cathedral.

22 September

This morning we climbed as far up the north tower as we could; only about half-way because of the scaffolding above. It

[393]

was raining fairly heavily while we were on the tower, and we were both wearing our bright yellow cycling capes. Under mine was the little blue knapsack which I take with me everywhere – filled with maps, books, chess, etc. – and as I was walking along a sort of stone gangway just under the great green slope of the roof S said, 'Now you look more like the Hunchback of Notre Dame than Don Quixote.'

A very slow perambulation of the aisles, transepts and ambulatory, stopping again for a prayer to the Black Virgin (who cannot be, for me, the mother of Jesus, but is very powerfully the Queen of Heaven; the Great Mother of antiquity, but made entirely gentle and loving by the Christian transformation).

When I first thought of coming here, about two years ago, I'd imagined us staying in Chartres for at least a week; but now we agree that we want to start the homeward journey tomorrow. It would have been easy enough, and perhaps continuously rewarding, to come to the cathedral seven days in a row. But after seeing two other churches and most of the old town this afternoon there seemed nothing much left to do in Chartres itself. We are not yet – probably never will be – the kind of keen students who could spend most of each day in the cathedral, carefully deciphering the windows.

I no longer enjoy French drinks very much, except for sweetish pink wine with our meals; and I long, with all my incurably insular heart, to be in one of our local pubs again. Some men become more physically adventurous with age; but I've followed the usual course and increasingly love best all that I know best.

I read in *Le Monde* that the slogan of the Nicaraguan revolutionaries is '*Notre vengeance est le pardon*'. If only it remains so!

To Le Mans by the most beautiful and comfortable train so far.

23 September

The cathedral here is very weird; beautiful but almost touching in its eccentricity. A rather squat Romanesque nave, but the transepts so long and so elegantly Gothic that one would take them for the main part of the building. This gives the cathedral a charm which Chartres altogether lacks – and rightly lacks.

At mass here a bearded young man in rough 'youth' clothes conducted a choir of schoolgirls, and a girl in blue trousers read the lesson. But quite enough of the traditional solemnity remained, and it seemed a very acceptable compromise. Certainly there was no sense of anything forced or unnatural about the mild and friendly informality.

Splendours of the old, hilltop town to the south of the cathedral. Beer and chess again in a café just outside it. (On this expedition we must have spent at least three times as much time in this occupation as in serious walking and serious cathedral-watching: fifty times as long as we've spent consciously at prayer. But this doesn't bother me in the least. Why should it, when the pleasure of sitting together like this is so great?)

But the pleasure was sharply removed when an old beggar woman came up and began mumbling and demanding unintelligibly at us. I gave her a few coins, and when she persisted in standing and demanding I felt an almost savage embarrassment. After a while I gave her some more coins; she bowed – low enough to make it a gesture of deep irony – and shuffled off at last.

This quite put me off my chess.

Memento Crucis, as a more deeply Christian man than I might put it. The poor we have always with us; but how easy it is, most of the time, to arrange our lives so as to keep them out of mind.

Back in St Malo after three more trains; and at this last French dinner I felt a thorough revulsion at the sight of those

[395]

great mounds of seafood and their greedy devourers. *La Grande Bouffe*. And our own more modest meal was certainly included in my revulsion.

I could emend what was said of Maria Theresa: '*Il prend et il pleure toujours.*'

24 September

A mild weariness of the spirit and feebleness of the body as we made our way to the boat this morning, bowed under our packs as if we'd indeed been on a genuine walking holiday.

A last, far-off view of Mont St Michel as the boat sailed out of harbour.

St Catherine's Point, the southernmost corner of the Isle of Wight. Long ago I settled three miles beyond it for what I thought would be the remainder of my life. A very premature paradise.

We had left the car in what we suspected was a forbidden park, and had almost resigned ourselves to its disappearance, either by stealing or by police action. So it was a positive joy to find it there, with nothing but a friendly police warning stuck to the windshield.

Supper – delicious tinned soup, cheddar and biscuits – and very early bed in a small hotel just south of Winchester.

25 September

Was Winchester Cathedral diminished by all the splendours that we'd seen in France? Well, it certainly seemed *homely*, particularly its unapologetic stump of a tower. But the nave, after all, is the second longest in Europe; and would have been as noble as ever if they hadn't hung great gaudy 'modernist' banners on every pillar. What crimes our poor Church too often commits in the name of keeping up with the times.

Then a quick mid-morning visit to our old friends Patrick

and Hermione O'Donovan at Alresford. Both of them are Catholic by birth and devout by faith, which made it all the greater pleasure to talk to them about our French experiences. When I said that we'd attended three masses Patrick sharply asked whether I'd taken communion. I admitted to it, expecting a rebuke; but he was very pleased. He is off to Ireland to cover the Pope's visit; and how much I admired the stamina he is still able to summon up for such exhausting assignments.

Considering how close we felt to them both it is strange indeed that we hadn't seen them for at least five years. True, Hermione is almost housebound with fearful arthritis; but we could reach them by the M4 in two and a half hours. I pray that this journey may have given me greater freedom of movement; for haven't I been almost as housebound as Hermione, by sickness of a different kind!

The best moment of coming home is when the car climbs that last rise on the motorway and we can suddenly see the towers of the bridge, the shining Severn itself and the line of hill under Tiddenham Chase. Just as I used to make it so much of a homecoming – and an escape – when I crossed on the ferry from Portsmouth to Ryde (1946–48) so the crossing of this great bridge, with a semi-expert scrutiny of the tide, now brings me safely back into my own country.

Stretched on my bed with the usual icons in front of me; the rosary in my hands; the well-tried prayers and meditations in my mind. Then the newspaper collected, as usual, from Mrs Birley's back door; the Orepool, as usual, with Harry behind the bar: the lights of St Briavels, as usual, when we are driving home, and the church tower against the sky.

I write, and feel, as if we'd just come back from two years in Tierra del Fuego.

30 September

After the first happiness at being back, two days of uneasiness as we settle down again. But a very cheerful group in The

Beaufort on Thursday: mass at Tymawr this morning. And now S has started to clean and paint the window frames and I've spent two afternoons weeding the garden. This winter, with the help of Mr Watkins, the builder, we shall set our house in order; and the garden will be well-prepared for the spring.

It is impossible to say what changes that little journey will have made in our lives: rash, I suppose, to assume that it will have made any changes at all.

I've pinned up a postcard of the Black Virgin of Chartres beside my bed, and I gaze at it without the faintest sense of idolatry.

4 October

'Everything that happens in the world takes place not only on the earth that buries its dead, but also in some other dimension which some call the Kingdom of God' (Pasternak).